P9-EEL-817

WITHDRAWN
UTSA Libraries

PIO BAROJA'S *MEMORIAS DE UN HOMBRE DE ACCION* AND THE IRONIC MODE: THE SEARCH FOR ORDER AND MEANING

MARSHA SUZAN COLLINS

PIO BAROJA'S *MEMORIAS DE UN HOMBRE DE ACCION* AND THE IRONIC MODE: THE SEARCH FOR ORDER AND MEANING

TAMESIS BOOKS LIMITED
LONDON

Colección Támesis
SERIE A - MONOGRAFIAS, CXXIV

© Copyright by Tamesis Books Limited
London, 1986
ISBN 0 7293 0252 0

DISTRIBUTORS:

Spain:
Editorial Castalia,
Zurbano, 39,
28010 Madrid

United States and Canada:
Longwood Publishing Group,
27 South Main Street,
Wolfeboro, New Hampshire 03894-2069, U.S.A.

Great Britain and rest of the world:
Grant and Cutler Ltd.,
55-57 Great Marlborough Street,
London W1V 2AY

Depósito legal: M. 43016-1986

Printed in Spain by Talleres Gráficos de SELECCIONES GRÁFICAS
Carretera de Irún, km. 11,500 - 28049 Madrid

for
TAMESIS BOOKS LIMITED
LONDON

LIBRARY
The University of Texas
at San Antonio

TABLE OF CONTENTS

This project was supported in part
by a New York University
Research Challenge Fund Grant.

INTRODUCTION

This book is a revised version of my doctoral dissertation on Pío Baroja's *Memorias de un hombre de acción*. My purpose was to achieve greater understanding of Baroja's concept of the historical novel, to rectify the relative critical neglect into which these novels have fallen, and to meet the need for reassessing their place in the author's overall literary production. But it soon became apparent that the series represents the author's most extensive and complex treatment of more universal preoccupations present throughout his work: his concern with order and meaning in the world, the nature of the hero, the artist, and self and society. From the very beginning Baroja fuses literary form and philosophical exposition to create a unique style that combines verbal simplicity, melodramatic plots, and metaphysical meditations — with results that often seem confusing and paradoxical. It is in this spirit of creating a broader and more illuminating context for the series that I have studied the novels in relationship to Baroja's earlier works, in terms of both literary genres and modes and as literary expressions of philosophical and existential ideas. These observations and analyses have, I hope, provided insight into Baroja's aesthetic and his entire literary production.

Of the seventy-six novels written by Pío Baroja, the twenty-two volumes of *Memorias de un hombre de acción* (1913-1935) have received by far the smallest amount of critical attention. The novels chronicle the adventures of Eugenio Aviraneta Ibargoyen, a minor Spanish historical figure whose career spanned roughly the first half of the nineteenth century, encompassing such events as the Spanish Napoleonic Wars, the struggle between Absolutists and Liberals during the reign of Fernando VII and the regent María Cristina, the First Carlist War, and the eruption of the Second Carlist War during the reign of Isabel II. Baroja's laborious investigation of historical documents and materials of all kinds in preparation for the series and his dedication of twenty-two of his greatest years of artistic productivity to the writing of these works, indicate the seriousness with which the author regarded the project. Two major books on *Memorias de un hombre de acción*, Carlos Longhurst's *Las novelas históricas de Pío Baroja* and Francisco Flores Arroyuelo's *Pío Baroja y la historia* have provided significant information on the genesis of the historical novels — the sources Baroja utilized, his attitude towards history, his organization and presentation of historical material, and his purpose in writing the books.[1]

Baroja's own novels attest to his fascination with historical material as the basis for fiction. Historical elements and situations appear in even the earliest novels. Fernando Ossorio's wanderings in *Camino de perfección* (1902) represent a failed attempt to translate a vital spiritual experience of the past, mysticism, into the present. In *El mayorazgo de Labraz* (1903), the struggles between Liberals and Carlists in an anachronistic, almost medieval city provide the background for a melodramatic love story. *La feria de los discretos* (1905), set in Córdoba before the Revolution of 1868, presents a hero who joins the Masons to work on a revolutionary plot. The action in *Los últimos románticos* (1906) and *Las tragedias grotescas* (1907) takes place in Paris towards the end of the Second Empire with a historical context that includes such events as the Franco-Prussian War, the Revolution of 1868, and the dethronement of Isabel II. Baroja utilized information from oral sources and his own childhood experiences to recreate the past of the Second Carlist War in *Zalacaín el aventurero* (1909), and the Basque seafaring days in *Las inquietudes de Shanti Andía* (1911). In these novels he begins to engage with historical material and his first adventure heroes appear.[2] The reading material in Baroja's personal library at Vera del Bidasoa offers additional evidence of his interest in history. More than half of the library books deal with nonliterary subjects and the majority of these relate to geography or history. Roughly a third of his historical books pertain to French and Spanish nineteenth-century history, including the *Memorias* of Godoy, *Historia de la guerra civil y de los partidos liberal y carlista* by Antonio Pirala, and *Historia del levantamiento, guerra y revolución de España* by the Count of Toreno.[3] These works were standard historical references in the latter half of the nineteenth century.

Furthermore, Baroja's interest in history typifies the spirit of his na-

[1] CARLOS LONGHURST, *Las novelas históricas de Pío Baroja* (Madrid: Guadarrama, 1974) and FRANCISCO J. FLORES ARROYUELO, *Pío Baroja y la historia* (Madrid: Helios, 1971). Other books from this recent phase of Baroja criticism are JOSÉ ALBERICH, *Los ingleses y otros temas de Pío Baroja* (Madrid: Alfaguara, 1966), BIRUTÉ CIPLIJAUSKAITÉ, *Baroja, un estilo* (Madrid: Insula, 1972), and CARMEN IGLESIAS, *El pensamiento de Pío Baroja: Ideas centrales*, Clásicos y Modernos, 12 (México: Antigua Librería Robredo, 1963). While my purpose and approach in studying *Memorias de un hombre de acción* are quite different from those of Longhurst and Flores, their books have been indispensable resources in the preparation of my study. Both authors have amassed enormous amounts of useful information that should provide a sound basis for further critical works on *Memorias de un hombre de acción* for some time to come.

[2] FLORES, pp. 50-54.

[3] JOSÉ ALBERICH, «La biblioteca de Pío Baroja», *Revista Hispánica Moderna*, 27 (1961), 102 and 108.

tional and European contemporaries. The nineteenth century was the age of historicism and the historical novel: the Waverley novels, *War and Peace, The Red and the Black, A Tale of Two Cities*. By the end of the century the historical novel had become a well established literary tradition in Spain. Translation of Sir Walter Scott's novels into Spanish began in 1825 in London, by the liberal émigrés, but publication of translations in Spain started shortly afterward in Madrid in 1830.[4] The 231 Spanish editions of these works that appeared between 1825 and 1899 indicate the enormous popularity of Scott's historical novels.[5] The publication of Francisco Brotón's *Rafael de Riego o la España libre* set a precedent as well for a tradition of national historical novels.[6] This initial phase of the historical novel in Spain merged between 1835 and 1850 with the serialized adventure novels, popularized in Spain by the works of Dumas and Sue.[7] As the nineteenth century progressed, then, the historical novel became increasingly an element of popular literary culture. A shift from an essentially tragic world view towards one of comedy and romance accompanied this general movement.[8] The forty-six historical novels of Galdós's *Episodios nacionales* (1869-1912), however, in terms of scope and seriousness of intention provided the most significant literary antecedent for the historical novels of Pío Baroja. Galdós combined the realistic, *costumbrista* strain of nineteenth-century Spanish literature and the conventions of the popular serial novels to present the history of contemporary Spain. The series implicitly represents the values and Progressivist views of the ascendant middle class in Restoration Spain. Baroja brought a different perspective to the historical novel in Spain. Although he appreciated the contributions of science to the technological advance of mankind, Baroja rejected the scientific, positivistic approach to history prevalent for much of the nineteenth century: «la historia no es ciencia, aunque puede y debe estar basada en ella», and later he says, «el elemento subjetivo del

---

[4] JOSÉ F. MONTESINOS, *Introducción a una historia de la novela en España en el siglo XIX* (Madrid: Castalia, 1966), pp. 59-63.

[5] JUAN IGNACIO FERRERAS, *El triunfo del liberalismo y de la novela histórica (1830-1870)*, Vol. II of his *Estudios sobre la novela española del siglo XIX* (Madrid: Taurus, 1974), p. 66.

[6] FERRERAS, p. 72.

[7] MONTESINOS, pp. 90-93.

[8] See FERRERAS, *El triunfo*, pp. 99-101, in which he describes the three types of historical novels that arose in nineteenth-century Spain: «novela histórica de origen romántico», «novela histórica de aventuras», and «novela de aventuras históricas». This progression in the development of the historical novel indicates a shift in sentiment towards melodrama, the contemporary displaced form of romance. This shift will be discussed in greater detail in chapter one in terms of its implications for Baroja's novels. James C. Simmons describes an analogous change in the English historical novel during the nineteenth century in *The Novelist as Historian: Essays on the Victorian Historical Novel* (Paris: Mouton, 1973), pp. 55-62.

historiador es demasiado importante en su obra».[9] His deprecatory attitude towards the notion of historical progress emerges in his ever-present ironic point of view, reminiscent of such turn-of-the-century European contemporaries as Joseph Conrad and Thomas Hardy.

This highly subjective and skeptical approach to history, and in fact to all of human experience, is one of the unifying characteristics of the Generation of '98. As witnesses of the aftermath of one of the most turbulent and decadent epochs in Spain's national history and the loss of all vestiges of her colonial power, the members of the Generation of '98 interrogated the past in search of the source of Spain's present problems and as a key to her future. The writer Antonio Azorín noted this historicizing tendency, «La historia nos tenía captados», and «La generación de 1898 es una generación historicista», and described the generational interest in the process of change through history:

> La generación del 98 es una generación histórica y, por tanto, tradicional. Su empresa es la continuidad. Y viniendo a continuar, se produce la pugna entre lo anterior y lo que se trata de imponer. El hecho es lógico. No hay verdadera y fecunda continuación sin que algo sea renovado. En este renovarse de las cosas, cobran las cosas mayor vitalidad. A lo largo de la Historia —en este caso la Historia de España— han existido diversos y múltiples momentos de renovación, es decir, de cambio. Han cambiado las costumbres y ha cambiado la manera literaria. Lo que interesa, en cada caso, es ver en qué se funda la pugna entre lo que venía viviendo y lo posterior.[10]

The historical novels of two of Baroja's contemporaries, Unamuno and Valle-Inclán, provide contrasting examples of this spirit of continuity and renovation. In *Paz en la guerra*, Unamuno depicts the Second Carlist War, most vividly the 1873 siege of Bilbao. He abandoned the chronicle-like treatment of the historical novel shortly afterward for the schematic, abstract portrayal of conflicting human passions in such novels of his artistic maturity as *Niebla* and *San Manuel Bueno, mártir*. The spirit behind his early historical novel, though, lies much closer to that of the progressivist view of history than that of either Valle-Inclán or Baroja. Unamuno derives significance from the bloody violence of the civil wars by placing it on another level where it becomes merely a part of the Darwinian struggle for existence. The Carlist War forms simply one more manifestation of this natural law, however, and does not represent a universal advance in moral values. Baroja, on the other hand, never could reconcile

---

[9] Pío BAROJA, «La historia», in his *Obras completas*, V (Madrid: Biblioteca Nueva, 1948, p. 1125). Subsequent references to this eight-volume edition, published between 1946 and 1951, will be cited by the title of the article or book, volume number, and page numbers.

[10] JOSÉ MARTÍNEZ RUIZ, *Madrid*, in his *Obras completas*, VI (Madrid: Aguilar, 1962), pp. 229, 231.

the brutality of the past with any vision of transcendent order, natural or divine. Valle-Inclán's representation of Spanish contemporary history in *El ruedo ibérico* presents a far more negative view of history than that of Unamuno. He employs satirical reduction by portraying major historical figures as morally-debased puppets. History does not appear as a linear, causally-determined progression of actions and events, but rather as a jumble of incidents — products of chance or whim in the debased Spanish society. Only Valle-Inclán's ironic viewpoint and literary technique hold the chaos together. Even the more conservative historical concepts of another member of the Generation of '98, Azorín, his *microhistoria* and «Vivir es ver volver», while acknowledging a potential for social change, contradict the predominantly progressivist optimism in Galdós's *Episodios nacionales*.[11]

A spirit of engagement with generic tradition, and particularly with Galdós, underlies Baroja's presentation of history in *Memorias de un hombre de acción*.[12] Baroja objected strongly to any association made between his approach to the historical novel and that of Galdós. He wrote in response to a critic's labeling of him as an imitator of Galdós: «No hay tal cosa. Yo, aunque conocí a Pérez Galdós, no tuve gran entusiasmo ni por el escritor ni por la persona» (*Divagaciones apasionadas*, V: 498). In another essay Baroja outlined the differences between their views of history in a more systematic fashion: 1) Galdós turned to history out of fondness for it whereas Baroja's curiosity about a type, the adventurer, drew him to history; 2) Galdós wanted to capture important historical moments, but Baroja's protagonist determined his choice of historical material; 3) Galdós saw the Spain of the War of Independence as separate and removed in time while Baroja saw the Spain of that period as closely tied to France by the movement of liberals and reactionaries and close in spirit to contemporary Spain; 4) Finally, Galdós had done little historical research for his novels, while Baroja had searched in the archives and had visited many of the sites for the action in his novels

---

[11] On the ideology behind the vision of history present through most of the *Episodios nacionales* see ANTONIO REGALADO GARCÍA, *Benito Pérez Galdós y la novela histórica española: 1868-1912* (Madrid: Insula, 1966), pp. 102-17. For additional information on the historical novels of the Generation of '98 see BIRUTÉ CIPLIJAUSKAITÉ, «The 'Noventayochistas' and the Carlist Wars», *Hispanic Review*, 44 (1976), 265-79. For Unamuno's ideas about history see PETER G. EARLE, «Unamuno and the Theme of History», *Hispanic Review*, 32 (1964), 319-39 and on *Paz en la guerra* see MANUEL GARCÍA BLANCO, «Sobre la elaboración de la novela de Unamuno *Paz en la guerra*», *Revista Hispánica Moderna*, 31 (1965), 142-58. Peggy Lynne Tucker discusses Valle-Inclán's attitude towards history in *Time and History in Valle-Inclán's Historical Novels and Tirano Banderas* (Valencia: Albatros Hispanófila, 1980). JOSÉ ANTONIO MARAVALL discusses Azorín's concept of *microhistoria* in «Azorín: idea y sentido de la microhistoria», *Cuadernos Hispanoamericanos*, Nos. 226-27 (Oct-Nov. 1968), pp. 28-77.

[12] See LONGHURST, pp. 247-61 and FLORES, pp. 354-68.

(*La intuición y el estilo,* V : 1074). These distinctions imply fundamentally different attitudes towards the historical novel. Baroja emphasizes his focus on an individual type as a point of departure for a study of an entire historical epoch. Galdós, on the other hand, moves from the more abstract historical level to a specific fictional representation of general concepts and historical events. Baroja actively pursues a subjective approach to history by having the actual experiences of his protagonist determine the incidents he will fictionalize. He even implies that his own methods provide a more truthful approach to history than those of Galdós. Baroja asserts that the subjective experience of events and ordering of the world forms a more valid approach to history than the imposition of a set of collective social values and beliefs on reality.[13] He also establishes a clear link between the past and the present and points out Spain's external ties with France while implicitly criticizing Galdós's more nationalistic, celebrative view of Spanish history. Baroja's careful delineation of differences indicates his own awareness of a profound shift in philosophical spirit towards a more modern view of the self as the basis for all human knowledge, for assessing the past, and planning for the future.

Despite all of these elements that indicate Baroja's great preoccupation with history, he maintained an emphatically negative attitude towards history in many of his essays. Baroja explained this position : «siento, creo que espontáneamente, una fuerte aspiración ética... Esta aspiración, unida a la turbulencia, me ha hecho ser más enemigo que amigo del pasado; por lo tanto, un tipo antihistórico, antirretórico, y poco tradicionalista» (*La dama errante,* II : 230). Baroja characteristically defines his position in terms of disagreement and denial.[14] In other essays he attacks the separation of fact and fiction, stating that little difference exists between history and the novel (*La caverna del humorismo,* V : 473). According to Baroja, subjectivity plays too great a role in the representation of history to consider it a science and determining the authenticity and importance of the facts on which it is based is always a difficulty («Los datos de la historia», V : 1125), similar to his assessment that the writing of history «no se ha hecho nunca a base de una documentación irrepro-

---

[13] Perhaps because the attitude towards history and the historical novel is so fundamentally different, Galdós's *Episodios* lend themselves much more readily to an analysis based on George Lukács's *The Historical Novel.* For analyses of the *Episodios* in relation to Lukács's ideas see MADELEINE DE GOGORZA FLETCHER, «Galdós», in *The Spanish Historical Novel: 1870-1970* (London: Tamesis, 1973), pp. 11-50, and REGALADO GARCÍA, «Los orígenes de los *Episodios nacionales* y la tradición de la novela histórica», *Benito Pérez Galdós y la novela histórica española,* pp. 133-38.
[14] For a study of Baroja's works from this point of view see LEO L. BARROW, *Negation in Baroja: A Key to his Novelistic Creativity* (Tucson: University of Arizona Press, 1971).

chable, sino a base de indicios y de intuiciones» («Los datos de la historia», V: 1140). Baroja states that techniques and limitations link the historian and the novelist. The historian begins to reconstruct an image of a historical figure from a preconceived notion of certain characteristics before doing research just as the writer assigns certain characteristics to a fictional character («Los datos de la historia», V: 1140). He goes so far as to assert that «la Historia es una rama de la literatura, no una rama de la ciencia» («Los datos de la historia», V: 1140). By subsuming history under the category of literature Baroja erased any pre-established barrier between fact and fiction, thereby permitting greater artistic freedom in creating the novels of *Memorias de un hombre de acción*. In addition, there is a striking similarity between this view of history and that of Schopenhauer. The philosopher also insisted on the non-scientific nature of history, pointing to its subjective and unsystematic qualities in support of his opinion. He stated that the individual and particular are the basis for history and reached the conclusion that poetry is more truthful than history.[15] Thus, a highly skeptical philosophical current underlies the novelist's position.

Baroja's iconoclastic attitude toward literary and historiographical traditions, as well as his ambivalence towards history in general, could only produce a unique and highly complex treatment of the historical novel. And it is my belief that to make the «historical novel» the central issue does not really reach the heart of the matter. Rather, I suggest that the author's project of writing a series of historical novels is a pretext for expressing a more universal concern for man's place in the world and his ability to give life meaning. In recent years hispanists have discovered that the Generation of '98's preoccupation with national problems mirrors the far-reaching issues of fin-de siècle European intellectual circles. The gradual breakdown of rational, positivistic philosophy that occurred throughout the second half of the nineteenth century led to a questioning of old values and of the social order and to the discussion of more profound ontological and epistemological issues such as the nature of man's being, his place and purpose in the world, and the meaning of life. The members of the Generation of '98, inspired by the philosophy of Schopenhauer and Nietzsche, engaged with these same existential concerns through the mediators of the Castilian landscape and Spanish national history. Pío Baroja's works, perhaps more than those of any of his contemporaries, provide evidence of the impact of these philosophers of the irrational and illogical on Spanish fiction. The turbulent epoch he chose as the historical focal point for the series *Memorias de un hombre de acción* offered him a means of addressing major existential issues: the

15 ARTHUR SCHOPENHAUER, *The World as Will and Representation*, trans. E. F. J. PAYNE, II (New York: Dover, 1966), pp. 439-46.

problematic relationship between illusion, truth, and reality; the question of man's moral responsibility; and the possibility of endowing a fundamentally chaotic, absurd world with order and meaning. But a genuine understanding of these concerns in the series and throughout his work must begin with the problems and paradoxes presented in his earlier novels.

I

MELODRAMA, IRONY, AND SATIRE: THE MORAL UNIVERSE AND THE CONTEMPORARY WORLD

> The life of man, as often seen in the world of reality, is like the water as seen often in pond and river, but in the epic, the romance, and the tragedy, selected characters are placed in those circumstances in which all their characteristics are unfolded, the depths of the human mind are revealed and become visible in extraordinary and significant actions.
>
> (SCHOPENHAUER, *The World as Will and Representation*)

APPROACHING THE EARLY WORKS OF BAROJA

Baroja's contradictions constitute perhaps the most difficult challenge to the critic who wishes to analyze his work in a meaningful way. Baroja dislikes history, but he researches and writes a series of twenty-two historical novels. He insists on visiting the sites for his books and writing about people he has met, and yet improbable people and events figure in almost all of his novels, and folk tales, ghost stories, horrifying scenes, and supernatural occurrences appear in many of them. He seems to view human existence in a pessimistic light, but few Spanish authors have written more celebratively of travel and human adventure or more lyrically of sunsets and landscapes. Rather than deciding which of these attitudes defines the «real» Baroja and provides the key to an understanding of his treatment of the historical novel, I would insist that all of these different aspects are part of Baroja and contribute to the fictional world of *Memorias de un hombre de acción*. This series, although constructed around a central historical figure, encompasses a variety of materials and concerns and moves along alternating between individual acts of heroism and massive betrayal, between tragic moments of loss and defeat and scenes of farce and happy reunions. The artistic mind behind the novels deals painstakingly with the minutiae of the organization of the Masons in early nineteenth-century Spain and the architecture of Bayonne, but also conveys the spirited conversation in fashionable salons and the

17

glitter of masked balls of that era. In addition to the variety of imaginative episodes and the vivid pictorial quality of *Memorias de un hombre de acción,* one senses Baroja's engagement with Spain's recent history and his preoccupation with profound existential problems, particularly the complex interaction between self and reality. In fact, the series presents an expansion of the literary techniques and philosophical concerns apparent in Baroja's earlier novels. In works such as *La casa de Aizgorri* (1900), *El árbol de la ciencia* (1911) and *Paradox, rey* (1906), Baroja examines the possibility or impossibility of achieving transcendent order in the world, either in the more abstract form of a moralistic conflict between good and evil or in the more concrete context of contemporary man's search for meaning in a world of flux and fallen values. Even in these early works Baroja emphasizes the individual, and the importance of will, self-discovery, and direction in life.

Yet as a rule, critics distinguish *Memorias de un hombre de acción* from the author's earlier and later novels by dividing his literary production into two or three major periods. Baroja seems to support this practice by separating his work into two phases: «una de 1900 a la guerra mundial; otra, desde la guerra del 14 hasta ahora. La primera de violencia, de arrogancia y de nostalgia; la segunda, de historicismo, de crítica, de ironía y de cierto mariposeo sobre las cosas» (*Galería de tipos de la época,* VII: 832). Donald L. Shaw, on the other hand, describes three phases in Baroja's evolution as a writer: 1) the vitalist phase in which life appears as a goal in and of itself, 2) the historical novel phase which encompasses two-thirds of *Memorias de un hombre de acción* written between *El mundo es ansí* (1912) and *La sensualidad pervertida* (1920), and 3) the phase of ataraxia, of achieving peace through self-limitation, which begins with *La sensualidad pervertida* and continues until the end of Baroja's literary creation.[1] On closer examination, however, Shaw's divisions do not account adequately for the facts. The exuberant adventures in *Memorias de un hombre de acción* and the adventurer-hero Aviraneta's devotion to an intense, active life could scarcely provide a more vitalistic impression. The notion of ataraxia as a solution to existential problems occurs as early as *El árbol de la ciencia* and emerges later in such characters from *Memorias de un hombre de acción* as Miguel Aristy in *La veleta de Gastizar* (1918), the fictional editor Pedro Leguía, and at times even Aviraneta. As previously mentioned, Baroja's preoccupation with history occurs quite early in *La feria de los discretos* (1905) for example, and much later in his unpublished novel *Los saturnianos* (set in pre-Civil War Spain). Francisco Flores Arroyuelo uses Baroja's differentiation as a point of departure, adding that elements of each period appear in the other so that the vali-

---

[1] DONALD L. SHAW, *The Generation of 1898 in Spain* (New York: Barnes and Noble, 1975), pp. 167-68.

dity of the distinction rests on a quantitative basis rather than a thematic one.[2] This assertion is difficult to prove and yields little in terms either of the essential themes and techniques of Baroja's works or his process of maturation as an artist. Carlos Longhurst approaches the matter from another angle:

> si antes Baroja había denunciado a la humanidad contemporánea desde un punto de vista moral o ético, ahora va a denunciar a la humanidad histórica desde un punto de vista parecido o igual. Pero es asimismo verdad que las novelas históricas revelan un alejamiento del tipo de novela en que consideraciones de índole filosófica son los que parecen predominar en la mente del novelista.[3]

While I agree with Longhurst that Baroja maintains his moralistic stance, I see no reason why the novels of *Memorias de un hombre de acción* indicate a departure from philosophical concerns. Instead of viewing Baroja's adventure novels in general and *Memorias de un hombre de acción* in particular as separate from his philosophical novels and somehow antithetical in nature, I see them as complementary works in which Baroja develops similar existential concerns and conflicts. Longhurst expands his ideas about the early novels: «todas estas novelas están profundamente imbuidas de un espíritu filosófico o reflexivo, son novelas cuyos temas giran en torno al significado de la existencia, de la orientación que podemos dar a nuestras vidas, y de la posición del individuo en la sociedad» (p. 12). True, but *Memorias de un hombre de acción* continues this philosophical preoccupation rather than ends it. Although Baroja envisioned the series from the very beginning as an enormous project of historical novels about Spain in the first half of the nineteenth century, he stated that «curiosidad hacia un tipo» (*La intuición y el estilo,* V: 1074) drew him to that period. A central historical figure provided him with the focus, the means of organization and the point of departure for spinning out volumes of personal and political, fictional and historical intrigue. Baroja clearly saw the historical world of *Memorias de un hombre de acción* as an analogue to the contemporary world and the temporal distance only provided him with greater freedom to mold the facts he discovered into a fictional world that reflects his own philosophical interests. It is misleading to avoid the contradictory aspects of Baroja's art by dividing his works into phases or labelling his novels and protagonists according to type. An understanding of *Memorias de un hombre de acción* emerges rather from examining the series as a logical outgrowth

---

[2] Francisco J. Flores Arroyuelo, *Pío Baroja y la historia* (Madrid: Helio, 1971), p. 63.
[3] Carlos Longhurst, *Las novelas históricas de Pío Baroja* (Madrid: Guadarrama, 1974), p. 11.

of the philosophical and artistic preoccupations apparent in Baroja's pre-1913 novels.

THE FORMATION OF A NOVELIST

The term «historical novel» implies the integration of historial «fact» —chronicles, memoirs, documents, eyewitness accounts— and fiction. This process of integration, however, is only a more specialized form of the interaction between fact and fiction that forms the basis for the novel as a genre. At the beginning of *The Nature of Narrative,* Scholes and Kellogg outline the breakdown of the epic into two antithetical types of narrative, the empirical, associated with the real, and the fictional, associated with the ideal. They point out that a new synthesis of the two occurred in *Don Quijote* to produce the first modern novel, but conclude by indicating the inherent instability of the combination and its tendency to split into its components. Scholes and Kellogg believe that signs of this breakdown have already appeared in the twentieth century.[4] They imply that, since Cervantes, consciously or unconsciously every novelist has had to come to terms with the conflicting pull between fact and fiction. Pío Baroja became a writer just at the time in which Western man grew acutely aware of this conflict as an existential problem as well as a literary one. Baroja's contemporary, José Ortega y Gasset, discovered precisely this aspect of *Don Quijote.* In his book *Meditaciones del Quijote* (1914), the philosopher discusses the dialectic between the imagination and reality in art and indicates the dual perspective essential to the novel as a genre, the shaping of reality by imaginative impulses and the shaping of the imagination by reality.[5]

Baroja's own writings reveal a tendency to blend freely fact and fiction. During 1903 he served as a war correspondent in Morocco for the journal *El Globo.* Although the journalistic standards for objectivity have undoubtedly changed with the passage of time, his seven reports present a marked predilection for imaginative narrative as opposed to mere informational reportage. In this case, he added imagination to experience to be conveyed as fact. In *Memorias de un hombre de acción,* on the other hand, Baroja combined historical fact with imagination to produce fiction. Regardless of the direction of movement in the dialectic, Baroja's tendency to blend the seemingly antithetical natures of fact and fiction provides

---

[4] ROBERT SCHOLES and ROBERT KELLOGG, *The Nature of Narrative* (New York: Oxford University Press, 1966), pp. 13-15.

[5] In Vol. I of his *Obras completas* (Madrid: Revista de Occidente, 1957), 309-400, at pp. 382-84.

a key to his later style, treatment of the historical novel, and to his total artistic production.[6]

The unique vision of reality present in Baroja's novels also grows out of a major philosophical shift that came to the forefront just as he was beginning his career as a writer. Around the turn of the century, positivism and its faith in progress through science gave way to a more skeptical, ironic world view that emphasized subjectivity instead of objectivity, man's will and irrational forces as opposed to his rational powers. It arose mainly from the influence of Schopenhauer and Nietzsche.[7] Nietzsche in particular had a great impact on the Generation of '98, especially on Baroja.[8] Gonzalo Sobejano points out that he first became familiar with the philosopher indirectly through a book by Henri Lichtenberger, *La Philosophie de Nietzsche* (1898),[9] although by 1902 all of Nietzsche's major writings had appeared in Spanish.[10] Baroja initially rejected many of Nietzsche's ideas, but by 1901 he developed a conciliatory, positive attitude towards the philosopher as a result of discussions with his friend Paul Schmitz, recorded journalistically in two articles entitled «Nietzsche íntimo» on September 9 and October 7 of 1901 in *El Imparcial* and fictionally in the conversations in El Paular in *Camino de perfección* (1903).[11] Nietzsche placed great responsibility on the individual, on self-perfection, and on self-overcoming. The will determines that self and its actions in a social context without aid from religion or other people.[12] Nietzsche felt that sensation provided the only reality and that any system of belief placed on reality produced a false sense of order: «To Nietzsche the form, meaning, and content of all science and all religion were aesthetic in origin, products of a human need to flee from reality into a dream, to *impose* order on experience in the absence of any substantive meaning or content.»[13] Despite their emphasis on the subjective aspect of reality, Nietzsche's ideas support a conscious encounter between the self and that reality, one composed of a flux of phenomena ordered only by the individual's perception. Baroja's own thoughts about art reveal a similar appreciation of the individual's vital experiences. He saw art

[6] JORGE CAMPOS, «Pío Baroja, corresponsal de guerra (1903)», *Cuadernos Hispanoamericanos,* Nos. 265-67 (July-Sept., 1972), pp. 279-88.

[7] HAYDEN WHITE, *Metahistory: The Historical Imagination in Nineteenth-Century Europe* (Baltimore: The Johns Hopkins University Press, 1973), pp. 321-22.

[8] GONZALO SOBEJANO, *Nietzsche en España* (Madrid: Gredos, 1967), 347-95, at p. 348. See also PAUL ILIE, «Nietzsche in Spain: 1890-1910», *PMLA,* 79 (1964), 86.

[9] SOBEJANO, pp. 50-51.

[10] ILIE, p. 80.

[11] SOBEJANO, pp. 349-51.

[12] EUGENE GOODHEART, «Nietzsche and the Aristocracy of Passion», in his *The Cult of the Ego: The Self in Modern Literature* (Chicago: University of Chicago Press, 1968), 114-32, at pp. 127-28.

[13] WHITE, p. 322, p. 87. See also ILIE, p. 87.

as a reflection of life, «Me interesa mi vida, la vida de la gente que me rodea, y el arte como reflejo de la vida» (*Divagaciones apasionadas,* V: 491). He insisted as well that reality endowed fiction with significance: «El escritor puede imaginar, naturalmente, tipos e intrigas que no ha visto; pero necesita siempre el trampolín de la realidad para dar saltos maravillosos en el aire. Sin ese trampolín, aun teniendo imaginación, son imposibles los saltos mortales» («Prólogo» to *La nave de los locos,* IV: 320). Both of these quotations indicate an unequivocal view of fiction as art that incorporates the world of experience, of everyday phenomena. Baroja never abandoned this position of the integral relationship between art and life and the contemporary philosophical currents reinforced his attitude. Schopenhauer, for example, viewed art as a reflection of reality, but made more meaningful by the artist's perception and interpretation.

Baroja also derived from Schopenhauer and Nietzsche his fascination with the human will. Schopenhauer formulated a philosophy that focuses on the will, that presupposes the separation of subject and object, will and representation. As in Nietzsche's writings, the will cannot be described in rational terms of time, space and causality, but is irrational in nature. Yet unlike Nietzsche, Schopenhauer felt that knowledge of one's nature would lead to denial and eventual annihilation of the will through self-limitation and castigation. The full force of the tug-of-war between Schopenhauer's nihilism and Nietzsche's vitalism in Baroja's own mind can be experienced through the ontological anguish of Andrés Hurtado in *El árbol de la ciencia.* There is no doubt that both philosophers were of great importance in the formulation of Baroja's own personal philosophy of art and life.

Baroja's life-long enthusiasm for popular literary forms of all kinds, from Basque folk songs and tales to serial novels and melodrama, is another major factor in his development as a novelist. He especially enjoyed the escapist adventure novels by authors such as Scott, Melville, Dumas, Stevenson, and Mayne Reid, and, as Alberich demonstrates, these imaginative works had great impact on his writing.[14] Baroja recognized the affective value of popular literature and lamented its disappearance: «Yo al menos, siento no vivir en la época en que se lloraba sobre las páginas de una novela, se estremecía uno de espanto en el melodrama y se reía bárbaramente en el sainete» («El folletín y el sainete», in *Vitrina pintoresca,* V: 841). He pointed out the influence of serial novelists like Paul de Koch and Montepin on the great novelists Victor Hugo and

---

[14] JOSÉ ALBERICH, «Baroja y la novela de aventura inglesa». in his *Los ingleses y otros temas de Pío Baroja* (Madrid: Alfaguara, 1966), pp. 103-20. See also BIRUTÉ CIPLIJAUSKAITÉ, *Baroja, un estilo* (Madrid: Insula, 1972), pp. 91-94, and EZEQUIEL GONZÁLEZ MÁS, «Pío Baroja y la novela de folletín», *Sin Nombre,* 2, No. 4 (Apr.-June, 1972), 58-67.

Honoré de Balzac (V: 838) and declared himself with pride a specialist in «literatura folletinesca» (*Las horas solitarias,* V: 233). The imaginative worlds of these literary forms, however, bear little resemblance to the world of human experience that Baroja asserted was essential to art. In fact, Northrop Frye has shown that most of popular literature is romance, an enduring, highly ritualized genre closely linked to the world of myth. Among romance's most basic features are polarized, moralistic characterization and a vertically-oriented plot that begins with a downward plunge into bondage, oscillates forward, and ends in an upward movement towards freedom, identity, and an idyllic world of more perfect order. Despite the varying accounts of displacement necessary to adapt the genre to different contexts, the fundamental elements of romance have remained the same for centuries. Frye associates the endurance of the genre with man's desire to recover sacred myth; man projects his wishes into fictional form.[15]

Baroja's enthusiasm for two apparently contradictory world views, on the one hand, the reality of everyday human experience supported by a complex contemporary philosophy of irony and skepticism, and on the other hand, the fiction of escapist adventure novels and melodrama ordered by human desire and its corresponding literary conventions, underlies the unique vision of man and history in *Memorias de un hombre de acción.* This paradoxical combination should be seen, however, as a natural development of antithetical tendencies already present in his earlier novels. In works such as *Camino de perfección* and *El árbol de la ciencia* Baroja engages with contemporary existential problems in the loose, episodic form characteristically associated with him. In *Paradox, Rey* he moves into the world of social satire and exhibits biting wit and an ironic perspective. But in two of his earliest novels, *La casa de Aizgorri* and *El mayorazgo de Labraz* (1903), Baroja displays total mastery of the conventions of romance. Despite the displacement necessary to make characters and context viable for the contemporary Spanish reading public, the simplified characterization and movement towards restored order and identity remain unmistakable. An abstract, moralizing tendency underlies this world view.

BAROJA AND ROMANCE

Baroja's moralistic stance emerges in *La casa de Aizgorri,* a melodrama, what Peter Brooks would call a displaced dramatic form of

---

[15] For a discussion of popular literature as romance see NORTHROP FRYE, *The Secular Scripture: A Study of the Structure of Romance* (Cambridge, Mass.: Harvard University Press, 1976), pp. 23-31. This book is the basis for my study of Baroja's novels as romances.

romance.[16] The novel maintains many stagelike elements: dialogue form, extensive scenery descriptions, and a vivid representational quality. As in its stage counterparts, *La casa de Aizgorri* depicts a conflict between the forces of good and evil, in which good ultimately triumphs. Peter Brooks has shown that in this regard melodrama represents the moral universe, a polarization of good and evil that symbolizes the desacralized vestiges of the world of myth. It appeals to one of the most deeply-rooted desires of man, the desire for transcendence.[17] Baroja reenacts the moral universe in this novel in which the perfect hero and heroine defeat strong enemies to obtain an idyllic existence.

He opens the novel with an examination of the economic and moral decay in a once-powerful Basque family. The Aizgorris own the distillery that employs most of the townspeople, but competition from new companies has driven them to bankruptcy, the workers to revolt, and the patriarch Don Lucio to alcoholic indulgences. Baroja sharply delineates the forces of good and evil in his characterization of the family members. The daughter Agueda, the young romance heroine, embodies virtue and innocence: «esbelta, delgada, algo rígida en sus ademanes, como es, parece evocación de las imágenes religiosas de la antigua Bizancio. Su tez pálida, sus párpados caídos, ... fuerzan a la imaginación a suponer alrededor de su figura una flordelisada aureola, como la de las vírgenes de los medievales retablos» (I: 3). Agueda's brother Luis is a worthless *señorito* drawn to womanizing and drinking. His distorted features symbolize moral deformity: «Se parece a su hermana Agueda; pero en él las facciones son borrosas e inexpresivas, la mandíbula desarrollada, los labios belfos, y los ojos, en vez de tener la expresión ensimismada y dulce de Agueda, parecen entontecidos, y sólo se animan con ráfagas de cólera» (I: 6). Both Luis and his father openly show hostility towards Agueda. Her daily torment from the family and financial worries lead to presentiments of doom and wild nightmares, as if she internalized the dark, threatening world outside her.

Other characters follow the same pattern of moral polarization as that of the Aizgorri family. The foreman Díaz occupies the role of the antagonist in the novel. He has lascivious designs on Agueda, indicated by his aggressive attitude, the rubbing of his hands, shining of his eyes, and showing of his teeth in her presence. He offers to save the distillery in

---

[16] PETER BROOKS describes melodrama as a form of romance in *The Melodramatic Imagination: Balzac, Henry James, Melodrama and the Mode of Excess* (New Haven: Yale University Press, 1976), p. 30. I will treat melodrama as a form of romance and will be using Brooks' work in conjunction with *The Secular Scripture* as a point of departure for my discussion of Baroja's early novels as romances.

[17] BROOKS, pp. 20-22. See also FRYE, «The Recovery of Myth», in *Secular Scripture*, pp. 159-88.

return for attention from Agueda, but she refuses. A subsequent argument with Don Lucio over bookkeeping leads to a vow of revenge from Díaz. He becomes the leader of the anarchic mob of striking workers who set fire to the factories at the end of the novel, a proponent of destruction and disorder. *La casa de Aizgorri* also has a powerful inanimate antagonist, the alcohol that forms the basis of the village's economy. The town doctor Don Julián, the wise old counselor who aids the romance hero and heroine, denounces alcohol for its effects on the community: «'Ese es el aspecto más triste de los efectos del alcohol; no mata, pero hace degenerar a la descendencia, seca las fuentes de la vida'» (I: 21). The evils of alcohol lie at the core of the town's degeneration and Agueda's family torment. As a result, Agueda's fate and that of the town blend into one. Mariano, a young man who owns the local foundry, aids Agueda in her struggle for survival. He acts as the romance hero, who rescues the heroine from the dark underworld and restores her to the world of light. At the same time, he tries to restore the town by purchasing Don Lucio's distillery and transforming it into an institution for the rehabilitation of diseased and crippled workers (originally Agueda's idea). Agueda will supervise the project, thereby relieving herself of the anxieties that torture her. Once again, Agueda's new identity as protector of the innocent merges with that of a new, regenerated society.

La casa de Aizgorri also displays the characteristic romance plot, common to melodrama as well. The romance opens with a downward plunge into a world of confusion and lost identity and moves upward towards anagnorisis —discovery of identity— and establishment or reestablishment of an ideal society. The plot reinforces the sharp distinction between good and evil apparent in the characterization by bringing about a resolution rewarding good, thus maintaining the perspective of the moral universe. Baroja's novel begins with a downward movement, with the romance heroine entrapped in a lower world. Besieged by financial worries and the moral and physical degeneration of her father and brother, Agueda even discourages Mariano's love for her for fear that she might pass the familiy's decay onto their offspring. The detailed descriptions of the Aizgorri home, a large, once opulent mansion now full of broken furniture, dark, half-empty rooms, and ghosts that roam at night, clearly indicate the imprisonment of this creature of light in a world of decay and death. Agueda interprets her recurrent nightmares as symptoms of madness creeping into her life. But in the course of the novel she learns that she has inherited her mother's strength rather than her father's weakness. Mariano aids Agueda's discovery of her true identity as a healthy and virtuous young woman by recognizing her as such and risking his foundry to purchase the Aizgorri distillery, to transform it into an asylum, and to bring Agueda home as his wife: «'Al cabo de cientos de años la savia enérgica de los Aizgorri no produce más que plantas enfermas y venenosas. Pero entre su floración malsana hay un lirio blanco y puro, y ése yo lo arrancaré de la casa de Aizgorri y lo llevaré donde hay sol y alegría y amor'» (I: 32).

The peripetal point occurs the night of Don Lucio's death. Luis has already fled to Madrid and Agueda remains in the house accompanied only by the faithful family servant Melchora and her loyal dog, a traditional underworld companion in romance. Her father lies dying in his room while she sees shadowy figures outside, not the ghosts she supposes they are, but rather the rebellious workers and the man paid by her father to commit arson in order to recover the insurance money for the distillery. When her father dies, Agueda's confrontation with death leads to self-discovery, the emergence of a new, strong-willed individual:

> al darse cuenta de que la muerte ha pasado por allí, cierra los ojos y espera algo, algo que va a caer sobre su alma, a hundirla para siempre en el abismo de la locura... de pronto, un impulso enérgico le dice que su razón no vacila, y ante lo inexplicable y ante la muerte, su espíritu se recoge y se siente con energía, y, victoriosa de sus terrores, entra con lentitud en la alcoba de su padre, se arrodilla junto a la cama y reza largo tiempo por el alma del muerto. (I: 37)

Brooks has defined melodrama as «an exciting and spectacular drama of persecuted innocence and virtue triumphant» and as «a drama of recognition» (pp. 26-27). At this moment in the novel, however, rather than the public, externalized, highly expressionistic recognition scene typical of melodrama and romance, Baroja presents a spectacular internalized moment of self-recognition and freedom from the bondage of her father, externalized in the charitable act of prayer for his soul. When confronted shortly afterward by the mob of striking workers who storm the house, Agueda displays her newfound will and courage by fleeing the place of bondage in the night with her dog Erbi to Mariano's workshop. Although the hero's support plays an important part in Agueda's freedom, Baroja does place the focus on the individual's confrontation with a dying, destructive world and her discovery of a reserve of inner strength to escape the dark world and enter a world of light. Baroja's concern with integrity of character, wholeness, solidity, and above all with the strength of will in facing a world of confusion and moral decadence appears in his first novel.

From this point onward the plot moves rapidly towards a happy conclusion in which virtue triumphs. In order to meet the conditions of his contract to obtain the Aizgorri property, Mariano must mold several iron machine parts by the next day. All of his workers desert him to go on strike with the exception of one, Garraiz. Eventually all of the positive characters in the novel, those who embody strength and integrity, meet in Mariano's workshop. Together Mariano, Agueda, Don Julián, and Garraiz forge the large iron wheel that insures a new life for the hero and heroine and symbolizes the virtues that they represent. This scene provides a novelistic analogue to melodramatic tableau, a visual representation summarizing emotional or moral states (Brooks, p. 62). Baroja renders this passage in a powerful expressionistic manner, not by detailed description, but rather by a striking contrast between the destructive fire of the mob outside the workshop and the fire in the forge that serves as an instrument of creation. He contrasts the violent shouts of the strikers with the harmonious collaboration of those within the workshop in founding the wheel. They successfully complete the task and *La casa de Aizgorri* ends up with Mariano's victorious entry into his house with Agueda in his arms to present her to his mother. The hero restores the heroine to her rightful place at the center of a warm maternal environment, a symbol of virtue and domesticity: «Mariano, tiznado, negro, que viene triunfante, trayendo a Agueda en sus brazos como un bárbaro que lleva robada la vestal patricial, y tras ellos, el mastín feroz, el perro, compañero eterno del hombre» (I: 49). This ideal society established at the end of the novel reaffirms the importance of a family based on love, loyalty, and personal integrity, that upholds the strength and newly-discovered will of Agueda, the individual, and promises help for the degenerated town, society, as well. The displaced ideal society of romance embodies the values of a morally-based, but middle-class perception of reality. Finally, the mob's fires of destruction blend with the light of dawn, as if to suggest that the lovers had transformed them into nightmarish illusions. This sign of hope and regeneration negates the discordant elements in the moral universe and reaffirms social order.

Along with the moralistic, simplified characterization and vertically-oriented plot common to romance and melodrama, *La casa de Aizgorri* also has the central conflict of the genres — the tension between the vision of the moral universe and the realistic details necessary for contemporary displacement (Brooks, p. 9). Such elements intrude on the romance world. For example, Don Julián's denunciation of alcohol and its hereditary effects raises the contemporary issue of determinism. Agueda's use of will to defeat the forces of decay around her indicates Baroja's belief that individual will denies determinism. Don Julián counsels her at one point, «'Sé fuerte. Ten voluntad'» (I: 25). Baroja's interest in the nature and strength of will appears throughout his works, although here in his first novel in an uncomplicated, totally affirmative context. One senses that in his very first novel he is engaging with naturalistic literature and the social Darwinism that informs it. This use of literature to explore philosophical and in particular, ontological issues, characterizes his entire literary production. Contemporary displacement also adds unusual elements

27

to the characterization of the romance hero and heroine. Agueda embodies not only the more traditional values of purity and domesticity, but also modern assertiveness and independence. The conventional trial of innocence of the romance heroine becomes in Agueda's case a trial of personal will. Similarly, Mariano reveres the ancient Basque family structure, but brings back modern metallurgical practices from his studies in England. He represents the educated young Spaniard of Baroja's time who, while he respects old customs, realizes the need for technological advance. Cases such as these provide a glimpse of an author with a keen interest in contemporary philosophical and sociological concerns despite the abstract, moralizing structure of melodrama and romance.

A scene in the town inn provides by far the most interesting example of a break with the world of romance. In short exchanges of dialogue among factory workers, townsmen, and farmers, Baroja presents some of the major problems facing Spanish society: agriculture vs. industry, Carlists vs. Liberals, and emergent organized labor vs. cottage industry loyalty. For a brief moment Baroja shifts focus from the conflict between good and evil to more topical matters, relevant socio-political concerns. This shift extends to the striking workers as well. Instead of placing them within the context of romance, he transforms them into objects of social satire. While they engage in highly energetic discussions, the Belgian anarchist Yann remains aloof and dismisses the political issues mentioned to him by Díaz. When asked by the foreman to define his position he simply describes himself as the son of Max Liebaert. Yann's mocking condescension makes the pretensions of the others seem ridiculous by comparison. Baroja puts him in the room to function as a satirist, to criticize the strikers through comic reduction. At the end of the scene, however, Yann becomes an object of satire, too. He agrees to accompany the strikers while listening distractedly to a song from a Verdi opera. He has the most unjustifiable reason of any of the workers to become involved in the strike, «'Si piensan ustedes pegar fuego a las fábricas, pueden contar conmigo'» (I: 41). Rather than hiding behind high-sounding motives, Yann reveals his sheer enjoyment of destruction. Although he assumes a superior critical position earlier, Baroja shows that Yann belongs on the same low level as the other strikers. Baroja takes the role of the social satirist by applying comic reduction to the fictional satirist.[18] The humorous effect emphasizes the pointlessness and hypocrisy of these characters' actions.

Although these contemporary preoccupations cause some tension with the moralistic world of melodrama, the idyllic conclusion of La casa de

---

[18] ROBERT C. ELLIOTT, «The Satirist Satirized: Studies of the Great Misanthropes», in The Power of Satire: Magic, Ritual, Art (Princeton: Princeton University Press, 1960), pp. 130-222.

Aizgorri ultimately neutralizes the discordant elements. The angry masses and the accompanying destructive outbursts of fire fade in the distance with the arrival of the dawn of the new society. Rarely (if ever), however, would the world of romance appear again in such pure form in Baroja's literary production. His engagement with reality made the maintenance of an idealistic moral vision of the world increasingly problematic. The harmonious integration of the individual and society became more difficult as the contemporary world intruded on the hopes and ideals of the protagonists. Happiness became more elusive and limited in scale than at the end of *La casa de Aizgorri,* in which Nature responds in kind to the optimism of the young lovers. But Baroja's moralistic vision never completely disappeared as he tirelessly explored the possibility for human happiness in a world he saw as chaotic and devoid of transcendent meaning.

The emerging conflict between the conventions of romance and the contemporary world continues in *El mayorazgo de Labraz* (1903), a more extensive treatment of the romance form. The novel exists in an earlier dramatic form, but Baroja revised it to its present narrative version.[19] I can only speculate about why he made the change, but I think Baroja realized that his art was moving in the direction of greater complexity — away from pure melodrama and towards a conscious engagement with the relationship between the individual and society, the moral universe and contemporary reality. A novelistic structure provides a better framework in which to develop these conflicts while maintaining the moralistic struggle that characterizes melodrama.[20]

The hero of this novel is Juan Labraz, the first-born son of a noble family identified with Labraz's glorious past. Like Agueda of *La casa de Aizgorri,* he finds himself entrapped in a lower world. He suffers from physical and psychological alienation on account of blindness, archaic social responsibilities, family problems, and the oppressive town of Labraz, dominated by greedy members of the clergy and selfish superstitious townspeople. Baroja represents the imprisonment of the hero visually by the town wall which, while it protects the town, locks out new ideas and progress. The Labraz house is as well a place of vast, empty rooms, darkness, and faded emblems of past splendor — the labyrinth of the romance

---

[19] FRANCISCO J. FLORES ARROYUELO, *Las primeras novelas de Pío Baroja: 1900-1912* (Murcia: La Torre de los Vientos, 1967), p. 35.

[20] BIRUTÉ CIPLIJAUSKAITÉ (in *Baroja, un estilo,* pp. 151-53) gives three major reasons for Baroja's transformation of *El mayorazgo de Labraz* from drama into novel: (1) a drama is more rigorous structurally and more limited and stylized, (2) a dramatist is at the mercy of public opinion whereas a novelist can be more individualistic in his expression, and (3) Baroja wanted to avoid the atemporalized abstraction of melodrama.

underworld. Juan Labraz appears as a morally superior hero entrapped in a morally inferior world, the falsely accused hero of romance.

Juan shows from the beginning of the novel a superior moral sense: «'Yo siempre he pedido a Dios que si me envía desgracias, deje mi alma limpia para sufrirlas. El conocer la tribulación, el analizarla, el meditarla, es ya un principio de consuelo, como el reconocer el miedo, el analizarlo y medirlo es ya un principio de valor'» (I: 79). His patient, stoic attitude has aided him in overcoming his blindness and his emotional loss of many years ago, when his sister Cesárea abandoned him to run off with Ramiro, the man taken in as a child by his mother. The same virtuous and long-suffering nature helps him endure the loss of his other sister Micaela, when she elopes with Ramiro after Cesárea's death. Juan takes the responsibility of replacing the bejeweled pieces stolen from the church by Ramiro and Micaela, sacrificing his land to pay for new ornaments. He thereby accepts the ancient obligation of the feudal lord to meet the needs of the people. Baroja associates the hero and his strength of character with Nature: «'tengo que volver al campo para encontrarme a mí mismo y para que mis inclinaciones recuperen su antigua fuerza'» (I: 124). Yet Juan Labraz also possesses a warmth of spirit easily destroyed by an insensitive world: «'Mi alma tenía el calor de las almas fuertes. El frío de fuera ha ido helándola poco a poco; era necesario que así sucediese. En medio del hielo de una Humanidad mezquina, las almas ardientes tienen que tiritar de frío... Yo, sin que nadie me quisiera, me he helado en este mundo glacial'» (I: 125). Don Juan exemplifies what Northrop Frye has described as the heroism of the romantic ethos, based on pain and endurance (*Secular Scripture*, p. 88).

Micaela and Ramiro take advantage of his goodness by committing the church theft and leaving him to deal with church and civil authorities as well as to take care of Cesárea's child Rosarito. The townspeople blame him for the crime by familial association. When Rosarito dies from an illness in spite of Juan's care, they consider it God's repayment for his sin committed with Marina, the innocent innkeeper's daughter brought to the house by the hero to care for the child. Juan Labraz undergoes a ritual death in the form of lack of will. His emotional suffering denies him the will necessary to break with the past and leave his torment behind him. The town doctor advises him on this matter: «'Deberías despertar, tener voluntad... Tienes la fortaleza de un santo o de un estoico; y lo que te pido es que seas hombre'» (I: 138). Once Juan leaves the town, however, he gradually emerges as a triumphant, strong-willed hero. He first exercises his will by burning the entire town harvest, a symbolic break with the past. On his journey to the house on the Mediterranean he exercises will once again by defending his companion Marina from the highwayman Melitón. When taken in by a shepherd and his family around Christmas time, Juan exercises wit and intellectual power by deciphering riddles and telling a story for the children after the Christmas Day banquet. The riddles and storytelling represent tests that the hero passes in order to break through the alienation and loneliness he experienced in the lower world of Labraz to ascend to a higher world. With the shepherd's family he experiences the warmth and the true sense of social communion denied him before in his life. Finally, he leaves behind his stoic, saintlike life in Labraz by recognizing and declaring his love for Marina at the end of the novel — a final exercise of will. Baroja suggests that a truly heroic figure must possess both strength of will and nobility of spirit to achieve human happiness.

Don Ramiro occupies the position of the evil antagonist in *El mayorazgo de Labraz*. Baroja's forceful portrayal of him as a creature of disorder and destruction gives him a demonic quality unmatched by any of the characters in *La casa de Aizgorri*. Ramiro describes himself as a person of pure instinct and will: «'Soy de otra raza despreciada, que no tiene más leyes que sus instintos y la libertad. He nacido del choque de pasiones salvajes, y esas pasiones rugen en mi alma como los leones en el desierto. Cuando encuentro un obstáculo en mi camino lo destruyo'» (I: 110). His combination of amorality and will contrasts sharply with the virtue and stoicism of Juan Labraz and his eventual exercise of will to protect, communicate and love. In addition to his role of antagonist, Ramiro acts as a demonic double for the hero, another conventional motif of the romance underworld (*Secular Scripture*, 117, 140-42). At the beginning of the novel, Ramiro and Cesárea arrive at the inn of Labraz in the middle of a cold, dark night. They both seem like mysterious figures bundled up in their cloaks, but when they arrive at the inn Cesárea's enfeebled condition reveals a sweet, pitiable individual whereas Ramiro's strength, aristocratic dress, handsome features, and bold flirtation with Marina, the innkeeper's daughter, lend him a Don Juanesque air of power over other people, and women, in particular. The Predicador (preacher) remembers Ramiro as a child when he first appeared in Labraz. He had traveled to the town with a band of gypsies and the King of the gypsies carried him on his shoulders. A year later the preacher found the boy wandering alone near the village, and Juan's mother doña Cesárea took him in and raised him as her own. Ramiro usurps Juan's place by gaining the affection of his mother, his sister Cesárea, and in the course of the novel his other sister Micaela. He breaks the ancient pact between the town, the clergy, and the ruling noble family that Juan strives so hard to uphold, by stealing the jeweled ornaments from the church. Ramiro's mere presence in Labraz transforms Juan into a helpless victim. But Ramiro and Micaela's departure from the city frees him from the paralyzing forces of darkness that Ramiro represents and he emerges as a heroic figure.

Ramiro unleashes his powers of disorder shortly after he arrives. Once Juan installs them in his house, Ramiro initiates a series of self-indulgent actions to satisfy his desires at the expense of others. He succeeds in ruining Marina's reputation, although the Predicator stops him from actually robbing her of her virginity. He recognizes Micaela's frustrated sensuality and pursues her with great attention. Baroja describes their affair as a struggle between two wills, each wanting to control the other. He goes to great lengths to indicate the perverted nature of their love and even utilizes setting to emphasize the fact. Micaela admits her love after sitting in a dry, abandoned garden parched by the summer heat. In one sense, the heat describes the intensity of her passion, but it also establishes a parallel between the sterility of the garden and the nature of their love: «Una sensación de sequedad, casi de ahogo, le hacía respirar con fuerza el aire de fuego que traía el aroma de las flores calcinadas por el sol» (I: 102). Ramiro, too, feels that their love has weakened him: «Sentía... que sus sentimientos, antes fuertes, inconmovibles, se deshacían, y que un principio de ternura, de necesidad de humillarse, trataba de reemplazar a su pasada frialdad» (I: 103). Although it might seem that the weakening of his will would humanize Ramiro, actually it drives him on to more monstrous actions. He devises the plan to murder his wife Cesárea by having Micaela give her an overdose of medicine. After the murder and the subsequent funeral, he develops the idea of stealing the family treasures from the chapel despite a nobleman's comment about their importance to the town: «'Si faltaran esas joyas, yo creo que la gente del pueblo le mataba a Juan'» (I: 127). This final action precipitates the hero's lowest point of cynicism and despair after the death of Rosarito and the town's abandonment of him.

The juxtaposition of hero and antagonist dominates the first half of the novel. While Juan withdraws more and more into himself suffering from isolation and lack of love, Ramiro's sphere of influence and power grows until he leaves the town of Labraz. Yet Baroja develops the conflict between the two men as more than an archetypal romance struggle between good and evil. Behind the characterization of Juan and Ramiro lies a literary response to contemporary philosophical views. In an 1899 article entitled «Nietzsche y la filosofía», Baroja shows a negative attitude towards Nietzsche's ideas, especially towards what he sees as an uncharitable lack of sympathy: «Para Nietzsche, la única misión de los pueblos es servir a sus genios, adorarlos y sacrificar ante ellos todo lo sacrificable; ésta es la moral buena; la mala es la ascética, la de piedad, porque perpetúa lo miserable y lo repulsivo» (VIII: 855-56). In the same essay Baroja describes what he sees as Nietzsche's reaction to the poor unfortunate people of the world: «Ante esos desdichados, el Zarathustra de Nietzsche tendría el supremo mérito de no dirigirles ni una mirada de compasión, ni una mirada de piedad; al contrario, se entretendría en hacerles sufrir más, o en desarrollar sus vicios y malas pasiones» (VIII: 856). Baroja's objection to Nietzsche's views has at its basis a moral ideal of compassion and love. In this early article on the philosopher, Baroja rejects what he sees as an amoral, elitist attitude towards life. Later he dramatizes his rejection of this point of view in the characterization of Ramiro and Juan Labraz. Obviously, the superiority of a strong will appeals to Baroja as his fascination with the evil powers of Ramiro illustrates. Yet the author also shows through this character that a perverted strong will appeals to the lower instincts in man and what they produce —passion, murder, and disorder— and he condemns the debased morality that drives that will. Ramiro represents Schopenhauer's notion of the «bad» man who uses his will to negate another man's will and usurp his sphere of influence. Baroja's sympathy clearly is with Juan's tender affection for his sister Cesárea and the child Rosarito, his honest commitment to satisfy the townspeople for the robbery, and finally, his acquisition of a strong will that he in turn utilizes to punish those who injured him, to protect Marina, and to share the joys of Christmas with the shepherd's family. When the hero slams his fist down on a table at the sight of a cat without an ear and a tail because some people burned them off for amusement, Baroja unquestionably strives to make the reader share Juan Labraz's moral indignation. He indicates the dangers that arise from a godlike will at the service of a morally debased man and the positive power of a strong will behind a morally sound man. Baroja exploits the conventional good/evil characterization of romance to comment on a contemporary concern, a moralistic rejection of what he perceived as Nietzschean amorality.

An analogous contrast in character exists between the romance heroine Marina and Micaela. Although flirtatious and girlish at the beginning of the novel, Marina proves herself loyal, compassionate, orderly, and loving in the course of the novel. After Micaela and Ramiro leave Labraz she cares for Rosarito and Juan tirelessly and after the child's death accompanies the hero into exile. He renames her Rosarito and she guides him on their way to the house on the Mediterranean.[21] Marina acts as the redemptive romance heroine who leads the hero out of his lower world captivity. She pulls him away from his former self and towards that of his new self, that of a strong-willed and compassionate hero. She awakens in Juan his first feelings of romantic love, realized in their kiss in the novel's final scene. Their tender love ends the novel on an affir-

---

[21] This may be a vestigial form of the incest motif, part of the underworld imagery of romance (Secular Scripture, p. 137).

mative note. Micaela, on the other hand, acts as a female counterpart to Ramiro. She appears from the beginning as snobbish, self-satisfied, and sexually repressed. Ramiro's appearance releases all of her negative energy as she becomes a willing accomplice in murder, robbery, and debauchery. Their criminal complicity points to moral decay as Ramiro and Micaela share their love in the most dusty, abandoned parts of the house inhabited by spiders and bats and littered with garbage and old clothes. Baroja emphasizes the perversion of the two lovers by indicating that their love feeds off this decay: «Subían los dos amantes a las habitaciones del piso alto y sentían como si su amor aumentase ante aquellos trastos desvencijados y polvorientos» (I: 123). Marina never abandons Juan despite the gossip of Labraz and the hardships on their journey, but Micaela gleefully falls into a lower moral state: «Sentíase, sí, hundida, rebajada ante su conciencia anterior; pero, en vez de encontrarse perturbada por esto, le sucedía todo lo contrario; hubiera querido hundirse más, encenagarse más. Al encanallarse, Micaela había encontrado su centro de gravedad» (I: 123). Baroja creates a strong archetypal distinction between the restorative, redemptive female and the sinful, destructive female in Marina and Micaela.

The opposing doubles Juan/Ramiro and Marina/Micaela establish a framework for doubling in the plot. This strengthens the ties between the romance genre and El mayorazgo de Labraz (Secular Scripture, pp. 140-44). The debased passionate love of Ramiro and Micaela generates a powerful struggle of wills that leads to a criminal partnership in murder, robbery, and abondonment of the weak and innocent. The growing love between Juan and Marina, on the other hand, creates a relationship of mutual respect and tenderness while generating strength, emotional healing, and self-discovery for them both. Ramiro and Micaela embody the dark, disruptive, evil forces of the universe while Juan and Marina represent the positive forces of love, compassion, and hope. The strength of the hero and heroine lies in their ability to break with the past and build a promising new life together. The doubling of the plot reinforces the dichotomy of the moral universe present throughout the novel.

In spite of Baroja's conformity with romance patterns in the characterization of his major characters, his treatment of the townspeople of Labraz shows an astute awareness of the problems of contemporary Spanish society. The pettiness and cruelty of the town provide a backdrop of social criticism for the conflict in the foreground of the hero with Ramiro, social conditions, and his own atrophied will. Baroja's characterization of the townspeople contradicts somewhat his criticism of Nietzsche for his lack of sympathy for ordinary people:

> Como la gente del pueblo no leía ni pensaba, todas sus energías eran únicamente vegetativas. La única ocupación moral que tenían era el denun-

ciarse y el armar pleitos. Los instintos brutales, a medias contenidos por el miedo al infierno, a medias irritados por el resquicio que la hipocresía deja a todos los vicios, habían hecho a los habitantes de Labraz de una inaudita ferocidad. (I: 99)

The narrator assumes a morally superior stance in describing the people of Labraz as mindless, brutal and bestial. Although Baroja may indicate something about the Spanish peasant and the nature of Spanish society, clearly in this passage social criticism merges with literary convention as the author sets up a collective, antagonistic force to oppose the hero.[23]

His social criticism appears most strikingly, however, in the funeral banquet following Cesárea's burial. The clergy and *hidalgos* present at the dinner indicate that Labraz has maintained the traditionally strong link between the nobility and the Church. The seating arrangement at the table suggests a hierarchic, archaic sense of social order. Baroja focuses especially on a member of the clergy, a dean whom he transforms into a grotesque, gigantic stomach. His detailed description reveals a mastery of caricature, an important element of his style throughout his career and more abundant in his satirical works. He classifies him as *clericus manducatoris* or *digestivus*: «Más que hombre, era un estómago; todos los demás órganos de su cuerpo se habían debido de atrofiar por falta de uso» (I: 116). The analogies proliferate and become more extreme as Baroja continues his satirical attack on this respected member of the community: «sus manteos y sus sotanas eran un mapamundi, en el que islas se convertían al instante en archipiélagos, y los archipiélagos en continentes» (I: 116). Baroja also presents in this scene a microcosm of the major conflicts facing Spanish society.[23] An argument arises during dinner between don Diego de Beamonte, a leading conservative *hidalgo* of Labraz, and his nephew Antonio, a young druggist and champion of social reform. Don Diego represents the old hierarchical values, belief in tradition, and rule by force and birthright. Antonio, on the other hand, believes in *regeneración* and the pursuit of liberty and justice. In these two figures Baroja dramatizes the contemporary Spanish struggle between generations and the values they uphold. In the discussion between Antonio and the Englishman Bothwell that follows the dinner, Baroja utilizes his skeptical fictional spokesman to indicate that he has little respect for either extreme position. Bothwell condemns material progress as a panacea for social ills, laments the lack of true heroes to guide society, and criticizes the ignorance of don Diego. The scene in which civil and religious leaders of the village insist that Juan Labraz finance replacements for the stolen chapel jewels provides evidence of Baroja's moral denun-

---

[22] ROBERT B. KNOX discusses the portrayal of Labraz as a collective villain in «The Structure of *El mayorazgo de Labraz*», *Hispania*, 38 (1955), p. 289.

[23] FLORES, *Las primeras novelas*, p. 38.

ciation of the archaic social order. The officials' visit forms a travesty of the ancient pact among civil leaders, church authorities, and the nobles to work together with mutual respect for one another, for the good of the people, and the community as a whole. The powerful men take advantage of the helpless, morally superior hero to protect their own reputations. Baroja attracts the reader's sympathy for Juan and the virtues he represents by placing the values he symbolizes at odds with those of the fallen, decadent world of Labraz.

Although I have pointed out the elements of social criticism and contemporary awareness in Baroja's treatment of the townspeople of Labraz and even in the emergence of certain satirical tendencies, this aspect of the novel clearly merges with the characterization and structure of romance. Just as the romance world incorporates the violent striking workers in *La casa de Aizgorri* despite their contemporary social relevance, the conflicts and decay of Labraz appear as part of the romance underworld in *El mayorazgo de Labraz*. As Marina and Juan move farther away from the town, the concern with contemporary society fades more into the background and the movement in the direction of an archetypal romance pattern towards deliverance and restoration becomes evident.

The plot of *El mayorazgo de Labraz* conforms with the traditional plot of romance. The novel begins with the hero's downward plunge into a disordered world. Ramiro's appearance in Labraz after many years transforms an already decaying society into depravity and social chaos and destroys the stable, though somewhat stoic existence of Juan Labraz. The low point of the downward movement occurs at Rosarito's death when the hero experiences the greatest alienation. The tragedy incites Juan to break his ties with Labraz by burning down the village's harvest and to set off for his Mediterranean home accompanied only by Marina. From this point onward the plot moves upward towards restoration as Juan and Marina go through a series of adventures, «trials», that culminate with the Christmas feast in the shepherd's house celebrating the birth of a child as well as the holiday. Juan and Marina's declaration of love for one another ends the final climactic scene of the novel.

Baroja employs changes of atmosphere and setting to heighten the effects of plot movement. The story opens with Ramiro's and Cesárea's arrival in Labraz on a cold winter night, an occurrence which initiates a series of mysterious, fateful events. The visit to the monastery during which Micaela and Ramiro fall in love occurs in the spring, traditionally the season of awakening desire. The scene of passion between the two in the deserted garden takes place in the summer heat. Cesárea's murder happens in the autumn, the season of decay and death. Finally, Marina and Juan flee Labraz in the fall and cross the snowy mountains during the bleak winter months, but declare their love for one another in spring, the season of love, rebirth, and renewal of hope.

As in *La casa de Aizgorri*, the romance pattern of the struggle between good and evil with the eventual triumph of good remains intact in *El mayorazgo de Labraz*. While contemporary socio-political issues appear in the background —the decay of cities and countryside, the lack of planning for the future, the conflicts between generations and between progressives and conservatives, the decay of an archaic class structure— Baroja asserts the power of a heroic will to overcome these limitations and attain a more idealized form of existence. Juan Labraz overcomes the obstacles in his path in his search for identity and self-fulfillment as the romance world upholds the moral universe and absorbs the problematic contemporary issues in the novel.

The structure of melodrama and romance that underlies *La casa de Aizgorri* and *El mayorazgo de Labraz* reveals the author's need to order the world in terms of the moral universe, as a struggle between good and evil. In these novels the protagonists' essential goodness and strong will prove sufficient to defeat the forces of decadence and evil present in the world around them. The abstracting quality of the genre neutralizes the more topical, intrusive material present in the texts and the narrative structure ends on an optimistic note with the restoration of identity and social order. *Camino de perfección* (1902), *El árbol de la ciencia* (1911), and *Paradox, Rey* (1906), however, reveal a different ordering impulse and attitude towards reality. Baroja no longer presents life as an abstract battleground for the forces of good and evil, but rather as an indomitable, varied process of conflict and change. Baroja maintains his novelistic focus on the individual and the assertion of will, but the relationship itself between man and the world becomes problematic. The destruction of evil, self-discovery, and the attainment of happiness no longer occur simultaneously if they occur at all. Instead, the desire for meaning and direction in life motivates the protagonists and often leads to ironic or tragic moments of defeat. In contrast to the heroes and heroines of romance, Fernando Ossorio and Andrés Hurtado struggle to cope with an everyday reality from which they feel alienated. Their search for vital fulfillment leads them through a series of crises, characterized by alternating phases of neurotic activity and paralysis, and ends ironically or tragically. The focus on individual growth and the episodic structure with philosophical underpinnings tie these novels with the *Bildungsroman* tradition. In essence, the quasi-autobiographical experiences of these agonized protagonists represent an education for life. A pessimistic view of the world emerges from the often despairing tone of these works, a reflection of Baroja's engagement with contemporary society and philosophical currents. In *Paradox, Rey*, Baroja enters the world of satire, a world of fantasy, irony, humor, caricature, and self-defeat. His biting tone, the debased nature of most of the characters, and the dislocation of the conventional sense of time and space, reveal his own critical moralistic vision of contemporary society. The three protagonists of these works exercise greater mobility than Juan Labraz or Agueda Aizgorri as their fictional lives become both a physical and spiritual quest for meaning in life.[24] As a result, the romance structure of the earlier novels either fades into the background or seems to disappear as Baroja strives to order the world in terms of a psychological and sensorial experience of everyday reality or in terms of the moralistic, but fantastic, distorting techniques of social satire.

THE SEARCH FOR IDENTITY

As the title suggests, Baroja's *Camino de perfección* (subtitled *pasión mística*) is a modern counterpart to Saint Teresa of Avila's 1583 guide to the perfect religious life and the way to God. Like Saint Teresa, Baroja employs the metaphor of the journey to represent an internalized spiritual quest, although he realizes the image literally in his protagonist Fernando Ossorio's wanderings about Spain. Ossorio's experiences describe an educational process of reconciliation with life in which the changing landscape provides an objective correlative for his secularized spiritual growth. His adventures inevitably lead to a confrontation with the mysticism of the past and a recognition that sixteenth-century mysticism remains only as an art form, not as a viable means of directing and defining one's life. Ossorio discovers that in the modern world only the embracing of vital experiences offers spiritual fulfillment for the individual. This tormented character embodies the existential problems facing the young Spaniards of Baroja's generation. In the introductory section narrated by an unidentified «I», Ossorio describes his present decadent state as the result of a childhood conflict between the influences of a fanatically religious, superstitious nurse and a Voltairean, skeptical grandfather. He cannot integrate these two opposing aspects of his personality and find peace and fulfillment in life. This is an indication of how painfully aware Baroja and his contemporaries were of the anguish that arises from the conflict between rational thought and irrational impulses within the individual.

Baroja indicates his purpose in writing *Camino de perfección* in the introductory section of the novel. The unidentified narrator encounters

---

[24] PETER EARLE discusses these three novels as part of the *Bildungsroman* tradition and as a group in which the journeys of the heroes lead inevitably to disillusionment in «Baroja y su ética de la imposibilidad», *Cuadernos Hispanoamericanos*, Nos. 265-67 (July-Sept. 1972), pp. 68-71.

the protagonist at an art exhibition displaying one of his paintings entitled *Horas de silencio*. The picture represents young people seated in poor middle-class surroundings. In the background, the profile of an industrial city looms threateningly, as if in anticipation of devouring the youngsters. Ossorio conveys through his artwork his sensibility to the plight of modern man, victimization by his own technology. In fact, he defines art as a response to life: «'no es un conjunto de reglas, ni nada, sino que es la vida: el espíritu de las cosas reflejado en el espíritu del hombre'» (VI: 12). Ossorio acts as a mouthpiece for Baroja with this definition.[25] Similarly, the spiritual message that lies behind *Camino de perfección* mirrors that of Ossorio's picture. Just as Ossorio uses pictorial representation to convey a contemporary man's anguish at the encroachment of machines on youthful vitality, Baroja uses the novel and the fictional experiences of his protagonist to express contemporary man's existential anguish in finding meaning in life and to supply a life-affirming model for his readers. Baroja emphasizes the contemporary relevance of the educational experience contained in his novel. Instead of abstracting human experience to the level of the moral universe, Baroja wants to capture everyday reality as it is reflected in the consciousness of a sensitive young man. His focus on the internal and external conflicts of individual experience gives *Camino de perfección* an intense, secularized spiritual quality.

The simultaneity of Ossorio's spiritual and physical journeys makes characterization and action in the novel inseparable. His process of self-discovery constitutes the entire book, in which the different phases of personal growth culminate in Valencia, where he attains spiritual equanimity. Fernando begins his journey in Madrid after the funeral of his grandfather's uncle when he moves into his aunts' house. He enters an initial period of asceticism in which he strives to nullify the world of physical sensations: «El ideal de su vida era un paisaje intelectual, frío, limpio, puro, siempre cristalino, con una claridad blanca, sin un sol bestial» (VI: 23). Despite these ideals, however, Ossorio becomes involved sexually with his Aunt Laura. Their relationship lacks any spiritual quality and Fernando finds himself suffocating in bestial pleasure. He feels enormous oppression and gradually slips into an agitated, enervated state in which his rational powers desert him as he attempts levitation and begins to imagine sights and sounds around him. Ossorio finally leaves Madrid to travel with the hope that physical exertion will cure him. This initial phase of Fernando's education sets up a paradigm for the rest of the novel's structure. Each episode or group of episodes explores the viability of certain philosophical or spiritual ideals as a way of

---

[25] JOSÉ ALBERICH, «Baroja: agnosticismo y vitalismo», in his *Los ingleses*, 13-35, at pp. 20-23.

endowing the individual's life with meaning and direction. The protagonist slips in and out of these episodes with varying degrees of success (usually failing) before eventually achieving vitalistic fulfillment at the end of the novel.

After Ossorio leaves Madrid, he wanders aimlessly about Castile encountering a variety of individuals and towns and seeing the arid landscape and the crumbling architectural structures within it as external counterparts to his internal emotional state. The next major step in his attempt to cope with the world occurs at the monastery of El Paular. The sight of a bishop's tomb stimulates thoughts about the cycle of nature: «¡Qué hermoso poema el del cadáver del obispo en el campo tranquilo! ¡Qué alegría la de los átomos al romper la forma que les aprisionaba, al fundirse con júbilo en la nebulosa del infinito, en la senda del misterio donde todo se pierde!» (VI: 41). This celebration signals a new awareness and awe before Nature. In the background, the image of the fountain endlessly renewing itself acts as a leitmotif throughout the episodes at the monastery. It reinforces Ossorio's awakening to the forces of Nature and life and emphasizes their cyclical pattern, «y seguía cantanto la fuente, invariable y monótona, su eterna canción no comprendida...» (VI: 43). Baroja indicates with these lines the fundamental inexplicability of life. But rather than trying to order and explain experience, he suggests that living and celebrating life endow it with the only meaning it can have. The German Schultze, whom Ossorio meets at the monastery, acts as his guide in learning this lesson. Schultze dismisses Ossorio's preoccupation with metaphysical problems as a waste of energy and recommends exercise as a means of overcoming his neurotic states. He introduces Nietzsche into the conversation and defends him when Ossorio accuses the philosopher of egotism.[26] Schultze's appreciation of the landscape awakens in Fernando a sensitivity to the beauty and grandeur of the natural world.

Ossorio, however, returns to his previous neurotic state after this introduction to vitalism. He becomes so obsessed with his problems that the heat and light of the bleak landscape drive him into a blind fever. In Toledo and Yécora he finally reaches the low point of his physical and spiritual degeneration. Fernando visits the El Greco painting *El entierro del Conde de Orgaz* several times during his visit to Toledo. He interrogates the artwork, a symbol of a viable life-directing force in the past, to see if it has maintained that viability. Ultimately his searching examination of the painting leads only to painful disillusionment. El Greco's work maintains solely an aesthetic appeal for the viewer, not a vital, spiritual one. As a result, Ossorio realizes that he cannot recapture that

---

[26] GONZALO SOBEJANO, «Componiendo *Camino de perfección*», *Cuadernos Hispanoamericanos*, Nos. 265-67 (July-Sept. 1972), pp. 475-76.

spirit of mysticism and falls into an even greater state of anguish. The social forces of the present fail him as well as the spiritual ones of the past. The architecture of Yécora bespeaks the artificiality of contemporary society. The buildings have a utilitarian, symmetrical air about them that denies Nature, and they even lack the aesthetic appeal of Toledo's buildings and religious artifacts. The Yécora visit leads to a denunciation of Spanish social institutions, especially the educational system that provides the basis for massive corruption: «De allí había brotado la anemia moral de Yécora; de allí había salido aquel mundo de pequeños caciques, de curas viciosos, de usureros; toda aquella cáfila de hombres que se pasaban la vida bebiendo y fumando en la sala de un casino».[27] The system brutalizes the individual and deprives him of the capacity for higher feelings.

Before he reached Yécora Fernando had decided that it would be his turning point: «esperaba que allí su voluntad desmayada se rebelase y buscara una vida enérgica, o que concluyera de postrarse aceptando definitivamente una existencia monótona y vulgar» (VI: 91). Once his search for meaning and direction in life totally fails in Yécora, he finally begins to find it. From Yécora he travels to Marisparza where physical labor and close contact with Nature make him forget his former preoccupations: «Todo lo que se había excitado en Madrid y en Toledo iba remitiendo en Marisparza. Al ponerse en contacto con la tierra, ésta le hacía entrar en la realidad» (VI: 98). As Fernando adopts the vitalist philosophy of Nietzsche introduced to him by Schultze he becomes capable of attaining human happiness. His appreciation of Nature leads to an all-embracing acceptance of life, and death as an aspect of life: «Si la muerte es depósito, fuente manantial de vida, ¿a qué lamentar la existencia de la muerte? No, no hay que lamentar nada. Vivir y vivir..., esa es la cuestión» (VI: 111). Ossorio completes his reconciliation with life in Valencia, where he falls in love with and marries his cousin Dolores.

Despite Ossorio's achievement of spiritual contentment at the end of the novel, Baroja undercuts that happiness with an ironic conclusion. In the final scene Ossorio contemplates his infant son. He plans to raise the child close to Nature and to his own instincts in order to spare the boy the existential problems he had experienced. Ossorio's mother-in-law plans otherwise: «Y mientras Fernando pensaba, la madre de Dolores cosía en la faja que había de poner al niño una hoja doblada del Evangelio» (VI: 129). This conflict of interests recalls Ossorio's own internal struggle at the beginning of Camino de perfección between the impulses derived from his religious nurse and those from his skeptical grandfather. Baroja

---

[27] Pío BAROJA, Camino de perfección, 3rd ed. (Madrid, 1920; rpt. New York: Las Américas, n.d.), p. 150. This passage is censored from the edition of the novel that appears in the OC.

ironically undermines the protagonist's final emotional stability by suggesting that Ossorio's son will have to face the same struggle. He indicates that each individual must find his own direction in life and that no preconceived system of values can resolve the essentially problematic nature of reality. Baroja's awareness of this difficult existential dilemma and his commitment to the celebration of life, its variety and vitality, give his work its peculiar paradoxical quality:

> Su obra se puede describir como una crónica de la vida en el campo de su experiencia, a la vez vasto y limitado; como una exaltación narrativa de los valores *naturales* de la vida en el marco de su pesimismo cósmico, de su visión intrascendente del mundo. Cogido en la trampa de su agnosticismo religioso y filosófico, trató oscuramente de reorganizar su jerarquía de valores dentro de los límites de ese agnosticismo, sin intentar forzarlos con ninguna metafísica.[28]

The structure of *Camino de perfección* reflects this vision of reality. Instead of the moralistic characterization of romance, and the complicated web of subplots, intercalated stories, and doubling effects of *La casa de Aizgorri* and *El mayorazgo de Labraz*, *Camino de perfección* exhibits a loose, rambling, episodic structure that follows the single plot line of an individual's educational journey. This structure permits Baroja to examine with a critical eye subjects like the nature of Spanish institutions, the structure of Spanish society, and the effects of industrialization on the modern world. Rather than abstracting vital experience to a level closer to myth, Baroja explores contemporary existential problems with psychological depth by focusing on the individual and on current philosophical ideas as a viable means of coping with everyday experience. The novel's ironic ending points out both the relevance and the relativity of the protagonist's solution to existential problems, a very different perspective from the optimistic, moralistic transcendence with which the other two novels end.

In spite of these contrasts, though, *Camino de perfección* maintains vestiges of the romance structure. The novel begins with Fernando Ossorio's entrapment in the nightmarish world of his aunts' house. There he succumbs to the nervous disorder that paralyzes him psychologically and physically. This phase corresponds to the underworld of romance in which the hero assumes a deathlike state. As Ossorio commences his journey, the episode at El Paular provides a glimpse of the way out of the underworld and into the world of light and life. This positive vision breaks the downward swing of romance and helps create the oscillating movement typical of the genre. The low point of the downward movement occurs at Toledo and Yécora where Ossorio's battle with heat and light, and his internal psychological struggle reach a climax. The fog transforms

---

[28] ALBERICH, «Baroja: agnosticismo», p. 34.

Toledo into the underworld symbol of the labyrinth: «Las calles subían y bajaban, no tenían alguna salida. Era aquello un laberinto; la luz eléctrica, tímida de brillar en la mística ciudad, alumbraba débilmente, rodeaba cada lámpara por un nimbo espectral» (VI: 78). The monotony of Yécora's architecture and the uniform mediocrity and brutality of the townspeople creates a similar underworld atmosphere. After Toledo and Yécora the upward movement of the romance structure begins with Ossorio's recovery in Marisparza. The protagonist's closeness to nature signal his awakening to vitality and beauty. The upward movement ends with Ossorio's reconciliation with life in Valencia where he gains a new identity as husband, father, and celebrator of the beauty of Nature. The two important women in Fernando's life indicate the direction of his movement in the novel. At the initiation of his education, Laura dominates his life. She is destructive and mannish, and possesses a sterile sensuality. Ossorio compares her at one point to a snake. His wife Dolores, on the other hand, displays the redemptive, restorative qualities of the romance heroine. Ossorio describes her in terms of the water imagery that functions positively in the novel: «pensaba que él era como un surtidor de la Naturaleza que se reflejaba en sí mismo, y Dolores el gran río donde afluía él» (VI: 124). One critic, F. G. Sarriá, has discussed the structure of *Camino de perfección* in terms of a movement from episodes centered on the sun and related symbols to episodes centered on water and related images.[29] As I have shown, however, these systems of symbols form only one aspect of the latent romance structure that underlies the novel. Baroja undercuts the potential for an optimistic romance ending, though, by limiting the vision of a transcendent reality to Fernando's experience alone and suggesting that the next generation will continue his existential struggle.

Andrés Hurtado, the anguished protagonist of *El árbol de la ciencia*, fails to attain the limited satisfaction and happiness of Fernando Ossorio. Like Ossorio, Andrés begins his educational journey in search of direction in life from deep dissatisfaction with career, family, and Spanish society in general. He undergoes a series of crises —professional disillusionment, the death of his younger brother, a stifling job in a small village, the death of his wife and child— that lead to his tragic suicide at the end of the novel. Hurtado's experiences provide ample opportunity for Baroja to offer a striking indictment of the brutality and mediocrity that pervade contemporary Spanish society, especially of the educational institutions that mold personal character. Baroja expresses through his protagonist a pessimistic view of human life, particularly of those ill-adapted to the materialism and impersonality that dominate society. Unlike the hero of

[29] F. G. SARRIÁ, «Estructura y motivos de *Camino de perfección*», *Romanische Forschungen*, 83 (1971), p. 248.

Camino de perfección, Andrés Hurtado cannot escape the despair that inevitably arises from a sensitive individual's encounter with a harsh reality.

Just as Ossorio's embracing of life represents Baroja's own vitalism and reassessment of Nietzschean ideas, Hurtado's experiences reflect Baroja's study of Schopenhauer's *The World as Will and Representation.*[30] As E. Inman Fox has pointed out, Hurtado's uncle and spiritual counselor, Iturrioz, offers him two solutions to the sensitive man's disillusionment with everyday life:

> ante la vida no hay más que dos soluciones prácticas para el hombre sereno: o la abstención y la contemplación indiferente de todo, o la acción limitándose a un círculo pequeño. Es decir, que se puede tener el quijotismo contra una anomalía; pero tenerlo contra una regla general, es absurdo (II: 493).[31]

Hurtado cannot find peace with either of his uncle's suggestions. His withdrawal into a contemplative life as a country physician in Alcolea del Campo ends in boredom and ultimately in an outburst of will in sexual activity. His life with Lulú, limited to the confines of their home, ends with life's intrusion in the form of his wife's pregnancy, life's corollary death (Lulú and the baby), and Andrés' final assertion of will in the act of suicide. The protagonist's entire vital experience in the novel provides a fictional representation of Schopenhauer's notion that life oscillates between suffering and boredom.[32] But this does not account completely for Andrés' existential dilemma. At the center of his internal conflict lies his inability to reconcile himself with life. Andrés possesses the absurd quixotism that Iturrioz mentions, the inability to accept the essential animal nature of human beings that he encounters daily as a doctor. Rather than compromise himself by striving for limited accomplishments in the human domain, under the symbol of the Tree of Life, Andrés rejects Nature to search for absolute truths, the domain of the Tree of Knowledge. Iturrioz warns him that his dogged pursuit of knowledge is a dangerous quest, «Estás perdido... Ese intelectualismo no te puede llevar a nada bueno'» (II: 507). In fact, Iturrioz draws to his nephews' attention the destructive potential of his devotion to truth, «'Yo, en el fondo, estoy convencido de que la verdad en bloque es mala para la vida. Esa anomalía de la Naturaleza que se llama vida necesita estar basada en el capricho, quizá en la mentira'» (II: 510). Iturrioz's insistence on the necessity of vitality and the relativity of truth indicates Baroja's

---

[30] On Baroja's vitalism see ALBERICH, «Baroja: agnosticismo», pp. 27-34, and CARMEN IGLESIAS, *El pensamiento de Pío Baroja: ideas centrales,* Clásicos y Modernos, 12 (México: Antigua Librería Robredo, 1963), p. 50.

[31] E. INMAN FOX, «Baroja and Schopenhauer», *Revue de Littérature Comparée,* 37 (1963), 355-59.

[32] FOX, p. 357.

acceptance of the life-affirming aspects of Nietzsche's philosophy.[33] The conclusion of *El árbol de la ciencia* confirms this. The voice of an unknown visitor indicates that Nature, scorned by Andrés, might have saved Lulú and the baby: «'Yo no conozco este caso, pero ¿quién sabe? Quizá esta mujer, en el campo, sin asistencia ninguna, se hubiera salvado. La Naturaleza tiene recursos que nosotros no conocemos'» (II: 569). Hurtado poisons himself in a despairing response to these words because science, the object of his devotion, could not save his wife and child. Ironically, he dies a victim of the Tree of Knowledge, from his own unwillingness to embrace the Tree of Life. Yet paradoxically, that act affirms life since as an act of the will it pulls the protagonist out of his contemplative existence. In typical Baroja fashion, the novel ends without resolving the central conflict between Life and Knowledge, Action and Contemplation, Nietzsche and Schopenhauer. Baroja merely addresses the problem in an apostrophic concluding statement by one of the doctors, «'Pero había en él algo de precursor'» (II: 569). He implies ambiguously that Hurtado is a forerunner either of those who will solve the dilemma or of a whole generation of men who will face the same problems — a typically paradoxical and ironic conclusion for a Baroja novel.

In *El árbol de la ciencia* as in *Camino de perfección*, Baroja explores fundamental existential problems and expands in fictional form his own engagement with contemporary philosophy as a means of dealing with everyday life. The young Baroja confronts his own existential dilemma by recreating his personal experiences and philosophical meditations in fictional form, just as Fernando Ossorio and Andrés Hurtado search for direction and meaning in life through personal experience and the guidance of their spiritual counselors Schultze and Iturrioz. The displaced mythical world of popular literature, the moral universe in which good always triumphs over evil, becomes the complex contemporary world of flux, uncertainty, paradox, relativism, irony, and tragedy.

BAROJA AND SATIRE

Some critics identify the inherently critical attitude of such a vision of the world as the perspective of the real Baroja. José Alberich describes him as a defender of truth above all, a destructive and critical agnostic who wishes to fight wrongs and delusion.[34] Carmen Iglesias extrapolates from Baroja's own comments about novels and writing that «la misión del escritor es criticar, satirizar, deshacer la falsedad y la mentira».[35] Both of these descriptions link Baroja's aesthetic view with satire: «The purpose

[33] IGLESIAS, p. 50.
[34] ALBERICH, p. 24.
[35] IGLESIAS, p. 158.

of satire is, through laughter and invective, to cure folly and to punish evil: but if it does not achieve this purpose, it is content to jeer at folly and to expose evil to bitter contempt».[36] In fact, when pushed to the extreme, Baroja's engagement with society and philosophical ideas and his accompanying ironic, pessimistic vision of the world produce satire. Satirical elements appear in all four of the previously discussed novels —reductive techniques, caricature, irony, pessimism— and Baroja's keen critical eye and awareness of the problematic nature of human existence lend themselves easily to this literary genre. Furthermore, Scholes and Kellogg have pointed out the dependency of satire on genres that support the existence of a higher world:

> Satire depends on notions of the ideal proper to epic, romance, and sacred myth, namely that the ideal world is good and the real world is bad; hence satire naturally flourishes when the world is in transition from an ideally oriented moral scheme of the cosmos to an empirically oriented non-moral schema. (p. 112)

This transition from romantic to positivistic impulses describes the intellectual shift that occurred over the nineteenth century, but especially during the latter half of the century as Baroja acquired intellectual and artistic maturity and as philosophers like Nietzsche challenged the entire system of values for Western civilization. Social criticism cedes to social satire in *Paradox, Rey,* in which Baroja assumes the moralistic point of view of the satirist to expose, judge, and tear down the degraded contemporary world rather than construct a moral universe from a very imperfect reality.

Paradox, Rey opens with a discussion between the eccentric inventors Silvestre Paradox and Avelino Diz de la Iglesia, in which they agree to leave Spain to colonize the Cananí region of Guinea. They depart on the ship Cornucopia, accompanied by crew members and other colonists from a variety of national backgrounds and professions: representatives of the government, soldiers, manufacturers, and scientists. During the voyage a storm blows up that washes the captain overboard. A sailor assumes command of the ship, but the ship drifts aimlessly in a dense fog for a week and the passengers separate into two opposing factions. One group takes a boat and leaves. Paradox and his friends remain onboard the vessel and eventually shipwreck on the shore of an unknown land. Natives capture and carry them to Bu-tata, the capital of Uganga, where they encounter a hostile, barbaric society ruled by the corrupt king Kiri and the superstitious high priest Bagú. In spite of their guards, the colonists recapture their guns and convince a group of natives to

---

[36] GILBERT HIGHET, *The Anatomy of Satire* (Princeton: Princeton University Press, 1962), p. 156.

aid their escape with promises of rum, salt pork, beans, and pretty women as rewards. With the help of these natives, Paradox and his companions establish Fortunate-House, an island fortress from which they sustain a subsequent attack by Kiri's followers. Eventually, a revolt in Bu-tata leads to the king's death, the founding of a new society run by the colonists, and Paradox's coronation. The colonists and natives live for a while in harmony in an idyllic society that brings prosperity and happiness to all. An invasion by the French Foreign Legion destroys the community, bringing it a more traditional Western civilization. The novel ends with a brief postscript describing Uganga three years later as a corrupt country in which syphilis, tuberculosis, and alcoholism run rampant. A clipping from the newspaper *L'Echo* summarizes a priest's speech in which he praises the army for its actions and offers thanks to God for bringing Christianity to Uganga.

In this brief dialogue novel, Baroja employs masterfully the conventions of satire to attack the pretensions of Western civilization in general and Spanish society in particular. He assumes a moralistic judgmental stance as he reveals the truth about modern society, its corruption, empty ideals, and debased nature through caricature, irony, lively humor, and flights of fantasy that include talking animals, incredible objects, and illogical actions.[37] Baroja's fundamental technique in expressing his satirical vision of reality in *Paradox, Rey* is the juxtaposition of sharply contrasting world views.[38] Certain incidents at the beginning of the novel establish the precedent for this procedure. The day before Paradox and Diz depart they join other guests at the hotel for an expedition on horseback. At a stop during the journey, General Pérez and a doctor force whisky down a rooster's throat for amusement. They laugh as the animal staggers about and exclaims, «'¡Que Dios castigue a estos desconocidos que así turban el reposo espiritual de un buen padre de familia!'» (II: 160). Paradox withdraws from the group in outrage at their cruelty. Although the rooster's describing himself as the head of a family gives the statement a ludicrous quality, the animal's humanized behavior emphasizes the debased actions of the human beings. The profession of the two men, one a representative of the powerful military structure and the other a member of a profession committed to helping others, heightens the reader's critical response to their actions. While riding back to the

---

[37] NORTHROP FRYE discusses the characteristics of Menippean satire on pp. 308-11 of the *Anatomy of Criticism*. He defines the satirical attitude as a combination of fantasy and morality (p. 310).

[38] HIGHET states (in *The Anatomy of Satire*, pp. 158-59) that the central problem of satire is its relation to reality. Satire strives both to criticize and to tell the truth. It achieves this goal in two ways: (1) By presenting a ridiculous, debased picture of the world as if it were real, (2) By contrasting our world with a vision of another world. In *Paradox, Rey* Baroja uses both of these methods.

hotel the group encounters a shepherd returning from a day's work. He strolls along singing and speaks with contentment about his life: «'El camino nunca es largo para el que tiene el corazón tranquilo'» (II: 162). The shepherd's humble existence, his closeness to the land, and inner tranquility contrast with the distasteful pretensions of the doctor and general. Baroja's deliberate placement of the shepherd in this episode provides an early indication in the text of where his moral sympathy lies.

The juxtaposition generates the larger contrast in Uganga between the two dystopias, the kingdom of Kiri and the French colony at the end of the novel, and the single utopia, the kingdom of Paradox. In Kiri's regime Baroja offers a satirical view of Spanish society, in which a small privileged class composed of the royal family, the nobles, and the military oppresses the masses. True to the conventions of satire, Baroja presents the characters in terms of their social functions rather than as distinct individuals (*Anatomy of Criticism,* p. 309). King Kiri is a bored, egotistical, lascivious lout who entertains himself by conquering large numbers of females and killing little birds. His prime minister Funangué, who wears a three-cornered hat and military epaulets, is characterized by stupidity and self-interest. Bagú, the high priest of Uganga, is a superstitious individual. He uses balls of dung to determine the future and worships the moon.[39] With these three figures Baroja denounces the three most powerful divisions of the Spanish ruling class, the king, the military, and the church, stressing their cruelty, self-interest, and lack of concern for the common people. The «civilized» Frenchmen who recapture Uganga at the end of *Paradox, Rey* bring back the corruption and oppression of Kiri's rule. Although a European power administers the new colonial government, Baroja shows that the «uncivilized» native government and the «civilized» government are equals in terms of amorality and social injustice.

Unlike some satirists, however, Baroja provides a glimpse of an ideal society among the negative worlds of the novel. Ironically, the eccentric, addled Paradox establishes the idyllic world and acts as a mouthpiece for many of Baroja's own views about morality and justice. In this respect he plays the role of the wise fool in satire.[40] In Paradox's kingdom, a benevolent monarch and group of officials rule the people with their best interests in mind. Everyone owns and works the land and neither slaves nor money is permitted. The schools offer only practical education and technology serves man rather than victimizes him. Paradox's chief

[39] JUDITH GINSBERG describes the structure of *Paradox, Rey* and the significance of the social structures in the fictional world in «Pío Baroja: The Transformation of Politics into Art (1900-1911).» Diss. City University of New York 1976, pp. 147-54.

[40] ALVIN B. KERNAN, *The Plot of Satire* (New Haven: Yale University Press, 1965), p. 82.

advisers embody positive social functions as well. The naturalist and geologist Thonelgeben respects Nature, but uses his knowledge to harness Nature's forces to help the people. The British manufacturer Sipsom possesses pragmatism and common sense, both qualities admired greatly by Baroja. He assumes the role of judge for the community and administers justice with fairness. Simplicity, good will, and closeness to Nature summarize Paradox's notion of government — all qualities represented by the shepherd in the opening scenes of the novel. The prosperity and vitality of his rule contrast with the brutalized, corrupt forces that destroy that idyllic world. At the heart of his society Paradox places a carousel, an object that paradoxically symbolizes both the innocent laugher and play of childhood and man's headlong, pointless rush towards death:

> ¡Oh, nobles caballos! ¡Amables y honrados caballos!... Allí donde vais reina la alegría. Cuando aparecéis por los pueblos formados en círculo, colgando por una barra del chirriante aparato, todo el mundo sonríe, todo el mundo se regocija. Y, sin embargo, vuestro sino es cruel, porque, lo mismo que los hombres, corréis desesperadamente y sin descanso, y, lo mismo que los hombres, corréis sin objeto y sin fin... (II: 216)

The carousel combines the comic and tragic aspects of life. Its central location at the plaza of Bu-tata suggests that this fantastic society has somehow captured the enigmatic, paradoxical quality of life itself. The carousel also symbolizes the world of *Paradox, Rey* in that like the play object, the central part of the novel projects a vision of an idyllic, peaceful world, but the overall structure reminds the reader of the futility of human existence. In the middle of a distorted, humorous interpretation of reality, Baroja places a more perfect world.

Paradox, Rey also presents a different way of ordering the world. Instead of the ascending movement towards discovery and restoration typical of romance, and the episodic, semi-autobiographical movement of the philosophical novels, this novel displays the disjunctiveness typical of the plot of satire.[41] In *Paradox, Rey* Baroja gives no sense of a logical progression, but rather juxtaposes contrasting scenes and social values. The intellectual content and humorous, ironic tone endow the scenes with meaning rather than psychological motivation or causality. Instead of change or movement in a particular direction, the satirical plot moves in a circle. The collapse of Kiri's reign and the success of Paradox's new government seem to signal growth in a positive direction, but the arrival of the French destroys the idyllic world and restores corruption and disorder comparable to that of the original government. The futility and self-defeating structure of the plot reinforces the pessimistic, ironic view that Baroja expresses throughout the satire. He

---

[41] KERNAN, pp. 100-03.

generates an overall impression of collapse and descent in *Paradox, Rey,* in which one society appears only to disintegrate into another. The instability and fragmentation in the narrative convey Baroja's negative moralistic attitude just as much as the implicit criticism in the societal contrasts and the explicit criticism in characters' statements within the text.

Paradox, Rey provides a fitting conclusion to this study of Baroja's earlier works. His vision of the world in both the earlier and later novels reveals a paradoxical attitude towards reality. As in the case of the carousel at the heart of Paradox's perfect society, Baroja sees both the idyllic, childlike aspects of life and its grim, fateful, futile qualities. The range of literary genres, tones, and themes in his earlier works reflects this paradoxical vision. In the romances, Baroja abstracts human experience to the level of the moral universe where an optimistic resolution offers a glimpse of a transcendent existence, reality on a higher moral plane. In his satire, Baroja looks down on the world in a skeptical, ironic way in which change ultimately leads to defeat, fragmentation, and a fall into decadence. The same moralistic vision, however, gives rise to these genres and in each there is an element of the other. Social criticism creates tension in the romance world and a utopian world contrasts with the debased underworld of satire. Finally, Baroja's philosophical novels, which give witness to a probing mind trying to come to terms with the problematic nature of life, reveal a profound personal concern with the contemporary world. In all these novels, Baroja places the individual at the center of the world. Whether or not his protagonists achieve victory, Baroja stresses human integrity, wholeness and trueness to self, as the key to life. This personal philosophy accounts in part for the paradoxical quality apparent in his own writing. Life in general may be a futile, self-defeating proposition for Baroja, but within this despairing view there is room for laughter, vitality, and assertion of one's self.

In these early works, Baroja's unique novelistic world begins to take shape. While he employs the popular literary genre romance as the basis for his first novels, he also adds more topical material in the form of socio-political criticism and starts to focus the text on the ontological development of a central hero and/or heroine. In *Camino de perfección* and *El árbol de la ciencia* Baroja complements the upper world (good)/ lower world (evil) dialectic of *La casa de Aizgorri* and *El mayorazgo de Labraz* with dialogue that successfully melds conversational speech with philosophical concepts. The discussions between Iturrioz and Hurtado typify Baroja's mature style in which characters who are essentially ideologues debate existential issues. The young Baroja is visible behind these protagonists as he struggles to forge Nietzschean vitalism and Schopenhauer's ataraxia into his own philosophy as a means of coping with the moral and political decadence around him. His novels become a vehicle for working out the existential problems facing himself and other young Spaniards, symptomatic of the existential crisis confronting all of Western society at that time.

To return to the relationship between the earlier novels and *Memorias de un hombre de acción,* perhaps Baroja himself provides the best way of labeling the shift between the two. The words «violencia, arrogancia y nostalgia» suggest the impetuosity, intensity, and innocence of youth. In Baroja's earlier novels, an implied author of firm moral conviction struggles to come to terms with the complex world around him. His Basque home life provided him with both a vision of a pastoral, innocent world and one wracked by the bloody upheaval of the second Carlist War. His first exposure to modern philosophy sharpens an already critical view of reality, shaped by his observations and experiences as a doctor, and his burgeoning artistic sensibility trying to combine the immediacy of experience with values and abstract ideas. The characterization by Baroja of his second epoch as one of «historicismo, crítica, ironía, y cierto mariposeo sobre las ideas» shows awareness of intellectual, artistic and existential maturity and the attainment of an ironic, critical attitude which corresponds with the initiation of his intensive historical research. The shift implies change, but change as a product of personal and professional growth. It implies continuity, a shift of tone and perspective, rather than an abandonment of earlier artistic and philosophical preoccupations. Baroja drew on both the moral universe and the contemporary world to recreate the historical adventures of *Memorias de un hombre de acción.* The series inevitably reflects the antithetical characteristics, paradoxical approach to life, dialectic of form, and dialogue of ideas already present in his earliest novels.

II

STORYTELLING AND HISTORYTELLING

> I mistrust all systematizers and I avoid them.
> The will to a system is a lack of integrity.
>
> (NIETZSCHE, *Twilight of the Idols*)

BAROJA AND HISTORICAL FICTION

In an essay entitled «The Storyteller», Walter Benjamin describes the storyteller in an oral tradition as an interpreter and communicator of experience.[1] Travel adventures or local traditions provide the basis for his stories, which contain wise and useful advice of a moral or practical nature. The storyteller's art does not expend itself, but rather lives on in man's memory. Benjamin implies that something in a story transcends the here-and-now of experience to be born again and again artistically as it speaks meaningfully to men across the ages. The storyteller's interpretation and reordering of experience ties him to literary tradition, and beyond that, to the world of myth. Benjamin distinguishes the storyteller's function from that of the historyteller, who explains the events which he relates. The historyteller need not go beyond the accurate ordering of his materials and explanation into the realm of interpretation, fictional patterns, and myth. Benjamin's distinction implies a dual perspective for the historical novelist, who assumes the role of both storyteller and historyteller. He wishes both to tell tales that entertain or instruct and explain history by projecting it onto a fictional world. But the historical novelist approaches historytelling with the mind of a storyteller. He may strive to convey the immediacy and specificity of historical experience without any indication of transcendent meaning, but inevitably his storyteller's perspective offers glimpses of underlying fictional patterns. A conflict can arise between the historical novelist's sense of obligation to historical fact and his desire to create an interesting story. Yet the resolution of the storytelling and historytelling tendencies

---

[1] WALTER BENJAMIN, «The Storyteller», in his *Illuminations,* ed. Hannah Arendt (New York: Harcourt, Brace, and World, 1968), pp. 83-109.

determines the nature of each historical novel's relationship to literary motifs and genres.

Baroja's choice of a historical figure's life as the point of departure for a series of historical novels imposed much greater limitations on him than he had faced before. He gives a humorous account in *La intuición y el estilo* (V: 1072-76) of his initial research on Aviraneta. Baroja began his study in the fall of 1911, after hearing the adventurer's name mentioned frequently by members of his family. He assumes a certain attitude of nonchalance towards the endeavor, undertaking it «no teniendo otra cosa mejor que hacer» (V: 1072), but points out the difficulties and frustrations he overcame in tracking down pertinent information. He even provides an amusing story, reminiscent of Larra's «Vuelva Vd. mañana», of his search for Aviraneta's service record. Baroja romantically labels the process of historical reconstruction as «una labor un poco de detective» (V: 1073). After assembling the details of Aviraneta's life, Baroja transforms historytelling into storytelling, giving «un carácter literario a la narración» (V: 1074). In the re-creation of the people and the atmosphere of early nineteenth-century Spain he freely adapts his contemporary experiences to the historical context. His frequent visits to a variety of cities and geographical locations in Spain and France gave him the background material for the settings of *Memorias de un hombre de acción*. For example, Baroja's observations of country life during a 1914 trip to Burgos provided the models for the guerrillas of 1809 in *El escuadrón del Brigante*. His intensive research work and desire for firsthand exposure to the locations of Aviraneta's activities indicate that Baroja felt a strong obligation to truth of historical fact and the immediacy of experience in this series.

Scattered comments among Baroja's critical essays provide suggestive information concerning the storytelling and historytelling in *Memorias de un hombre de acción*. He emphasizes flexibility and multiplicity as the major features of the novel as a literary form: «La novela, hoy por hoy, es un género multiforme, proteico, en formación, en fermentación; lo abarca todo; el libro filosófico, el libro psicológico, la aventura, la utopía, lo épico; todo absolutamente» («Prólogo» to *La nave de los locos*, IV: 313).[2] Baroja denies the novel's adherence to classical principles of unity. Instead, he associates it with the temporal continuum of history: «La novela, en general, es como la corriente de la Historia: no tiene ni prin-

---

[2] This prologue (IV: 308-27) is one of the most important texts for understanding Baroja's concept of the novel. It is to an extent a response to Ortega y Gasset's *Ideas sobre la novela* and *La deshumanización del arte*. For more information on their dispute over the novel see Donald L. Shaw, «A Reply to *Deshumanización*—Baroja on the Art of the Novel», *Hispanic Review*, 25 (1957), 105-11 and Carmen Iglesias, «La controversia entre Baroja y Ortega acerca de la novela», *Hispanófila*, No. 7 (Sep., 1959), pp. 41-50.

cipio ni fin; empieza y acaba donde se quiera» (IV: 326). This association explains the open-ended, fragmented quality of many of his novels. In the few instances in which Baroja specifically mentions the historical novel, he does so within the context of literary history rather than in terms of generic classification. He strongly denies that he modeled *Memorias de un hombre de acción* after Galdós's *Episodios nacionales* and rejects the notion that Galdós initiated the historical novel of the recent past:

> Antes que él habían escrito novelas históricas Espronceda, Larra, Patricio de la Escosura, Cánovas, Trueba, Navarro Villoslada, Bécquer y otros muchos, a la manera de Walter Scott. Cierto que casi todos estos autores habían escrito relaciones de tiempos remotos; pero se habían hecho también novelas históricas contemporáneas de las guerras carlistas y de las conspiraciones liberales, por Ayguals de Izco, Villergas y por otros muchos autores de escasa importancia, hoy desconocidos por la generalidad, que tomaron como personajes de sus novelas a Cabrera, a Zurbano, a María Cristina, al conde de España, a sor Patrocinio y hasta mi pariente Aviraneta, a quien yo he intentado sacar del olvido en mis últimos libros. *(Divagaciones apasionadas, V: 498)*

Baroja stresses rather the impact of popular literary forms on his writing: «se nota, sí, la de las novelas de aventuras, porque yo he sido en mi juventud gran lector de folletines de evasiones célebres, de relatos de viajeros y espectador de melodramas truculentos» (V: 499). These particular influences, the romances and the episodic, first-person narratives with an emphasis alternately on action or description, indicate the fictional patterns that underlie Baroja's own peculiar blend of storytelling and history-telling in *Memorias de un hombre de acción*. Baroja associates the historical novel with the Romantic movement. According to him, Classicist literature looks to history for models, but tends to equate present and past, minimize differences, and stress the universal. Baroja considers Romanticism's emphasis on national peculiarities and the incomprehensibility of one epoch to another a fundamentally more honest historical approach. In response to a critic's assertion that in *Memorias de un hombre de acción* he deliberately chooses to explore an especially unspectacular period of Spanish history, Baroja utilizes the argument of comprehension to defend his choice of historical period. The temporal proximity of early nineteenth-century Spain to the date of writing the *Memorias de un hombre de acción* novels permits easy comprehension of the individual psyche and social structure of that time:

> Yo encuentro que en una época cercana se puede suponer, imaginar o inventar la manera de ser psicológica de los hombres que vivieron en ella. En cambio, el modo de ser de los hombres de hace doscientos, quinientos o más años, a mí, al menos, se me escapa. (V: 499)

As usual, Baroja emphasizes the importance of understanding the human element in the re-creation of a historical world.[3]

This preoccupation carries over into his views on history. Baroja feels that history should focus more on the psychological make-up of people from a certain period than on historical events:

> La Historia, que afirma el nexo de la Humanidad antigua y moderna en el tiempo y en el espacio, debe de ser, seguramente, más bien el conocimiento de los procesos psíquicos de las masas y de los hombres que la relación de sus agitaciones externas, que a veces son vanas y no indican nada positivo. («La historia», V: 1126)

In another essay, Baroja describes three types of history. In universal histories, sociological historians present generalized observations organized in a schema with labels assigned, but ignore details. Integrated history mixes the approaches of a variety of intellectual disciplines in a study of the past. Baroja criticizes these types of history, the former, for its pedantry, and the latter, for its unpleasing, grab-bag quality. Both lack *humorismo,* a term that encompasses humor, wit and the entertainment derived from capricious events, a quality Baroja defined and sought in his own work. Baroja finally describes the kind of history he respects: «La historia de hechos particulares, escrita por el no profesional, y aquí suelen aparecer el humor, los contrastes, las causas pequeñas, sirviendo de motivo a hechos trascendentales» (*La caverna del humorismo,* V: 474). Baroja prefers the historical interests of the amateur historian, with his focus on personal matters, historical obscurities, and events in which the disproportion between cause and effect defies logical causality, to the grandiose histories of pretentious professional historians. His historical interest reveals an affinity for that rejected or ignored by more ostentatious historians and a great curiosity for unusual historical events and characters. «La introducción de elementos oscuros, personales, capricho-

---

[3] This statement reinforces my belief that Baroja created the historical world of *Memorias de un hombre de acción,* among other reasons, for its relevance for contemporary society. It reveals a latent Romantic impulse to present the past as a key to understanding the present and the future. Jean Molino discusses this particular aspect of the Romantic historical novel in «Qu'est-ce que le roman historique?», *Revue d'Histoire Littéraire de la France,* 75, Nos. 1-3 (Jan.-June 1975), 195-234, at pp. 217-19. For more information on *Memorias de un hombre de acción* in relation to Galdós's *Episodios nacionales* see FRANCISCO J. FLORES ARROYUELO, *Pío Baroja y la historia* (Madrid: Helios, 1971), pp. 354-68, CARLOS LONGHURST, *Las novelas históricas de Pío Baroja* (Madrid: Guadarrama, 1974), pp. 247-59, JOSÉ ANGELES, «Baroja y Galdós: un ensayo de diferenciación», *Revista de Literatura,* 23, Nos. 45-46 (Jan.-June 1963), 49-64, JOAQUÍN CASALDUERO, «Baroja y Galdós», *Revista Hispánica Moderna,* 31 (1965), 113-18, JULIO CARO BAROJA, «Confrontación literaria o las relaciones de dos novelistas: Galdós y Baroja», *Cuadernos Hispanoamericanos,* Nos. 265-67 (July-Sept. 1972), pp. 249-69, and BIRUTÉ CIPLIJAUSKAITÉ, «The 'Noventayochentistas' and the Carlist Wars», *Hispanic Review,* 44 (1976), 265-79.

sos, y la de la casualidad, bastan ya para darle a la historia un carácter de humor» (V: 474), he says. Baroja probably derives his notion of *humorismo*, at least in part, from Schopenhauer. According to the philosopher, laughter arises from incongruity and paradox as a suddenly perceived difference between a concept and the real objects put in relation to it. This kind of ironic humor forms an essential part of the novelist's style and permeates the fictional world of *Memorias de un hombre de acción*.[4] By Baroja's account, then, the novels of *Memorias de un hombre de acción* would seem to be a type of history, the historytelling of an *historia humorística* combined with the storytelling impulses of popular literary forms. He proudly asserts the superiority of his amateur approach to history to that of the professional historians by implying that *historia humorística* gives a more truthful impression.

Baroja's tendency to merge the notions of novel and history, apparent in his comparison of the novel with history in terms of openness and in his concept of *historia humorística,* finds support in recent discussions about the nature of history and historiography. In an analysis of historical discourse, Roland Barthes indicates that historical narrative, like fictional narrative, is a linguistic construct. Historical texts as well as realistic fiction tend to eliminate an indicator of the enunciator (such as a subject pronoun) and to identify completely the referent with that which is signified. This creates the illusion of objectivity in which the historical texts and the actual historical events seem the same. Barthes stresses the illusory nature of this effect and the fact that historical discourse *represents* historical reality, but can never be identical with it.[5] Barthes' analysis of history as discourse provides a linguistic basis for Baroja's intuitive insistence on the subjectivity of historical texts. Lionel Gossman notes that only towards the end of the eighteenth century did history appear as separate from literature. Since both are forms of narrative and susceptible to change, at times history and fiction enrich each other by providing a model for change:

> But the tension between the requirements of system and those of change, between order and adventure, will usually persist in all kinds of narrative practice (historical or fictional) and may at certain moments become acute enough to become themselves the principal theme of narrative works. At such times, history may come to be associated, as it was in the *Poetics*, with the singular, the unexpected, the uncontrollable, the unsystematic, and fiction, on the other hand, with the ordered, the coherent, the general or universal. We may then discover that while historians are striving to achieve maximum narrative coherency and to approximate to the forms of

---

[4] ARTHUR SCHOPENHAUER, *The World as Will and Representation,* trans. E. F. J. Payne, I (New York: Dover, 1966), p. 59.
[5] «Le Discours de l'histoire», *Information sur les Sciences Sociales,* 6, Pt. 2, No. 4 (Aug. 1967), 65-75, at pp. 72-75.

fiction, certain novelists are trying to undercut these very forms and conventions by an appeal to «history».[6]

Although Baroja reverses the associations by connecting order and coherence with history and the unexpected and unsystematic with fiction, he does recognize how the two can influence each other: «No hay gran diferencia entre la historia y la novela, y así como un Chateaubriand o un Flaubert han podido convertir la novela en una obra seria de construcción y de técnica, Carlyle ha podido hacer de la historia una novela fantástica y caprichosa» (*La caverna del humorismo*, V: 473). Hayden White's *Metahistory* offers further evidence of the collapsing boundaries between history and fiction. White's book has a twofold purpose: (1) to provide a history of the historical consciousness in nineteenth-century Europe, and (2) to examine the historical thinking and methodology of that period in order to set forth a method of describing historiographical style. White considers a historical work a form of narrative prose discourse distinguished by its attempt to explain past structures and processes by representing them linguistically. In his analysis of styles, he utilizes techniques from literary criticism (as well as others), such as the types of tropes in figurative language and modes of emplotment adapted from Northrop Frye's *Anatomy of Criticism*.[7]

Although Baroja mentions the historical novel only in terms of a literary tradition, modern critics have failed in their attempts to establish the historical novel as a literary genre with distinct characteristics. The persistent failure to do so raises doubts about the validity of distinguishing it as such. George Lukács' book *The Historical Novel* (1936-37), still the major critical work on the historical novel as a genre despite serious problems in the presentation and exposition of its central argument, examines the historical novel as an artistic reflection of social and historical transformations, an outgrowth of the new awareness of historical process as a mass experience and an emergent class consciousness that appeared as a result of the French Revolution.[8] He uses the *Waverley*

---

[6] LIONEL GOSSMAN, «History and Literature: Reproduction or Signification», in *The Writing of History: Literary Form and Historical Understanding*, ed. Robert H. Canary and Henry Kozicki (Madison: University of Wisconsin Press, 1978), 3-39, at p. 10. On pp. 3-9 Gossman discusses the changing attitudes towards the relationship between history and literature through the ages.

[7] HAYDEN WHITE, «The Poetics of History», in his *Metahistory: The Historical Imagination in Nineteenth-Century Europe* (Baltimore: The Johns Hopkins University Press, 1973), pp. 1-42.

[8] GEORGE LUKÁCS, *The Historical Novel*, trans. Hannah and Stanley Mitchell (London: Merlin Press, 1962). For a revew of Lukács' book see Peter Demetz, «The Uses of Lukács», *The Yale Review*, 54 (1964-65), 435-40. Demetz has two major objections to Lukács' book. He sees Lukács as a prisoner of the rigid antithesis of Hegelian dialectics, closed to the pluralities of life (p. 436). Demetz also views Lukács' collapsing of the distinction between novel and historical novel as a weakness in his argument (p. 437). JEAN MOLINO, «Qu'est-ce que le

novels of Walter Scott as the model for the classical historical novel, in which the artistic form provides a vehicle for re-experiencing history as a series of crises and changes affecting every aspect of life and in which fictional characters represent historial and social types. After the Revolution of 1848, Lukács says, the historical novel became a decadent literary form that denies historical process and offers only escapism into an exotic world. He ends by lamenting the bourgeois alienation from the progressiveness of history and asserting that in its proper perspective there is no distinction between historical and realistic fiction. Lukács' major contribution to the study of the historical novel is his recognition that the artist engages with the historical consciousness of his time and inevitable projects this engagement onto the fictional and historical world of his novel.

Herbert Butterfield takes a different approach to the question of

roman historique?», pp. 200-01, criticizes Lukács for the following reasons: Lukács bases his study on Scott, who had a traditional philosophy of history that had virtually no relationship to the French Revolution; Lukács is steeped in the purely human phenomenon of historicism, which forces a pattern of birth, decline, and death on literary forms; and finally, Lukács' view creates a mythological history, just as mythological as a more traditional intrepretation of history. I add my own objections to those previously stated: By eliminating the distinction between the historical novel and the realistic novel, Lukács constructs a circular argument that undermines the premise on which the argument is based, i.e. that there is a separate, identifiable literary form the historical novel, with its own problems of form determined by certain socio-historical conditions. Lukács' use of Scott as the classical historical novelist raises problems, too, because his interpretation of the material is questionable. A recent dissertation (William D. Darby, «Sir Walter Scott and the Historical Novel: Intellectual Values and the Definition of a Genre», Diss. Wayne State University, 1974) supports some of Lukács' ideas, notably that Scott does try to capture history as it was to those who experienced it (p. 181) and that Scott believes that history records the emergence and progress of human civilization (p. 237). On the other hand, Darby indicates that Scott presented a complex and not totally optimistic view of Edmund Burke's unfavorable reaction to the French Revolution (pp. 220-21). Darby also points out that Scott did not examine history as strictly a product of objective historical forces. There is always a religious and moralistic concern in Scott's novels as he observes historical forces from the perspective of forces greater than himself (p. 263) and he assumes a moralistic attitude towards human motivation (p. 288). In labeling post-1848 historical novels «decadent», Lukács ignores the fact that these works may be a reflection of a new historical consciousness just as much as Scott's. He refuses to recognize that there may be forms of historical consciousness other than his own. Finally, Lukács' distinction between classical and decadent historical novels constitutes a nomative, prescriptive approach to the historical novel. He does more towards establishing an evaluative system for separating good books from bad than in terms of providing a descriptive literary analysis of the historical novel as a genre. For a more favorable assessment of Lukács' contribution to the study of the historical novel see JACQUES MÉNARD, «Lukács et la théorie du roman historique», La Nouvelle Revue Française, Nos. 237-40 (Sept.-Dec. 1972), pp. 229-238. Ménard rightly stresses Lukács' recognition that the historical novel incorporated a historical consciousness in its form (p. 232) and his new awareness of the potential of the hero as a collective representative of socio-historical types (pp. 232-33).

genre in *The Historical Novel* (1924).[9] While Lukács emphasizes the historical aspect of the literary form, Butterfield focuses on its fictional aspect by attempting to describe the unique feeling that the genre produces. He stresses the pictorial quality of the historical novel and the Romantic sensibility of nostalgia, irrecoverableness, and temporal distance that pervades these novels. Butterfield sees escapism as an essential characteristic of historical fiction and notes that its form can merge with that of the episodic travel narrative or the novel of adventures. History offers material for constructing stories, but at times the stories go beyond a historical context to present a more cosmic view of man at odds with his destiny. The strength of this work lies in Butterfield's descriptive approach to historical fiction and his awareness that it assumes certain literary forms and possesses specific characteristics.

In the years that have passed since the appearance of these early twentieth-century critical works, the terminology has changed, but the complexity and difficulty of identifying the historical novel as a distinct literary form remain. Jean Molino, after dividing the historical novel into macro- and micro-genres, abandons an attempt to arrive at a theory of the historical novel because of the lack of a sufficiently broad comparative text.[10] Similarly, Joseph Turner acknowledges the historical novel's resistence to generalization as a genre after jeopardizing its state as such by asserting that content more than form sets it apart from other fiction.[11] Other critics' analyses of the historical novel continue in the vein of either Lukács or Butterfield. Claude Mettra views the historical novel, irrespective of its lyrical, social-realistic, or mythical perspective, as an interrogation of history whose nature varies with the times. André Daspre, following Lukács, views it as a form of realistic fiction that can provide an objective analysis of history and make the reader more aware of his place in history.[12] On the other hand, Pierre-Jean Rémy, like Butterfield, notices that history incorporated into fiction adds an element of both dynamism and fatality to the text. Northrop Frye continues along the line of Butterfield's association of escapism, a Romantic sensibility, and the novels of adventure with the historical novel by suggesting that most historical novels are romances. Finally, Zoé Oldenbourg envisions the historical novel as a means for man to get back in touch with the world

[9] HERBERT BUTTERFIELD, *The Historical Novel* (Cambridge: Cambridge University Press, 1924). While Butterfield's study has the advantage of being descriptive rather than prescriptive, it seems impressionistic rather than analytical.

[10] «Qu'est-ce que le roman historique?», pp. 232-34.

[11] JOSEPH TURNER, «The Kinds of Historical Fiction: An Essay in Definition and Methodology», *Genre*, 12 (1979), 333-55, at. p. 335.

[12] CLAUDE METTRA, «Le Romancier hors les murs», *La Nouvelle Revue Française*, Nos. 237-40 (Sept.-Dec. 1972), pp. 5-29, at p. 19; ANDRÉ DASPRE, «Le Roman historique et l'histoire», *Revue d'Histoire Littéraire de la France*, 75, Nos. 103 (Jan.-June, 1975), 235-44, at pp. 238-39.

of myth and as an expression of a deep psychological need to realize the universal human experience of life and death in the form of a hero's adventures.[13] Neither of these major approaches justifies the consideration of historical fiction as a separate literary genre. The distinction they make and the characteristics they describe are unconvincing in this regard. Whether the critic indicates historical consciousness as the basis for the historical novel, stressing the importance of historytelling, or fictional patterns as the basis, stressing storytelling, the fact remains that the two are inseparable in the actual literary text. For the most part it seems that the historical novel can best be described in terms of other more established genres, such as romance and satire, as in Baroja's case.

PRECURSORS OF «MEMORIAS DE UN HOMBRE DE ACCIÓN»

Baroja's *Las inquietudes de Shanti Andía* (1911) and *Zalacaín el aventurero* (1909) reveal a storyteller's tentative steps towards rapprochement with historytelling. The ordering of the fictional world, the variety in tone and point of view, and the emergence of the adventurer-hero in these novels indicate their importance as precursors for the *Memorias de un hombre de acción* series. Baroja sets the action of the novels in the past, although he provides almost no specific historical data in the texts. He continues his focus on the individual, but the introspective quality present in novels such as *Camino de perfección* diminishes as his heroes turn outward in asserting their will in action. Both novels present the life stories of adventurers, which implies an ordering of events in terms of chronological growth, and yet the nature of the heroes' lives lends itself to a fragmented, episodic development. Baroja avoids the limitations imposed by historical fact by using fictional characters as protagonists. The antithetical impulses analyzed in Chapter I continue in *Shanti Andía* and *Zalacaín*. In the former novel, Baroja re-creates the world of romance while invoking the atmosphere of pre-industrial Basque society and the world of its sailors. The life stories of Shanti Andía and his uncle Juan de Aguirre take the form of memoirs written by Shanti

---

[13] PIERRE-JEAN RÉMY, «L'Histoire dans le roman», *La Nouvelle Revue Française*, Nos. 237-40 (Sept.-Dec. 1972), pp. 156-60, at pp. 158-59; FRYE, *Anatomy of Criticism* (Princeton: Princeton University Press, 1971), pp. 306-07. ZOÉ OLDENBOURG, «Le Roman et l'histoire», *La Nouvelle Revue Française*, Nos. 237-40 (Sept.-Dec. 1972), pp. 130-55, at pp. 154-55. I remain unconvinced that there is evidence or a need for distinguishing the historical novel as a separate genre. Although another possibility is to define the historical novel in terms of reader response, Käte Hamburger has shown that the individual perceives the historical past of a historical novel in the same way he does the world of any fictional text, and therefore reader response does not provide a means of defining the historical novel as a genre. See *The Logic of Literature*, trans. Marilynn J. Rose (Bloomington: Indiana University Press, 1973), pp. 110-16.

after he has retired from his days at sea. The narrator's retrospective position generates a Romantic sense of the Basque past and a tone of nostalgia and heightened sensibility deprive the historical world of concrete chronological and historical characteristics. As a result, the historical world of *Shanti Andía* blends indistinguishably with the abstract, polarized worlds of romance, the underworld and the idyllic society. In *Zalacaín,* set in the Basque country during the second Carlist War, Baroja continues in the ironic vein present in some of his earlier works. The ironic tone with which he treats his hero and his adventures adds a humorous and subversive element to the text that undercuts the traditional concept of heroism. Instead of a fictional text full of specific references to historical events, Baroja gives a fast-moving, entertaining account of a fictional adventurer's life. The influence of adventure novels and popular literary forms is apparent in both novels and supports the tie that critics like Butterfield, Molino, Rémy, and Frye have seen between such works and the historical novel.

In *Las inquietudes de Shanti Andía* Baroja presents literally a storytelling, the memoirs or life story of a fictitious Basque sea captain, Santiago Andía. The captain narrates the adventures of his youth in the first person. All of Baroja's narrators have a strong awareness of self and, as the narrative progresses, Shanti reveals different facets of his own personality. At the beginning of the novel, he points out that he writes his memoirs only at the insistence of a friend: «Desde la muerte de don Blas de Artola, el teniente de navío retirado, la plaza de hombre ilustre está vacante en nuestro pueblo. Cincunegui excita mis sentimientos ambiciosos, ... según él no puedo dejar a mis paisanos en la orfandad en que se hallan» (II: 997-98). The lighthearted tone of self-deprecation prepares the reader for the playfulness and bemused affection with which Shanti regards many of his youthful exploits. His retrospective position of maturity enables him to assess his attitude as an innocent young man: «Yo no comprendía que había en mí una exuberancia de vida, un deseo de acción; ... yo necesitaba hacer algo, gastar la energía, vivir» (II: 1044). Shanti's impulse for action gives way later in life to what he himself describes as nostalgia, sentimentality, and complacency. He manifests these particular qualities in several lyrical passages in which the Romantic themes of mutability and identification with Nature appear, as well as at the end of the novel, where he expresses longing for the old days of adventure. At one point, Andía identifies himself as the quintessential observer, all eyes: «Muchas veces me he figurado ser únicamente dos pupilas, algo como un espejo o una cámara oscura para reflejar la Naturaleza» (II: 1002). The adventurer disappears in these lines, as if he had become a disembodied spirit with only a voice and eyes. His self-awareness extends to the recognition of the strange effects produced by autobiographical writings: «El ver mis recuerdos fijados en el papel me daba la impresión de hallarse escritos por otro, y este desdoblamiento de mi persona en narrador y lector me indujo a continuar» (II: 997). Shanti notes the distancing effect created by transforming oneself into a persona and the feeling of dividing oneself into two. This fascination with the division of self permits him to treat himself and his life as a literary creation. Shanti Andía also responds to the temporal distance between the moment of narration and the moment of his adventures, between himself as narrator and actor. At one point, he separates his life into active and contemplative epochs: «Extraña exigencia la mía y la de los hombres andariegos. En una época, todos son acontecimientos; en otra, todos son comentarios a los hechos pasados» (II: 1055). Shanti divides his life into one period of experience and another one of storytelling and reflection on those experiences. This duality appears in many of Baroja's protagonists and narrators and suggests that the two phases are complementary rather than antagonistic aspects of vital experience.

The temporal distance also generates a series of Now/Then comparisons, typical of Sir Walter Scott's novels and for the most part atypical of Baroja's historical fiction: «Antes, el barco de vela era una creación divina, ... hoy, el barco de vapor es algo continuamente cambiante, como la ciencia...» or «Antes, el capitán era un personaje sabio, ... hoy es un especialista injerto en un burócrata» (II: 1001). The nostalgic comparisons create a certain tone, an attitude towards the past in which the world removed in time and space seem more appealing. There is little sense of history in this view; the Basque seafaring world of Shanti seems far from the people and events of history and an explanation of them. Instead, Baroja produces in the novel a pictorially-rich, highly imaginative vision of the past linked more closely to the world of romance than to his own historical consciousness. But Baroja himself has little respect for the pretensions of great historical texts and his notion of *historia humorística* suggests that perhaps romance does represent a type of historical consciousness. Shanti echoes Baroja's skepticism about history as an objective, scientific discipline:

> Esta colaboración espontánea adorna los grandes hechos y los grandes caracteres. El uno insinúa: «Podía ser»; el otro añade: «Se dice»; un tercero agrega: «Ocurrió así», y el último asegura: «Lo he visto...» De este modo se va formando la Historia, que es el folletín de las personas serias. (II: 998)

He expresses a critical, ironic view of history, suggesting that beneath a thin veneer of logic and factual appearance lies the complicated web of unidimensional people and implausible incidents typical of serial novels. Shanti undermines the notion of causality and rational motivation usually associated with history. He accordingly applies his skepticism to men who have a definite purpose and direction in life: «¡Qué ilusión! No hay fin en la vida. El fin es un punto en el espacio y en el tiempo, no más trascendental que el punto precedente o el siguiente» (II: 999). The directionlessness expressed in these lines grows logically out of the undermining of rational motivation present in the earlier comments.

Shanti narrows the boundary between storytelling and historytelling by equating history and serial novels in his statements, but the novel itself bears out Baroja's belief that very little distinguishes history from fiction. At the beginning of the novel Shanti speaks of his exposure to the tales of an old salt named Yurrumendi who sparks the imagination of the boys of Lúzaro and inspires them to go to sea. Yurrumendi mixes fantastic stories of sirens, seahorses, and encounters with sea snakes and the Flying Dutchman, with tales that have a modicum of truth. He speaks of the maelstrom as a hideous monster that gobbles up ships. While the maelstrom is not an animal, it is a natural phenomenon that generates a dangerously strong suction effect. Similarly, Yurrumendi asserts that in the Sargasso Sea one sails on land. Although one undoubtedly is still in water, the dense seaweed makes the water appear like land. Yurrumendi's tales of pirates and slave ships especially fascinate the children, although he also has more fanciful stories such as miracles in his repertory. Shanti comments: «Sus cuentos no se diferenciaban gran cosa de las historias que él tenía por verdaderas» (II: 1023). Andía notes that the old sailor tried to add verisimilitude to the fanciful stories: «Le gustaba a Yurrumendi, cuando relataba esos cuentos extraordinarios, documentar sus narraciones con una exactitud matemática, y así decía: 'Una vez, en Liverpool, en la taberna del Dragón Rojo...'» (II: 1023). In Yurrumendi's storytelling process fictional and real elements move easily in either direction. He fictionalizes real experiences by exaggerating and adding the marvelous and makes extraordinary narratives more realistic by introducing precise concrete references. In the course of the novel, Juan de Aguirre's manuscript describing his adventures aboard the slave ship El Dragón presents true events that rival those of Yurrumendi's stories. Aguirre's real experiences with pirate-like individuals, buried treasure, and exotic locations come to life as a fictional world made real by human experience. Reality, history, and fiction blend together in these episodes.

The multiple narrators in the novel have an interesting impact on the sense of order in the fictional world. Although Shanti performs the role of the central narrator, Fermín Itchaso (a man who had sailed with Aguirre) narrates some of Aguirre's experiences aboard El Dragón, the village doctor tells the story of La «Shele» (Juan de Aguirre's first love), Aguirre recounts his own adventures in his manuscript, and the Englishmen Small and Smiles describe the search for the treasure of *El Dragón*. At times Itchaso's and Aguirre's stories overlap and create different perspectives of the same events. The multiple narratives also cause multiplicity and diffusion of narrative threads. Initially Shanti focuses on his own life story, but the focus shifts to his uncle Juan de Aguirre, and back and forth during the novel between the two. Baroja weaves other life stories into these two major narrative threads: those of Mary Sandow (Shanti's wife and cousin), La «Shele», and Juan Machín (the son of La «Shele» and Juan de Aguirre). The mass of interrelated narrative lines creates an overall impression of disorder in the novel. The interruptions of several narrators contribute to this subversion of order and undermine the sense of chronological order, a presupposed method of narrative organization for memoirs. Shanti begins with his childhood adventures, education, first experiences as a sailor, and his discovery of Juan de Aguirre and Mary before Itchaso's story interrupts this narrative sequence. After the old sailor's lengthy account, Andía describes his struggle with Juan Machín over Mary, which leads to another extensive narrative interlude with various narrators concerning Juan de Aguirre's first love, Juan's own story of his experiences, and the ultimate fate of the treasure-hunters, before Shanti ends his memoirs with a description of his contemplative life as an elderly man in Lúzaro.

The narrative segments themselves sometimes run counter to chronological order. The reader often learns of the actions leading up to an event after it has occurred, almost as if in a flashback sequence. Juan de Aguirre's servant Patrick Allen leaves in search of buried treasure immediately after his master's death. Only in the next section of the novel during Itchaso's story does the reader learn the history and nature of the treasure. Similarly, Juan Machín's true identity as Mary Sandow's half-brother is revealed only after competing with Shanti for Mary's love. In the final section of the novel, Shanti Andía jumps from his wedding to thoughts about his grandchildren, a chronological leap that subverts the reader's sense of temporal logic. The strong elements of coincidence and fate in the novel also add to the impression of disorder. In fact, the plot of the novel turns around chance rather than causality, psychology, or any sort of rational motivation. Shanti happens to run into people who sailed with his uncle and can tell him about Aguirre's life. Juan Machín meets and falls in love with his half-sister by chance. During their search for the treasure, Small and Smiles encounter two Dutch sailors from *El Dragón* who are looking for the same thing. The importance of fate in Shanti Andía recalls Baroja's discussion of chance and caprice as a means of giving history *humorismo*.

Despite the appearance of disorder created by multiple narratives, fragmentation, chronological disorder, and the lack of rational motivation, the internal order that arises from conformity to the conventions of romance endows the curious web of interrelated people and events in *Shanti Andía* with artistic coherence. The two major plot lines follow the patterns of romance. Shanti escapes entrapment and death on a number of occasions. During his youth he nearly drowns on a sinking ship. He narrowly misses death twice during his courtship: once, when kidnapped and left stranded by Machín on the rock-island Frayburu, and second, when caught in a sudden storm with a group of fishermen out in a small boat. Machín's great strength of will and violent temperament born of interior turmoil (from the Aguirre family) lend him a demonic quality. The discovery of his true identity and the subsequent emergence of the incest motif reverse his role as the principal adversary of the hero and permit Shanti to marry Mary Sandow. The generous wedding gift of Machín aids Shanti in acquiring a new identity as a prosperous man in Lúzaro. The village's tranquility and closeness to nature and the glimpse of domestic bliss at the end of the novel provide a vision of the hero and heroine in an idyllic society.

Juan de Aguirre's life story conforms even more closely to the romance plot of descent into a lower world, escape from bondage, and attainment of a new identity and a superior society. After he leaves Lúzaro, Juan enters the lower world of the slave ship *El Dragón* by switching positions and names with Tristán de Ugarte, a ruthless, amoral cutthroat. The ship's cargo is a metaphor for the debased world of Aguirre and his sailor companions, who are slaves to their own impulses and savagery. This band of social misfits consists of an unharmonious, orderless group of Basques, Dutchmen, Englishmen, and Portuguese. Each group speaks its own language and bands together accordingly. Captain Zaldumbide, an avaricious thief, and the ship's medic «Doctor Cornelius», a hunchback who practises homeopathic medicine and whose constant companion is a black cat named Belzebuth, set the example for the demonic society of the ship. Aguirre recounts a number of horrifying adventures of violence and cruelty. Eventually his demonic double, Ugarte, returns to the ship. A hideous scar marks Ugarte's face and he dogs Juan's footsteps from the moment he boards the ship. Both bear the name Ugarte and for every courageous, superior action of Aguirre's, Tristán commits an act of treachery. During the course of a voyage, a mutiny arises from the normal chaos of ship life. The mutinous crew kills the captain while Aguirre and a handful of loyal sailors barricade themselves in a cabin. They manage to hold out until the rebellious group recognizes the need for their expertise. Aguirre assumes command of the ship and squelches a plan by Ugarte to seize *El Dragón* and transform it into a pirate ship. Just as Juan seems to emerge from this underworld society, a British vessel attacks the ship and the crew escapes in a whaleboat and manages to bury the captain's treasure before the English capture them. Aguirre descends into another lower world, a pontoon (prison ship). During his period of imprisonment, Juan undergoes a trial of his moral fibre and a sort of conversion that prepares him for the acquisition of a new identity and deliverance from bondage. On board *El Dragón* he exhibited superior moral strength and leadership potential. In prison, he cultivates the rational side of his intellect by studying mathematics and acquires inner tranquility from newborn stoicism. Aguirre, Ugarte, and Allen manage to escape from prison and experience a number of difficult times as they move about the countryside. A retired sea captain, Sandow, and his daughter Anna take them in at one point. Juan and Anna fall in love and after a time he travels to France, where Anna and Allen later join him. In the meantime, Allen kills Ugarte in a tavern fight, which symbolizes Aguirre's definitive break with his darker self, a rupture underlined by the fact that Ugarte dies under the assumed name of Aguirre. Juan assumes the role of the romance hero, who rescues the captive maiden and his loyal friend to attain a simple, tranquil life in Lúzaro.

The adventurer-heroes of *Shanti Andía* provide the model for the *Memorias de un hombre de acción* hero Aviraneta. The narratives of Shanti and Aguirre indicate that they divide their lives into active and contemplative epochs. During their mature, quiet years, both feel the need to reflect on their former lives and preserve their experiences in an articulate and more permanent form. As individuals they exhibit moral superiority. Shanti has a developed Romantic sensibility, as well as sensitivity to the plight of the poor and unfortunate men of the world. Aguirre displays courage and nobility of spirit in his love and loyalty. But Baroja's greatest interest lies in exploring the active side of their lives that emerges from an inner exuberance and vitality, a strength of will that endows them with superior energy. The vitality manifests itself in the form of adventures, extraordinary experiences and events that challenge the adventurer's courage and resourcefulness and sometimes endanger his life. These adventures usually occur on the margin of society, and therefore the adventurer often explores the darker side of life. Characters like Shanti and Aguirre move comfortably in and out of storms, prisons, and underworld societies. Yet because of their energetic lives, they seem especially susceptible to the forces of fate. They easily become victims of plots and circumstances beyond their control, but these situations arouse their will and courage. Baroja also makes a Romantic association between the adventurer and Nature. Shanti and Aguirre maintain their closeness to the sea even when they retire from the sailor's life. Despite the complacency of old age, Shanti cannot forget the appeal of the adventurer's life: «Sí, yo me alegro de que mis hijos no quieran ser marinos..., y, sin embargo...» (II: 1158).

In *Zalacaín el aventurero* Baroja places the life story of another adventurer in a historical context. He develops the hero's exploits episodically, but in a linear fashion, without the fragmentation and chronological shifting and disorder of *Shanti Andía*. Baroja drew on the experiences of his father and his friends during the second Carlist War for the historical backdrop: «Los detalles históricos no están tomados de libros, sino de viva voz. Algunos los oí de labios de mi padre, que estuvo en la guerra carlista de voluntario liberal; otros los escuché de mis amigos» (*Divagaciones apasionadas,* V: 501). Baroja's sources had already transformed historical experience into storytelling material and the artist's work inevitably reflects this blend of storytelling and historytelling. Baroja does not employ the first-person narration of the memoirs in *Shanti Andía,* but rather assumes the position of a third-person omniscient narrator who distances himself from his fictional characters and feels free to utilize the narrative distance to manipulate them and to generate a pervasive tone of wit and irony. Instead of the romance world of *Shanti Andía,* which seems more akin to the dimly-remembered world of childhood dreams and experiences, *Zalacaín* partakes of an escapist adult world with a somewhat removed, but present, underlying set of concrete historical facts.

At first glance, the historical details seem to have little importance in the novel. During Martín Zalacaín's childhood, his great-uncle and mentor in roguery, Tellagorri, sings little ditties celebrating the Treaty of Vergara (which marked the close of the first Carlist War in the North) and the reign of Isabel II, and criticizing María Cristina. Tellagorri foresees the outbreak of war and on his deathbed counsels Martín not to support either side, but rather to exploit both for profit as a neutral businessman. As the war begins, Zalacaín silently notes the organization and victories of the Carlists while secretly he agrees with Liberal principles and feels annoyance with Liberal rhetoric and lack of action. As a dealer in contraband for the Carlist army, he witnesses the reactionary, archaic nature of the Carlist forces and the ineptitude of Carlos VII. Zalacaín's adventures take him into the Carlist stronghold at Estella, an encounter with a guerrilla band, and the rout of the Carlist army as it attempts a retreat across the border into France. His life is inscribed within the historical context of the second Carlist War. In the first part of the novel, *La infancia de Zalacaín,* the hero grows from childhood to youth just as Tellagorri predicts war. In Part II, *Andanzas y correrías,* Zalacaín acquires fame and fortune and performs his greatest acts of daring as the war progresses. His enmity with Carlos Ohando (an enemy since childhood) increases since Ohando supports the Carlist cause.

Finally, in Part III, *Las últimas aventuras,* Zalacaín leads the Liberal forces up Peñaplata to close the retreat of the Carlist army. His death at the hands of Ohando's henchman coincides with a definitive end to the war. Baroja carefully weaves the life of his fictional hero into the historical circumstances. As the story progresses, the historical elements become more intertwined with the plot. The dynamism of the hero becomes more inseparable from the turbulence of the historical context.

A certain attitude emerges from Baroja's treatment of historical material in the text. The fact that the hero openly defends the Liberal cause towards the end of *Zalacaín,* that his archenemy fights for the Carlist cause, and that Carlos VII receives only negative comments (such as the mention of the epithet *don Bobo*), reveals Baroja's own Liberal sympathies. The author goes on to some length to satirize the Carlist forces. At one point in the novel the guerrilla band of El Cura seizes Zalacaín and his brother-in-law Bautista. The barbarity of El Cura and his men, who commit such acts as beating schoolteachers, tar-and-feathering women, and recruiting guerrillas by force, belies the Carlists' reputed devotion to Church, Honor, and Country. The fact that Baroja selects a band led by a priest for this episode heightens the implicit irony. The «Historia casi inverosímil de Joshé Cracasch», embedded within this adventure, contributes to the ironic treatment of the Carlists. Joshé Cracasch is an enamoured, simple, village musician who happened to stumble onto El Cura's men during a walk outside his hometown. Prior to his forced joining of the guerrilla forces, Cracasch had made a series of clownlike, foolish attempts to gain the approval of the family of his beloved by donning outlandish costumes and playing practical jokes. Just as he has begun to mend his ways, Joshé becomes caught up in a war that he is much too simple-minded to understand. Cracasch and his story are amusing and absurd, but Baroja implies that his fate and the historical form that it assumes share that absurdity. The Carlist forces become an object of ridicule, a satirical target. Baroja expands his satire of the Carlists in a dialogue between the Count of Haussonville and a Basque named Asenchio, the servant of a Carlist soldier. The Frenchman complains constantly about Spanish food while mixing French and Spanish phrases: «'¡España! ¡España! ¡Jamais de la vie! Mucha hidalguía, mucha jota; pero poco alimento'» (I: 226). Asenchio garbles Spanish, too: «'La guerra' —añadía Asenchio, metiendo la cucharada— 'es cosa nada *bueno*'» (I: 226). Baroja presents the supporters of the Carlist cause as pretentious and ridiculous buffoons who cannot even speak the language of the country they pretend to defend. His ironic undercutting of a historical cause and revelation of his own political sympathies represent a very different approach to the past from the abstract, Romantic vision of *Shanti Andía.*

The satire of the Carlists forms only one aspect of the pervasively ironic tone that operates in the text at a variety of levels. Verbal ironies arise in such scenes as the conversation between Haussonville and Asenchio in which their linguistic confusion contributes to the humor of the text while on another level it transforms them and their cause into objects of satire. Baroja also makes humorously ironic comments about the characters of his novel. The narrator mentions the class consciousness of Tellagorri's dog Marqués: «participaba del odio de Tellagorri por los ricos, cosa rara en un perro» (I: 170). He points out the individualism of Tellagorri's social attitudes: «'Cada cual que conserve lo que tenga y que robe lo que pueda' —decía. Esta era la más social de sus teorías; las más insociables se las callaba» (I: 170-71). In passages such as these Baroja's ability to manipulate narrative distance for ironic effect becomes apparent. He also generates irony in the text through incongruous comparisons. After his escape from Estella and his rescue of his beloved Catalina from a convent, Martín encounters a childhood friend, Linda, the circus girl, who has become a wealthy courtesan. Zalacaín stays with her for awhile to recover from a minor gunshot wound, which prompts the following comment from the narrator: «De conocer Martín la *Odisea,* es posible que habría tenido la pretensión de comparar a Linda con la hechicera Circe, y a sí mismo con Ulises; pero como no había leído el poema de Homero, no se le ocurrió tal comparación» (I: 230). The ridiculous nature of the comparison creates an explicitly ironic contrast between the liaison of the sorceress Circe, gifted with supernatural powers, with Ulysses, the crafty epic hero of an ancient heroic age, and that of an elegant, experienced female with an adventurous contraband dealer who has a weakness for women, in a less than heroic time. The irony of the passage cuts in another direction as well. The narrator emphasizes the fact that Zalacaín would be incapable of making such a comparison and does not subsequently do so. He draws attention to the fact that he, the narrator, puts in the extraneous comparison, which not only creates humor because of its incongruous and flippant quality, but also draws attention to his own superior, removed stance. The narrator emphasizes his distance from the text by assuming a humorously judgmental tone towards the fictional world.

The ironic tone widens in *Zalacaín* to become a general attitude towards the world. In the story about Joshé Cracasch, Baroja stresses the absurdity of the character, his actions, and the circumstances in which he finds himself a member of a guerrilla band. In fact, Baroja's satire of the Carlists, his ironic word plays and asides, and his manipulation of narrative distance for ironic effect, all contribute to a vision of the world as irrational and absurd. The strong presence of both chance and fate in the novel adds to this impression. During Martín's childhood, Tellagorri and a former city official uncover a fifteenth-century manuscript that relates how an ancestral Martín Zalacaín married a daughter of the Ohando family, quarreled with a member of the same family, and was killed by a friend of his enemy. History repeats itself in the nineteenth-century Zalacaín's life. Martín fights with Carlos Ohando, marries Catalina Ohando, and dies from a wound inflicted by Cacho, one of Carlos's accomplices. Although Zalacaín imposes his will on the world in the form of courageous deeds, a historical document fatalistically predetermines his life. Martín breaks out of jail and escapes death from the Carlists several times, but he cannot elude his ultimate fate. In addition, chance encounters play an important role in Martín's life and subsequently in the movement of the plot. He happens upon Carlos Ohando in Estella while delivering letters to the Carlist commander of the army. He runs into Linda after the escape from Estella. But by far the most interesting are his chance encounters with the foreign journalist, a war correspondent who decides to chronicle his life story. Martín meets the journalist for the first time during an attempt to ambush a stagecoach by El Cura's men. The hero later meets him at three crucial moments: in Estella, where he delivers the letters to the Carlists; in Urbía after the war, where he recounts his adventures to the journalist amidst the rubble; and in Roncesvalles, where he dies. These accidental meetings undermine the sense of causality in the fictional world and represent another aspect of the ironic world view in the novel. The process by which the journalist transforms Zalacaín's life story and the historical experiences implicit within it into chronicles and stories, storytelling and historytelling, mirrors Baroja's transformation of the oral narratives of his father and friends into the storytelling and historytelling of the novel. The coincidence of the adventurer and the chronicler implies inseparability, that the writer needs material from the world of experience in order to create. But Baroja also points out that the remembrance of history or experience is shaped and in effect *made* by the storytelling and historytelling of the writer. He emphasizes the importance of the writer's role in this regard, but in addition he stresses the element of chance in connecting writer and subject. In this way Baroja underscores the arbitrary nature of human experience in the world.

Zalacaín represents a more complex version of the adventurer-hero than Shanti Andía. He possesses the same strength, courage, and force of will that drive him to accept difficult and dangerous challenges. The narrator comments on the hero's strong sense of self: «tenía ambición, amor al peligro y una confianza ciega en su estrella» (I: 244). Martín lacks, however, the conscious self-awareness of many of Baroja's heroes: «'yo siento en mí, aquí dentro, algo duro y fuerte...; no sé explicarme'» (I: 214). Zalacaín lives in a state of constant disquiet, an instinctive, innate part of his character. He himself associates his impulses with the wild, anarchic forces of nature:

«Es usted la inquietud personificada, Martín» —dijo Briones.
«¿Qué quiere usted? He crecido salvaje como las hierbas y necesito la acción, la acción continua. Yo, muchas veces pienso que llegará un día en que los hombres podrán aprovechar las pasiones de los demás en algo bueno.» (I: 249)

The last sentence indicates a nascent idealism on the part of Zalacaín. Baroja makes a tentative move towards adding conscious thoughts and principles to the intuitive character of the adventurer. In fact, he expands the adventurer's perspective to encompass an attitude towards life. Zalacaín expresses the following world view: «Yo quisiera que todo viviese, que todo comenzara a marchar, no dejar nada parado, empujar todo al movimiento: hombres, mujeres, negocios, máquinas, minas; nada quieto, nada inmóvil» (I: 249). Baroja adds a philosophical dimension to the adventurer with this vision of the ideal world as a dynamic, vitalistic one of flux — a universe of perpetual Brownian movement. Even here the adventurer's force of will comes through in the imposition of his own vitalistic attitude onto the world.

Baroja complicates his characterization of the adventurer, however, by making him an object of the text's pervasive irony. One chapter of the novel, «Como Zalacaín y Bautista Urbide tomaron, los dos solos, la ciudad de Laguardia, ocupada por los Carlistas», seems to announce an account of an especially heroic deed. Actually, the protagonist and his companion undertake this adventure as a response to offensive statements about Basques made by an officer under the command of the Liberal Captain Briones. Their wounded pride drives them to volunteer for a suicide mission. They scale the city wall only to discover that the Carlists have almost abandoned Laguardia. They display a rag as a sign of their success. A small enemy patrol sends them flying back to Briones and his men, who welcome them as heroes. Zalacaín appears more comic than heroic in this episode. He acts like a juvenile daredevil in attempting the deed, but the fact that he and Bautista «take» a nearly empty city heightens the ironic contrast between the title and the action. Baroja makes his hero a victim of dramatic irony, too. In the escape from Estella, Zalacaín flees from the Carlists in a stolen Carlist uniform only to be taken prisoner by the Liberals when he arrives at a place of safety. The greatest irony of all, however, takes place at the end of the novel, when after successfully completing many dangerous tasks and engineering numerous ingenious escapes, Zalacaín dies of a gunshot wound in the back fired by his childhood enemy Cacho. The inescapable irony of fate, prefigured by the fifteenth-century manuscript, brings about the adventurer's death. Once again, Baroja punctuates the irony of the event with an incongruous comparison:

> A lo lejos, un clarín guerrero hacía temblar el aire de Roncesvalles. Así se habían estremecido aquellos montes con el cuerno de Rolando.
> Así, hacía cerca de quinientos años, había matado, matado también a traición, Velche de Micolalde, deudo de los Ohando, a Martín López de Zalacaín. (I: 251)

The author establishes an initial contrast between the death of the epic hero Roland and Zalacaín's ancestor. Although both die as a result of treachery, Roland dies a warrior's death in battle after exhibiting extraordinary prowess. The ancestral Zalacaín, on the other hand, dies from a crossbow wound in the eye before he can enter combat to defend the family honor. The temporal distance at least ennobles the episode somewhat. Yet the juxtaposition of Roland's death and that of the modern Zalacaín in a roadside inn after demanding that Carlos Ohando kneel and and beg his sister's forgiveness for insulting her, seems utterly ludicrous. Finally, the aggrandizement of the adventurer in the form of an elegant epitaph and poem in his honor, both parodies of honorific literary forms, contributes to an ironic vision of the hero. The ironic distance with which Baroja and the narrator view Zalacaín adds a troubling element to the characterization of the adventurer. The subversive nature of the irony threatens to undercut the portrayal of the adventurer as a hero. Although Baroja doubtless intended Zalacaín to be an exceptional individual, a hero, he generates an ambivalent attitude in the text by playfully and ironically undermining the adventurer's heroic stature. This ambiguity attests to Baroja's ability to add dimensions to a type of character and to his humorous and subversive impulses as an artist.

«MEMORIAS DE UN HOMBRE DE ACCIÓN»

The combining of storytelling and historytelling culminates in *El aprendiz de conspirador,* the first volume of the *Memorias de un hombre de acción* series. The novel provides a microcosm of the fictional historical world of *Memorias de un hombre de acción* in terms of historical range and focus and literary techniques employed. The multiple narrators, chronological disorder, and episodic, fragmentary plot of *Shanti Andía* and the critical, ironic tone of *Zalacaín* recur in *El aprendiz* and elements of both Shanti and Zalacaín resurface in the hero Eugenio Aviraneta. Baroja introduces the reader to the subject of the series, Aviraneta and his life story, and to the fictional editor Pedro Leguía, whose research efforts, transcription of pamphlets, inclusion of newspaper clippings and letters, and rearrangement and addition of material, mirror Baroja's own creative and investigative endeavors. Baroja clearly derives Leguía from the foreign journalist of *Zalacaín,* but makes him a more complex and important character.

The title of the series, *Memorias de un hombre de acción,* recalls Shanti's retrospective personal recounting of his adventures and those of his uncle. The «hombre de acción» identifies Aviraneta as a type, the adventurer, but suggests a more philosophical approach to the hero. *El aprendiz de conspirador* prepares the reader for the storytelling and historytelling to come by explaining the relationship between the editor and Aviraneta and providing the background information leading up to the hero's participation in the War of Independence. Leguía initially meets Aviraneta in Laguardia in 1837. The two men become friends and Leguía accepts Aviraneta's offer to join him in his intrigue for the Liberal cause. Eventually Aviraneta tells Leguía about the secret notebook in which he has recorded facts and observations about his past experiences in case he should write his memoirs as a defense against his enemies. Aviraneta narrates episodes from his youth to Leguía and describes Enlightenment Spain, including comments on education, the progressive clubs, the Masons and other secret societies of the times. He even outlines the activities of the Inquisition. Later the notebook comes into Leguía's possession and he pieces together the memoirs. He investigates and reconstructs what Aviraneta has not developed earlier.

Although the basic action and purpose of *El aprendiz* seem simple enough, Baroja makes the introduction to the fictional and historical material of *Memorias de un hombre de acción* as complicated as the rest of the series and almost as complex as nineteenth-century Spanish history. Shifts in perspective and multiple narratives much more involved than those of *Shanti Andía* contribute to this effect. Baroja opens the novel with the voice of a third-person omniscient narrator, which permits the reader to meet both Leguía and Aviraneta from an external and internal viewpoint. But as the narrative progresses the narrator almost imperceptibly moves into the point of view of Pello Leguía, who does not know the identity of Aviraneta at first, but feels great curiosity about this anonymous man who mixes freely with both Carlists and Liberals.[14] The narrator deliberately withholds this information so that the reader shares Leguía's confusion. The shift in point of view adds to the aura of mystery about Aviraneta and two embedded narratives increase the ambiguity. A man identified only as «el hombre de la zamarra» recounts a tale from the past in which Aviraneta appears as a treacherous character. A later narrative by a friend of the hero, Zurbano, portrays Aviraneta as a

---

[14] This is a situation in which point of view, that of Leguía, differs from narrative voice. For an explanation of the distinction between mode and voice see GÉRARD GENETTE, «Mode», in *Figures III* (París: Editions du Seuil, 1972), 183-224, at pp. 203-06.

patriotic defender of personal liberty and the Constitution of 1812. The counterbalancing of these two accounts prepares the reader for the contradictory viewpoints ahead in *Memorias de un hombre de acción* about historical events and the hero. Baroja places yet another narrative within Aviraneta's first person account. Aviraneta's relative and spiritual mentor Etchepare describes his adventures as a republican during the French Revolution. The technique of embedding creates a Chinese box effect of storytelling in the text.[15] This deliberately confusing mass of perspectives and narrative voices embodies in fictional form some of Baroja's attitudes towards history as developed in his essays. Baroja presents his belief in the subjectivity of history in the form of numerous interrelated first-person narratives not masquerading as objective accounts. He stresses that history arises from an intuitive development of facts and clues. Leguía reconstructs Aviraneta's history from facts and clues. Baroja emphasizes the understanding of psychological types as the key to comprehension of another historical epoch. He focuses on «a man of action» as a means of understanding nineteenth-century Spanish history in *Memorias de un hombre de acción.* Finally, Baroja insists that history is a type of literature. He demonstrates this conviction in *El aprendiz* by making the entrance into the fictional historical world of *Memorias de un hombre de acción* a web of personal narratives that fuse storytelling and historytelling. The narrators simultaneously tell stories and history, literary constructs forged from personal experience and historical reality.

As in *Shanti Andía,* the multiple narratives create a variety of chronological perspectives. Unlike the earlier novel, however, each temporal locus has specific historical reference points in terms of dates, locations, and important events. The progression of narrative voices corresponds to an ever-widening chronological vista moving back in time to the French Revolution and forward again to 1808 on the eve of the War of Independence. *El aprendiz* opens in 1837 during the First Carlist War. In the subsequent accounts by Aviraneta's two acquaintances, the temporal orientation shifts to 1820-30, during which time the Liberals lose power and attempt to regain it under the command of General Mina. In his own narrative, Aviraneta moves back in time to 1792, the year of his birth, and leads up to 1808. Etchepare relates events that go back to the 1780s. In Scott's novels, the specificity of historical dates and events helps guide the reader in his understanding of the text. But the variety of voices and times in *El aprendiz* has just the opposite effect. It disorients the reader and challenges him to reorder the narratives and time sequences in a more readily comprehensible form. Baroja complicates matters

---

[15] For an interesting study of the Chinese box effect created by the embedded narrative see Tzvetan Todorov, «Narrative-Men», in *The Poetics of Prose,* trans. Richard Howard (Ithaca: Cornell University Press, 1977), pp. 66-79.

further by abruptly truncating some of the narrative threads. He leaves unresolved the story of Leguía's exploits and his love affair with Corito Arteaga until volume thirteen of *Memorias de un hombre de acción, El amor, el dandismo y la intriga.* The glimpse of Aviraneta's activities in 1820-30 raises questions about his political ties during that time. Baroja obviously uses this literary device to create suspense and heighten reader interest in the rest of the series (something which he may have picked up from serial novels), but the temporal shifts have their own internal coherence as well. They represent a sequence of flashbacks that provide personal and historical information leading up to the current moment of narration. For example, the novel begins on the road with Corito and Leguía in a stagecoach bound for Laguardia. The narrator immediately moves backward in time to tell about Leguía's family, childhood, and meeting of his beloved. On a broader scale, Aviraneta's and Etchepare's accounts function as flashback sequences outlining the historical events leading up to the Spain of divided loyalties in 1837, with which the novel opens. The variety of temporal foci also has the effect of blurring distinctions, producing a chronological montage. Regardless of the date —1837, 1820, 1808, or 1789— Leguía, Aviraneta, and Etchepare all champion the cause of freedom and Liberalism. The circumstances and names of the factions change, but the principles remain the same. Each man passes on the legacy of the active life on behalf of liberty to his apprentice, from Etchepare to Aviraneta, and from Aviraneta to Leguía. This initiation process in which an older man, a repository of wisdom, introduces the younger man to the ideals and ways of an elite society, recalls the romance pattern in which a wise old man instructs and aids the hero in his quest for self and a more perfect society. Baroja also draws attention to the fact that continuity across historical epochs is generated by human relationships, not by the progression of time itself or by the linear march of historical events.

Since he does not use a single, linear plot, a sole narrator, or temporal movement to order the fictional world, Baroja relies on the patterns of romance and satire present in *Shanti Andía* and *Zalacaín* to organize the episodes of *El aprendiz.* Aviraneta ends his narrative with a description of how he and his friends form a secret society, *El Aventino,* plan and execute the elopement of a Frenchman, Frassac, with a young Spanish woman, Paquita Zubialde. The episode has all the qualities of a comic opera — a jealous, possessive father opposed to his daughter's suitor, different nationalities as an additional blocking element, a group of loyal and clever friends who aid the lovers, a flamboyant and almost farcical midnight escape, and a happy ending in which the lovers are reunited. At one point Aviraneta makes a humorous reference to the underlying romance plot in speaking of Paquita's father, the dragon hoarding the treasure (and by implication of the hero's quest and acquisition of the treasure), «cuando se enteró de que Paquita tenía relaciones con un teniente de dragones, se convirtió él en el dragón de su hija» (III: 109). The lighthearted word play of the statement indicates the bemused attitude of the narrator towards the romance plot, which approaches parody. The daring escape plan, which involves Aviraneta's crawling across a rope ladder from a window to a roof, descending a drain pipe, gathering up the young woman (whose excessive weight threatens to injure him), and traveling secretly in a hidden boat across a river to the next village for the wedding ceremony, amuses as much as it highlights the courage and cunning of the hero. Even in such a clearcut development of a romance pattern as this, the comic elements introduced by Baroja tend to reveal the sardonic smile of an implied author in the background. The tone differs significantly from the sentimental treatment of romance in *Shanti Andía*. Baroja's dissection of the *tertulias* of Laguardian society openly reveals the satirist's impulse to strip away appearances and expose the inner core of truth. The narrator begins with the conservative, aristocratic salon of *Las Piscinas* — a stronghold of the Carlists. A satirical portrait of one of the ladies of the group, the snobbish, horsey Graciosa San Mederi, shows the pretentiousness of that social class. Graciosa's sensibility has never overcome its exposure to the novels of Ann Radcliffe:

> desde entonces no pensaba más que en situaciones extraordinarias y espantosas, en bosques incultos y llenos de misterio... y, sobre todo, en lagos, en esos lagos sombríos y poéticos en los que se puede navegar una noche de luna sobre un ligero esquife mientras se escuchaba a lo lejos el rumor de las locas serenatas.
>
> Desgraciadamente para ella, vivía en un pueblo asentado en lo alto de una colina, en donde no había más lago que aquellos dos charcos que se llenaban con lluvias del invierno, y en las que no se podía navegar más que en un cajón y empujando con un palo en el fondo cenagoso, cosa terriblemente antipoética. (III: 35-36)

Baroja's sarcastic deflation of the Romantic images by contrasting them with their real counterparts unmasks the lady's illusions and her ignorance of the harsh realities that surround her. Baroja proceeds down the social ladder, examining each *tertulia* as representative of a certain segment of society. He ends with an analysis of the rebellious villagers, who simply band together on impulse, according to their own desires and hatreds. Two old women lead these groups, Dolores «la Montaperras» (a Liberal supporter) and Saturnina «la Gitana» (a Carlist supporter). Each receives a detailed description in the text and despite their apparently different political affiliations, Baroja points out their sameness in terms of bestiality: «Estas dos arpías representaban la parte turbia que hay en todas las sectas y en todos los partidos; en ellas, el odio al enemigo era lo principal; un odio frenético, sin cuartel» (III: 39). Baroja's anatomy of the Laguardian *tertulias* functions as a critique to all of Spanish society. His observations transcend the 1837 context to include the contemporary social structure, in which hypocrisy, personal interest, and instinct take precedence over ideological concerns and social well-being. This episode provides just one example of observations made about the historical world of *Memorias de un hombre de acción* that have serious implications for contemporary society as well.

In *El aprendiz de conspirador,* Baroja gives just enough information about the hero to arouse reader interest in his exploits. He briefly outlines Aviraneta's record of participation in major historical events in the introduction: he fought with Merino against the French in 1809, with the Liberals against Merino in 1821, with Byron in Greece, in support of the Constitution in 1823, and with the exiles under Mina in 1830. The sketchy summary gives an idea of the extent of his political activism and the seriousness of his commitment to the Liberal cause. Like Shanti Andía and Zalacaín, courage, strength of will, cleverness, and adaptability characterize Aviraneta rather than brute strength and passion. Significantly, Baroja compares him in the novel with animals associated with astuteness and cold meditation, «A Pello le pareció un pajarraco, una verdadera ave de rapiña» (III: 55) and «pareció un aguilucho resistiendo las embestidas de un jabalí» (III: 69). Aviraneta demonstrates his skills in his reconnaissance of Laguardia and in his escape from the ambush arranged by «el hombre de la zamarra» and his friends. Baroja expands the ideological aspect of the adventurer he first explored in *Zalacaín,* in Aviraneta. The hero acts on behalf of a cause and with an ideal Spain in mind as an ultimate goal:

> «España no necesita más que una dictadura: la de la justicia, la de la libertad. Nada de fuerza, nada de soldados que quieran imitar a Napoleón. El Poder civil debe estar siempre por encima del Poder militar. El Ejército no debe ser más que el brazo de la nación, nunca la cabeza.» (III: 67)

Aviraneta envisions a future utopia, «un mundo de justicia y de bondad, sin guerra, sin enemigos, sin violencias» (III: 69). Behind the ideals of the hero, of course, lie Baroja and the Generation of '98's vision of a collectively sick society and their desire for major moral and social reforms. In this way, Baroja projects his own preoccupations onto Aviraneta and his historical world. Aviraneta shares Shanti's self-awareness and Zalacaín's victimization by people and fate. When he begins his narrative, he presents his philosophy of life:

> «Mi filosofía, si es que a un político aventurero se le permite tener filosofía, ha sido siempre ésa: trabajar con entusiasmo para conseguir las cosas, y cuando no las he conseguido, quedarme tranquilo y renunciar a ellas sin dolor alguno.

> Como hombre de mala suerte, he sufrido bastantes desgracias; he presenciado catástrofes, derrotas, incendios, matanzas; patriota entusiasta, he sido testigo de dos invasiones extranjeras y del desmoronamiento del imperio colonial español; liberal y progresista, he visto a mi país padeciendo las reacciones más bárbaras; me ha herido la calumnia y el descrédito, privándome de todas las armas cuando necesitaba más de ellas; he pasado por casi todas las cárceles de España; he estado muchas veces a punto de ser fusilado..., y, sin embargo, si volviera a vivir, volvería a hacer lo mismo que lo que hice.» (III: 79)

The hero expresses a retrospective, matter-of-fact attitude of resignation towards the hardships and disappointments he has suffered and an uncompromising, dedicated reaffirmation of his actions and his cause. The stoic tone reveals the philosophical and intellectual side of his active life. Aviraneta reflects on his actions and assesses them. Baroja also instills within his hero the importance of being aware of reality and of being able to see through illusion. Aviraneta shares Baroja's belief that fiction must reflect reality:

> «... únicamente la realidad, de chico y de hombre, ha llegado a apasionarme. En la misma literatura no he podido nunca comprender las obras basadas en frases bonitas; si detrás de la ficción poética o dramática no he sentido la realidad, no me ha interesado el libro o el drama.» (III: 90)

> «... sólo allí donde he vislumbrado la realidad, aunque sea a través de un velo espeso de ficción, he podido sentir interés.» (III: 90)

The high value Aviraneta and Baroja attach to the presence of reality behind fiction has greater significance than as a statement of aesthetic preference. Baroja makes a plea for the recognition of the reality behind the fictional historical veil of the works of *Memorias de un hombre de acción,* a vision of contemporary man's place in the world. He also appeals for recognition of his «hombre de acción» as an embodiment of profound philosophical concerns.

The fictional prologue that frames *El aprendiz de conspirador* provides the most important key to understanding Baroja's reasons for writing *Memorias de un hombre de acción.* Baroja employs the often-used literary device of the discovered manuscript to explain his interest in Aviraneta's life. He mentions his Aunt Ursula's references to a relative who had been a spy and conspirator. As in his non-fictional essay account, Baroja initially expresses indifference: «oía con indiferencia estos relatos de cosas viejas que, por mi tendencia antihistórica y antiliteraria, o por incapacidad mental, no me interesaban» (II: 9). Some time later Aunt Ursula informs him of Pedro Leguía's death and the discovery of their relative Aviraneta's memoirs among his papers. After more time has passed, Baroja reluctantly admits to having examined the material and gained interest in it: «Me pareció, a pesar de mi tendencia antihistórica, que algunas cosas no dejaban de tener interés» (III: 11). Although the tone of these statements is light, humorous, and playful, Baroja's insistence on his anti-historicism is consistent with the attitude expressed in his essays.[16] Instead of a case in which the emphatic quality of a speaker's denial serves to affirm that which he apparently wishes to deny, I think Baroja wants to emphasize the fact that his approach to history in the novels that follow differs greatly from that of professional historians he disdains. It is a response to and rejection of the professional histories. He puts distance between himself and the historians by not even feigning objectivity, but rather indicating his subjective interest in Aviraneta: «no sé si por razón de parentesco familiar y espiritual, o por verlo tan maltratado en algunos libros viejos, me determiné a publicar estas Memorias» (III: 12). In Baroja's own mind, he, Leguía, and Aviraneta all blend together: «los tres formamos una pequeña trinidad, única e indivisible» (III: 12). Baroja also points out his desire to vindicate Aviraneta, to reverse the judgement of him as a traitor attached to him by historians:

> Aviraneta quiso ser un político realista en un país donde no se aceptaba más que al retórico y al orador. Quiso construir con hechos donde no se construía más que con tropos. Y fracasó.
> Entre tanto charlatán hueco y sonoro como ha sido exaltado en la España del siglo XIX, a Eugenio de Aviraneta, hombre valiente, patriota atrevido, liberal entusiasta, le tocó en suerte en su tiempo el desprecio, y después de su muerte, el olvido. (III: 12)

Baroja's desire to reveal the truth about Aviraneta, and his negative attitude towards nineteenth-century history, identify him once again with the satirist. He must reverse the accepted values attached to that period to vindicate the hero. He must reveal the mediocrity and chaos of the epoch, if necessary by dismantling the positivistic, causality-based historical approaches and unmasking the false heroes of the age to exalt his own hero. Baroja's desire to vindicate Aviraneta, however, is far from a purely altruistic motive. His tendency to identify with Aviraneta and Leguía indicates that in a sense his vindication of Aviraneta is a vindication of himself and of his philosophy of life. At the beginning of the prologue, Baroja states his preference for the present and the future over the past, but comments: «cosa absurda en España, en donde, por ahora, lo que menos hay es presente y porvenir» (III: 9). Baroja expresses his nonconformity with the prevailing attitudes of his culture, but by rewriting nineteenth-century Spanish history from the point of view of his downtrodden hero Aviraneta, he exorcises the demons of his own historical past. Storytelling about history becomes a means of establishing

---

[16] For more information concerning the apparent contradiction between Baroja's antihistoricism and his writing of *Memorias de un hombre de acción* see FLORES ARROYUELO, pp. 64-71, and LONGHURST, pp. 126-27.

oneself in an integrated temporal continuum of past, present, and future. As Baroja said, speaking for himself and others of his generation, «Si tuviéramos una idea clara y exacta de lo que hemos sido, conociéramos nuestra historia sin leyendas ni ficciones no sólo en períodos anormales, sino en el período normal de la vida, podríamos comprender fácilmente lo que podemos ser» (*El tablado de Arlequín*, V: 30).

III

THE DEMYTHIFICATION OF HISTORY

> Verily, my friends, I walk among men as among
> the fragments and limbs of men. This is what is
> terrible for my eyes, that I can find man in ruins
> and scattered as over a battlefield or a butcher-
> field. And when my eyes flee from the now to
> the past, they always find the same: fragments
> and limbs and dreadful accidents —but no human
> beings.
>
> (NIETZSCHE, *Thus Spoke Zarathustra*)
>
> The material of history is the transient com-
> plexities of a human world moving like clouds in
> the wind, which are often entirely transformed
> by the most trifling accident.
>
> (SCHOPENHAUER, *The World as Will
> and Representation*)

ORDER, HISTORY AND FICTION

Baroja's concept of *historia humorística* and the complex, confusing,
disorderly form that it takes in *Memorias de un hombre de acción* provide not only a subversion of more traditional, grandiose histories and
a continuation of the paradoxical conflict between romance and satire
in his earlier works, but also a reversal of more traditional philosophical
attitudes towards historical figures and events as part of a broader, more
general pattern of meaning. For archaic man, history as we know it,
as a succession of unique dates and events, did not exist. Occurrences
only derived meaning from their transhistorical significance, as analogous
repetitions of divine archetypes realized within the cyclical time of the
cosmos.[1] Although the historians and historical novelists of later ages
have abandoned cyclical time, they share with their ancestors what
Scholes and Kellogg have called «man's strongest impulse», the desire

---

[1] MIRCEA ELIADE, *Cosmos and History: The Myth of the Eternal Return* (1954:
rpt. New York: Harper Torchbooks, 1959). See especially chapter one, «Archetypes and Repetitions», pp. 1-48. On the reappearance of cyclical theories in
modern times see chapter four, «The Terror of History», pp. 139-62.

M. SUZAN. 6

to transform the empirical world into a mythical one.[2] Whether authors of fiction, historians, and literary critics view history as a collection of great men and deeds within a heroic tradition, as a steady march towards improvement of the human condition or simply as a series of cause-effect relationships, the same mythifying impulse of attaching transcendent meaning to the here-and-now of experience, of viewing the particular in terms of a significant whole, animates their desire to explain the people and happenings of the past. A historical novelist like Galdós, for example, presents nineteenth-century Spanish history in the *Episodios nacionales* in a coherent, simplified fashion by maintaining a limited number of fictional narrators, a linear concept of time, high selectivity in choosing historical figures and events, and by making the fictional historical world consonant with an overview of Progressivism, nationalism, and a certain standard of heroism. As for formal histories, Hayden White shows in *Metahistory* that historical texts have recognizable structural patterns, among them a mode of emplotment, identifiable in terms of a combination of four general categories of characteristics. Northrop Frye notes that when the historian deals on a metahistorical level, in a more general, universal context, he draws closer to the position of the fictional writer: «We notice that when a historian's scheme gets to a certain point of comprehensiveness it becomes mythical in shape, and so approaches the poetic in its structure.» In the literary sphere of activity, the attempt of modern formalist criticism to describe texts in terms of basic narrative patterns, whether they are called *mythoi,* narremes, or simply structural paradigms, indicates the need to identify literature as the repetition and variation of certain basic constructs.[3] In each case, mythification arises from transcending the particular by viewing it on a more abstract and meaningful level in which the significance that underlies the specific form of the text becomes evident, which in turn enables the reader and critic to compare and contrast it with other related material. In each text, too, the concept and presentation of order are fundamental to understanding the world view that underlies the form that the mythifying process takes. It is not surprising that romance, the literary mode closest to myth, has the most clearly delineated and enduring system of order, and that satire,

---

[2] ROBERT SCHOLES and ROBERT KELLOG, *The Nature of Narrative* (New York: Oxford University Press, 1966), p. 135.

[3] HAYDEN WHITE, «Introduction: The Poetics of History», in *Metahistory: The Historical Imagination in Nineteenth-Century Europe* (Baltimore: The Johns Hopkins University Press, 1973), pp. 1-42. NORTHROP FRYE, «New Directions from Old», in *Fables of Identity: Studies in Poetic Mythology* (New York: Harcourt, Brace, and World, 1963), 52-66 at pp. 53-54. The attempt to identify and describe diverse literary forms in terms of a limited number of patterns is, of course, nothing new. Such varied works as Propp's *Morphology of the Russian Folktale,* Kristeva's *Texte du roman,* and Frye's *Anatomy of Criticism* are different responses to the same classifying impulse behind Aristotle's *Poetics.*

that farthest from myth, has the most fragmentary and disjunct presentation of order.

Baroja constantly denies the existence of any transcendent order or meaning in history or in the universe. He believes only in the intranscendent particular in its disordered, unpredictable, and paradoxical natural state as reflected in his term *historia humorística,* and not as part of a general pattern of meaning. Perhaps his approach to history, in contrast to the more traditional one, can best be described as the demythification of history. But to see Baroja as merely a pessimist or nihilist, as some would have it, shows a serious lack of understanding of his world view, and of the intentions of any ironist or satirist.[4] The examination of order in *Memorias de un hombre de acción* as both theme and form provides the most revealing method of understanding Baroja's demythification of history.

The question of order in Baroja's novels has always been a problem for his critics. Some have actually become upset over the loose construction, the element of caprice, and the apparent lack of asthetic coherence:

> De ahí esos frecuentes viajes que encontramos en sus narraciones, sin unidad, ni trama ni verdaderos conflictos; sólo pretextos en que apoyar el incesante peregrinar de sus criaturas, el constante hormigueo más afín al folletín que al género novela, hasta el punto que se diría que su lenguaje sólo sirve al objetivo de la información.[5]

Others comment on the lack of order, but try to account for it in some logical fashion. Ortega y Gasset, one of the author's earliest and most astute critics, criticizes Baroja for the disjunct and disorganized quality of his novels, but regards it as a result of the author's attempt to capture the speed and variety of life. Similarly, López Estrada attributes his lack of structure to a faithful representation of the indeterminacy and disorder of real life. Eugenio de Nora sees disorder in Baroja's works as a response to the internal aesthetic demands of the novel, i.e. the sacrificing of structural order to the independent movements of the characters within that novelistic world, which atmosphere and rhythm counteract as unifying factors. José Alberich accounts for the looseness

---

[4] FRANCISCO CARENAS refers to Baroja's works as the product of «un innato mal genio» and describes his art as «radical anarquismo y dolorido pesimismo» and «un callejón sin salida del escepticismo» in «La abrumadora concreción del lenguaje barojiano», *Cuadernos Americanos,* 202, No. 5 (Sept.-Oct. 1975), 117. JOSÉ ORTEGA Y GASSET feels that according to Baroja «una idea no es digna si no es una idea contra algo o alguien». He refers to Baroja's «culto del yo un poco nihilista» and identifies the most elementary aspect of Baroja's work as the «nostalgia del orangután», in «Una primera vista sobre Pío Baroja», *El Espectador* (1916-1934), Vol. II of his *Obras completas* (Madrid: Revista de Occidente, 1957), 103-25, at pp. 112-13.

[5] CARENAS, p. 123.

and fluidity of Baroja's construction as an expression, on the one hand, of his skepticism towards any theory or dogma and subsequent emphasis on the particular and concrete, and, on the other hand, of his desire to bring writing closer to spoken language, with its arbitrary starts and stops, associational logic, and rapid flow. Finally, María Embeita views Baroja's «estructura deshilvanada» as a reflection of his concept of the world as «confuso, caótico, sin sentido».[6]

Order as structure and as a theme in *Memorias de un hombre de acción* has to date been dealt with inadequately. Jaime Pérez Montaner discusses the structure of the series only in terms of Baroja's organization of the historical material. Although he feels that the volumes may be read as one continuous novel, he divides the twenty-two works as follows: (1) *El aprendiz de conspirador* (Vol. I) —End of the eighteenth century and beginning of the nineteenth century; (2) *El escuadrón del «Brigante»* (Vol. 2) —Guerra de la Independencia (Spanish Napoleonic Wars, 1808-1814); (3) *Los caminos del mundo* (Vol. 3) —First period of Absolutism (1814-1820); (4) *Con la pluma y con el sable —Los contrastes de la vida* (Vols. 4-7) —«Triennium» of the Constitution (1820-1823); (5) *La veleta de Gastizar* and *Los caudillos de 1830* (Vols. 8-9) —Ominous Decade (1823-1832); (6) *La Isabelina —La venta de Mirambel* (Vols. 10-20) —Regency of María Cristina (1833-1840), focuses on the conflict between Liberals and Carlists, Court intrigue and conflicts, and the Carlist War; (7) *Crónica escandalosa* and *Desde el principio hasta el fin* (Vols. 21-22) —Reign of Isabel II (1843-1868). Pérez Montaner points out Baroja's emphasis on the period 1833-1840 as the period of greatest activity for Aviraneta and that of the growth of Liberalism, notes chronological gaps in the series, and labels a certain similarity between the first and last volumes as an attempt to give a circular form to the series. Flores Arroyuelo treats order in *Memorias de un hombre de acción* only in terms of structural content by describing the first novel as a frame tale and summarizing the plots and divisions within the rest of the novels. Carlos Longhurst shows the greatest understanding for the problems of order in *Memorias de un hombre de acción* by recognizing that the structure and themes of the works —chronological order, organization within the novels and of the novels, and Baroja's concept of history— are inseparable and must be considered together

---

[6] See JOSÉ ORTEGA Y GASSET, «Ideas sobre Pío Baroja», *El Espectador* (1916-1934), Vol. II of his *Obras completas* (Madrid: Revista de Occidente, 1957), 69-102, at pp. 96-97. FRANCISCO LÓPEZ ESTRADA, *Perspectivas sobre Pío Baroja* (Sevilla: Universidad de Sevilla, 1972), pp. 47-53; EUGENIO DE NORA, «Pío Baroja», Vol. I of his *La novela contemporánea (1898-1927)* (Madrid: Gredos, 1958), 97-229, at pp. 123-25. JOSÉ ALBERICH, *Los ingleses y otros temas de Pío Baroja* (Madrid: Alfaguara, 1966), pp. 84-87; and MARÍA EMBEITA. «Tema y forma de expresión en Baroja», *Cuadernos Hispanoamericanos*, Nos. 265-67 (July-Sept. 1972), p. 145.

to understand the series. Longhurst stresses that Baroja's view of history as chaotic, arbitrary, and without transcendent meaning explains the apparent freedom with which Baroja treats his historical material and his lack of concern for causality and logical development of plot. He points to the trajectory of Aviraneta's life as the fundamental unifying factor of the series, along with the prologues, which help orient the reader, and the reappearance of fictional characters in various novels of *Memorias de un hombre de acción,* which also gives a sense of continuity to the whole. Longhurst himself, however, realizes that the structure of *Memorias de un hombre de acción* deserves closer analysis, especially in relation to the themes of the series.[7]

In just such a closer analysis I now propose to show that Baroja's demythification of history is achieved through the subversion of those procedures that normally unify, endow with meaning, and mythify in historical fiction —the fixing of the point of view and tone, the accounting of time, the implications of causality, and the threading together of episodes. His ironic undermining of these aspects in the texts produces a chaotic, disjunct, dark vision of Spanish nineteenth-century history that resists any attempt to provide it with transcendent meaning. The disorder of this historical world ruled by self-interest, hypocrisy, and unrepressed violence has its analogue in the structure and literary technique of the novels themselves.

POINT OF VIEW AND TONE

An author's use of a consistent point of view and tone in a novel provides one of the most effective methods of unifying the text and shaping a reader's response to the fictional world; i.e., it communicates certain values and attitudes and makes the work more coherent and intelligible. In historical novels, point of view and tone lend themselves to the simplification and consolidation of complex and contradictory historical situations and occurrences rendering history much more accessible and systematic than it is in reality. Of course, history books share with historical fiction the subjective selection and presentation of material, but most historical novelists do not even maintain the pretense of objective research and development of historical information. Historical fiction consciously

---

[7] JAIME PÉREZ MONTANER, «Sobre la estructura de las *Memorias de un hombre de acción*», *Cuadernos Hispanoamericanos,* Nos. 265-67 (July-Sept. 1972), pp. 619-620. I have added the dates and some of the historical information to the divisions. See also FRANCISCO FLORES ARROYUELO, «Estructura y contenido de las *Memorias de un hombre de acción*», in *Pío Baroja y la historia* (Madrid: Helios, 1972), pp. 127-83, and CARLOS LONGHURST, «El significado de la historia» and «*Las memorias* como ciclo novelesco: cronología y estructura», in *Las novelas históricas de Pío Baroja* (Madrid: Guadarrama, 1974), pp. 125-58 and pp. 161-99.

admits its subjectivity and fictional nature from the start, and conse-quently, it is several degrees further advanced in terms of patterning itself after fictional models than are historical texts (but it remains a matter of degree, not of fundamental nature).

Galdós's use of point of view and tone in the *Episodios nacionales* shows how this aspect of literary technique creates order in the novels and contributes to the mythification of history. The series consists of five major divisions with ten volumes in each division. (Galdós died after finishing six of the novels in the fifth division, although he had already planned the four remaining works.) The novels within each division are narrated by one or more main characters, so that the reader is provided with a familiar guide and representative from the current social structure to order and present the historical world to him. Through the eyes of the young Gabriel Araceli, Galdós transforms the resounding defeat of the Spanish at Trafalgar into a triumphant celebration of the patriotic fervor and unity of the Spanish people in which ordinary men become heroes. While Galdós does not spare the reader any of the unpleasantness of naval warfare, the violence, gore and the terrible pain of loss of the loved ones, the tone of exaltation and admiration for these new common heroes and of Spanish national pride comes through on every page without any insinuation of doubt or ironic undercutting. Galdós's use of a youth-ful, inexperienced witness as the storyteller gives him the freedom to convey the impact of such an emotionally intense experience on an un-formed, impressionable mind with as yet none of the sophistication or pre-judices of an adult. Similarly in *Zaragoza,* now filtered through the con-sciousness of a more mature Araceli, Galdós carefully develops the towns-people's heroic actions under siege as analogous to the experience of Christian martyrdom, spiritually triumphant in their physical defeat, by skillfully drawing clear moral lines in the text and borrowing motifs from hagiographic literature. The community maintains a unified heroic front of self-sacrifice and ultimately rejects the evil miser Candiola, a traitor to the common cause. In these novels Galdós molds history into myth, the apotheosis of the Spanish people, as their spirit of unity, bravery, and patriotism triumphs over trial after trial of historical defeat. The reader shares in the emergence of a collective hero through the eyes of a pro-tagonist who himself embodies this new national attitude.

The point of view and tone in *Memorias de un hombre de acción,* however, produce just the opposite effect, one of uncertainty, ambiguity, and demythification. As with Shanti in *Las inquietudes de Shanti Andía,* Aviraneta the narrator is removed in time and space from the Aviraneta who instigates and participates in historical deeds. This gives two differ-ent perspectives of the hero, as an actor, and as a meditative mature individual who analyzes history retrospectively. Aviraneta criticizes the Liberals' failed attempt in 1830 to reenter the country and reestablish

86

a foothold in the Spanish government: «Las precauciones del Gobierno eran tales y su presteza y actividad tan extremadas, que hacían imposible que una acción tan desperdigada, tan anárquica y tan mal dirigida como la de los emigrados pudiera tener éxito» (*Los caudillos de 1830*, III: 940-41). He describes the atmosphere in Madrid after María Cristina abdicates and Espartero assumes the regency (1840-1841):

> Ni por las ideas ni por el temperamento se podía saber con claridad quiénes eran los liberales y quiénes los reaccionarios.
> La envidia y la intriga lo dominaban todo; por cuestiones personales cambiaban de política los militares y los reaccionarios. *(Desde el principio hasta el fin,* VI: 1122)

Aviraneta's commentary contrasts sharply with his eyewitness accounts of historical events. He narrates his experience as a cavalry officer in the battle of Hontoria, a skirmish between Spanish guerrilla forces and the French army during the Napoleonic Wars:

> Tuvimos un momento la certidumbre de que habíamos arrollado al enemigo; una descarga cerrada nos recibió; silbaron las balas en nuestros oídos; respiramos un aire cargado de humo de pólvora y de papeles quemados; cayeron diez, doce, quince caballos y jinetes de los nuestros; sus cuerpos nos impidieron seguir adelante; hundimos las espuelas en los ijares de los caballos; era inútil; al pasar la nube de humo nos vimos lanzados por la tangente. *(El escuadrón del «Brigante»,* III: 198-99)

Baroja's style captures the difference between the analytic, retrospective Aviraneta and Aviraneta the man of action in this succession of actions and reactions expressed in short, choppy phrases that convey the immediacy and swiftness of the events and an excited individual's perception of them. This double point of view creates a dual vision of history, too, with distance as the mediating agent. When Aviraneta's perception of history acquires temporal or critical distance, the reader receives historical analysis, historytelling. When he becomes the eyewitness narrator, the reader perceives history as action, as immediate experience conveyed through storytelling. Baroja apparently felt that this dual vision was necessary to present a more honest perception of history in the novels, and his hero embodies as well as provides this duality. Interestingly, one of the first items that Aviraneta buys when he leaves home to go off to war is a spyglass. The object accompanies him throughout his lifetime adventures and Baroja makes references to it throughout the series. The spyglass becomes so closely identified with the hero that in *La ruta del aventurero,* narrated by another character (J. H. Thompson) and in which Aviraneta is disguised as an English naval officer called simply «el capitán», it provides the major clue by which the reader recognizes his true identity. The spyglass symbolizes the adventurer's instinctive ability to distance himself from, or engage himself at will with any situation facing him.[8] It represents the multiple perspectives from which one can view an event and the multiple selves that each individual possesses. Baroja indicates that contemplation transforms the hero into another man and that all men have the potential to become another self:

> A don Eugenio le gustaba contemplar el paisaje; le producía, momentáneamente, un olvido de todo; le recordaba los días de su infancia, cuando iba a la peña de Aya y al monte Larrún a ver el mar a lo lejos. Ese germen ahogado que tenemos todos de otro hombre o de otros hombres despertaba en él con la contemplación. *(Los recursos de la astucia, III: 620)*

Other characters in the series assume a spectator's stance and repeat the dual perspective of Aviraneta. Leguía peers out of his window into the moonlight to see his English friend Jorge Stratford Grain making love in the garden to a young noblewoman, which goes counter to Grain's cynical comments about sentiment and reveals the superficiality of Leguía's own relationship with Delfina in *El amor, el dandismo y la intriga*. Paco Maluenda, a young Carlist soldier, witnesses a brutal murder from a hiding place in *Las mascaradas sangrientas* and his moral as well as spatial distance seal his own fate by tying him forever to the thieves and murderers of Bertache's band. The spatial distance created by crossing the border into France contributes a critical perspective, too. Aviraneta sets in motion from France a number of his plans for political change, including the plan of the Simancas documents, a scheme to split the Carlist camp between the religious zealots and the moderate faction represented by the Carlist Commander-in-Chief Maroto. The orderly world of France helps Alvaro Sánchez de Mendoza assess his visit to Spain in the wake of the Carlist War in the North:

> Al llegar a la frontera, al notar la tranquilidad y el orden que reinaban en Francia, llevó su imaginación inmediatamente, con melancolía, hacia las tierras de España, aquella *nave de los locos*, desgarrada, sangrienta, zarrapastrosa y pobre que era su país. *(La nave de los locos, IV: 472)*

Alvarito's observation creates an image of a man divided in two, alienated from his other self, that associated with his family, country, and cultural heritage. Yet he cannot sever himself completely from what he has witnessed in Spain. He is both part of that nightmare world and separate from it. Leguía's narration of his adventures in *El amor, el dandismo y la intriga* mirrors Aviraneta's retrospective temporal position with his memoirs. While in the course of the novel Leguía's actions appear unmediated by temporal distance, an occasional critical comment about changes in his own character or about his relationship with Aviraneta reminds the

---

[8] BIRUTÉ CIPLIJAUSKAITÉ is of the opinion that *humorismo* and seeing things from a distance are the two constants in Baroja's work in *Baroja, un estilo* (Madrid: Insula, 1972), pp. 249-50.

reader of the Leguía who presents the novel, the disillusioned, elderly man who writes about his youth as therapy for sadness and boredom. All of these references indicate how Baroja uses distance to create multiple perspectives in the series, by doubling the focus of an individual character into spectator/actor, narrator/actor.

Baroja's use of multiple narrators in the series compounds the multiple points of view on history that Aviraneta's and the other narratives provide, and it enables the author to distance himself from the fictional world. A variety of characters assume the narrative task as Aviraneta slips into the background: Ignacio Arteaga, an *afrancesado* friend of Aviraneta's in *Los caminos del mundo;* J. H. Thompson, a Dickensian vagabond Englishman in *La ruta del aventurero* and part of *Los contrastes de la vida;* Pepe Carmona, a businessman from Málaga for part of *Las furias;* the editor Leguía, who continues his own life story in *El amor, el dandismo y la intriga,* and many others whose less extensive accounts are intercalated into the longer narrative divisions. As a result, the reader perceives history filtered through the consciousness of different personalities, nationalities, and political persuasions, and this produces a view of historical characters and events that is not only multiple and ambiguous but, at times, contradictory, as Baroja presents the same historical event from different points of view. Aviraneta presents the battle of Hontoria as a heroic victory for the Spanish achieved through clever strategy and extraordinary courage, but his friend Ganisch, when questioned by Leguía about the encounter, sums up the battle in a few sentences and dismisses it as of little importance. Leguía intervenes here to comment on Ganisch's obvious jealousy, but on other occasions Baroja lets the contradictions stand and does not guide the reader's response. Pepe Carmona's account of the Barcelona uprising in 1835, in which a mob scaled the walls of the fortress and massacred a large number of Carlist prisoners, implies Aviraneta's involvement in planning the deed, but Aviraneta proclaims his innocence and blames the barbaric actions on enemies of the Liberals who attempt to discredit the Constitutionalist movement. A similar juxtaposition of different points of view leaves in question the cause of, and Aviraneta's involvement in, the 1834 murders of the monks of St Isidore in Madrid. Baroja prefers to keep the implications of these events and their bearing on the reader's perception of the hero's character undecided and mysterious, rather than presenting them from a single point of view and thereby placing them within a consistent general historical pattern.

The ambiguous light Baroja casts on historical events extends to historical figures as well. In *Humano enigma* and *La senda dolorosa* he presents a portrait of the Count de España, commander of the Carlist forces in the East (Cataluña), from the point of view of Hugo Riversdale, a young Englishman working as a Liberal secret agent for Aviraneta and sent to observe the Carlist forces from the inside. Riversdale hears numerous accounts of the atrocities committed by España: jailing or shooting people for minor or imagined offenses, arbitrarily loading the guns of a firing squad with blanks just to enjoy the terror of the victims. Yet when Hugo interviews the Count, he discovers a congenial, witty man of considerable charm who distinguishes in his own mind between his true character and the public role he must assume. Riversdale emerges from the encounters totally confused by the man he sees —«violento, contradictorio y enigmático a cada paso» (*Humano enigma,* IV: 687). And Baroja denies the reader a definitive perspective of not only the Count de España, but also of Bessières, Riego, Lord Byron, and a number of other well-known historical figures.

Baroja's shifting points of view portray history on a variety of levels. In *Los recursos de la astucia,* Leguía recounts a story entitled «La canóniga» as told to him by a coffinmaker of Cuenca. In the tale, an evil penitentiary denounces Miguelito Torralba's intentions to deliver the city to the Absolutists in 1823 after assuming the young man has composed an anonymous ballad making fun of his affair with a wealthy townswoman. The Liberals arrange a night ambush for Miguelito and his friend in which he is killed and his love for Asunción thereby tragically ended. The political issues of 1823, the conflicts between Liberals and Absolutists, figure in the tale only as tools used by individuals to wound or destroy personal enemies. Ideology succumbs to the darker side of personal interest. In the second half of the novel, Aviraneta narrates the historical events of 1823, the collapse of the Liberal government and the invasion by the French. Baroja juxtaposes two different perspectives of a single historical period: one, a more intimate vision of the intertwining of human tragedy and historical forces, and the other, a personal perspective of an individual who forms part of those historical forces. Baroja shows throughout the series a preoccupation with presenting the human side of history, how a person's life becomes caught up in and shaped by historical forces. Through these individualized conflicts, Baroja reveals history as a subjective experience, not as an abstract, mythified construct, but as a part of ordinary life. The recounting of sentimental educations comprises much of *Memorias de un hombre de acción,* and Aviraneta's process of education and growth provides a *Bildungsroman* pattern for other such histories —Leguía's in *El amor, el dandismo y la intriga,* J. H. Thompson's in *La ruta del aventurero* and *Los contrastes de la vida,* Alvarito Sánchez de Mendoza's in *Las figuras de cera, La nave de los locos,* and *Las mascaradas sangrientas,* and many others. Various aspects of the historical period in Spain are inscribed within the context of their lives just as Aviraneta's life-story embraces half a century of Spanish history.

From the preceding observations, one can readily see that Baroja's use of point of view undercuts the reader's attempt to derive a consistent, coherent pattern of meaning from the historical events recounted in *Memorias de un hombre de acción*. As in most cases where subversion provides the norm of the text, Baroja's attitude is difficult to discover as well. Like point of view in the series, the tone is varied, changeable, and inconsistent and even his attitude towards the hero Aviraneta seems somewhat ambiguous. One moment the author tries to invoke sympathy for the hero as a great historical figure, mistreated and maligned by more powerful, but much inferior characters. Baroja presents Aviraneta as a valiant cavalry officer, a clever, resourceful spy, and an astute strategist, but periodically and abruptly he submits his hero to comic reduction. Aviraneta figures out an elaborate scheme to get out of prison only to find himself wading through piles of manure to make good the escape. He shows bravery and cunning in foiling a trap set by Absolutists who have uncovered his secret society and its plan to murder Fernando VII, but then acts like a ridiculous, drunken buffoon by running from the police across the rooftops of Madrid dressed as a monk and stopping to relieve himself onto the streets below. Aviraneta, as the «Robespierre» of Aranda during the Liberal triennium, manages to impose his will on a resentful town, but the infirm, elderly father of his former beloved sends him flying into the street in panic after a chance encounter. Baroja's own attitude towards his protagonist does not permit him to be seen as a larger-than-life individual who transcends the here-and-now through extraordinary deeds to be incorporated into the world of myth.

Baroja's tonal shifts in his depiction of other characters and events add to his ambiguous presentation of history. In the story of the Count de España's actions in Cataluña, his fall from favor in the Carlist camp, and his subsequent betrayal and murder by the Junta de Berga recounted in *Humano enigma* and *La senda dolorosa,* Baroja changes tone so many times that it is impossible to derive any conclusion about his intentions. The Count first appears as a violent megalomaniac deserving of loathing and fear. Then, through Hugo Riversdale's accounts he becomes a congenial, though mysterious figure, who merits respect for his astuteness and amusement for his wit and caricaturesque qualities. When he becomes the victim of the Junta's treachery in Aviá, the Count's fear reduces him to an impotent child, worthy of scorn. But as his betrayers seem ever more evil and cruel, the Count de España begins to appear a tragic victim worthy of sympathy and pity. When the Junta forces him to exchange his general's uniform for peasant rags he asks a poor old man to bless him in a village they ride through on his way to his own murder and an unknown grave. In this scene, the formerly monstrous general becomes a pathetic, Christlike figure. Finally, the tragic tale collapses into a macabre farce in which a phrenologist and his assistant Llusifer visit the Count's grave at night, dig up the body, sever the head from the rest

91

of the corpse, analyze the skull, and send it on to a professor for more study. Eventually the skull becomes a church relic used for funerals and for celebrating All Saints' Day. Baroja ends the tale on a bemused, but moralistic tone with this reminder of the insignificance of all human life before its final, inevitable comic reduction to a skeleton. The comic episode signals the author's distancing himself from the Count de España after drawing close to him and showing compassion for him as a victim of human treachery.

Bleakness and despair before the spectacle of Spain ravaged by wars and mediocrity constitute Baroja's most consistent tone in *Memorias de un hombre de acción*. Aviraneta recounts scene after scene of violence and barbarity: «Guerrear es suprimir durante un período la civilización, el orden, la justicia; abolir el mundo moral creado con tanto trabajo, retroceder a épocas de barbarie y de salvajismo» (*El escuadrón del «Brigante»*, III: 162). And the other narrators make similar comments as witnesses of the effects of war. Alvarito Sánchez de Mendoza sees the devastation of the Spanish landscape during the last days of the Carlist War as a product of the most base instincts in man:

> En todas partes era el mismo espectáculo; las calles sucias, las iglesias cerradas, los cementerios abandonados, llenos de zarzas y de cardos; en ninguna parte gente; todo silencio, sombrío... No era sólo la necesidad estratégica de ataque o de defensa la que produjo el montón desordenado y confuso de tejados abiertos, paredes agujereadas, ventanas desvencijadas y caídas, con los cristales rotos; era más bien aquello la consecuencia de la brutalidad, del rencor y de los malos instintos de la fiera humana.
> (*La nave de los locos*, IV: 358)

Throughout the historical world of *Memorias de un hombre de acción*, Baroja inundates his readers with horrible scenes of bestiality and loss. The material destruction pales in comparison with the wrecked hopes and lives of the people that they leave behind. The frustrated lovers in «La canóniga», the disillusionment and death of young Lacy during the Liberal attempt in *Los caudillos de 1830*, the drifting apart of Manón and Alvarito after the Carlist War in *La nave de los locos*, the total debauchery of an innocent young man put in jail in *El sabor de la venganza*, and the constant failure of any individual or group to effect large-scale socio-political reform in Spain all attest to the destructive effects of history. Baroja presents no vision of the Spanish people as heroic or as having leaders of great moral character. *Memorias de un hombre de acción* lacks those great moments of transcendence when individuals or groups rise above historical circumstances, so prevalent in the *Episodios nacionales*. The characters that escape the bleak world of *Memorias de un hombre de acción* do just that, they give up one reality for another, and Baroja often leaves in doubt the success of that evasion. Alvarito of *La nave de los locos* leaves behind the devastation of Spain to settle in France, marry a woman he likes but does not love, find material success and domestic comfort, but live alienated and withdrawn from the woman he once loved as if she were a total stranger. One of Aviraneta's agents, nicknamed «El Rostro Pálido», after spending part of his life as a *señorito* and a spy, falls in love with a young woman, and decides to reform his ways, but he ends up having to emigrate to America to have a chance to realize that dream in *Los confidentes audaces*. Aviraneta never hears from him again. Many characters in *Memorias de un hombre de acción* end up withdrawing from an active life and finding some measure of inner tranquility, but only at the expense of great personal suffering —the loss of a loved one, total disillusionment with their former ideals or society in general— and by learning to face adversity with indifference or stoic resignation. Aviraneta himself ends up completely isolated from the government he tried so hard to serve after numerous persecutions and exiles. He adopts a spirit of resignation and spends his time reading, writing his memoirs, and collecting insects and shells since «había quedado reducido a ser un hombre escéptico y burlón» (*Desde el principio hasta el fin,* IV: 1152), «reducido» being the key word in this statement. Baroja's predominant presentation of man in *Memorias de un hombre de acción* as victimized, alienated, or destroyed by historical forces and his own base instincts undermines any attempt to see man as the mythmaker, as one who goes beyond everyday realities by reshaping the particularities of existence into a general, unified whole of transcendent meaning.

TIME

The concept of time presents another important ordering element in historical novels. A horizontal line symbolizing an irreversible movement in one direction best represents historical time. Each historical event follows the next successively and they are often linked by causality. An individual may attribute an overall significance of progress or decadence to the series of historical events or simply place them in chronological order. Historical time stands in opposition to cosmic time, a concept associated with archaic man and with myth, and in which a cyclical temporal paradigm represents the alternating creation and destruction of the universe. Archaic man endowed this time construct with a sacred meaning whereas historical time symbolizes for the most part a secularized, demythified concept of time. While irreversibility characterizes historical time, eternal repetition typifies cosmic time.[9]

[9] On cosmic and historical time see MIRCEA ELIADE, *Cosmos and History* and *The Sacred and the Profane: The Nature of Religion* (New York: Harcourt, Brace, Jovanovich, 1959). On the rejection of cyclic time by the Christians see C. A. PATRIDES: «The Phoenix and the Ladder: Gentiles and Jews», in *The Grand Design*

As an organizational principle, historical time in the form of the narration of unique historical events accompanied by specific successive dates creates the impression of an orderly flow of time and events and provides the reader with easily accessible temporal reference points, and this in turn contributes to an easier comprehension of historical events. In some cases the temporal reference points become the major source of order. Sir Walter Scott's repetition of «sixty years hence» and his frequent mention of dates in *Waverley,* and Mary Renault's introductory time line giving the major dates in the life of Simonides in *The Praise Singer* provide examples of the historical novelist's concern with making clear the linear progression of time. This progression is especially evident in the *Bildungsroman* historical novels, such as *Waverley,* in which the author fuses the succession of historical events with the growth and development of the hero.[10] The emphasis on linearity might seem to undermine the mythification process, but, in fact, when historical time is combined with such storytelling elements as adventure, romance, and exotic settings, then the perception of time in the novel is altered, too. The historical novels, in which action and incident tend to dominate, engage the reader readily with the novel as temporal reference points slip into the background, and the historical novel is transformed into a romance or novel of adventures which leads back to the world of myth.[11]

Baroja, on the other hand, treats historical time in an ironic, subversive manner that contributes to the general demythification process in *Memorias de un hombre de acción.* The temporal shifts present in *El aprendiz de conspirador* continue throughout the series to such an extent that one easily loses track of temporal reference points and any sense of the progression of time. The chronological succession of historical events can only be determined by reconstructing it in retrospect. This emphasizes the relative unimportance of historical time for Baroja as an organizing force. For example, Aviraneta supposedly writes the text for *El escuadrón del «Brigante»* (as Leguía reports at the beginning of volume two) in 1834 while he serves time in jail for organizing the secret society La Isabelina. Baroja does not pick up this episode in Aviraneta's life until

---

of God: The Literary Form of the Christian View of History (Toronto: University of Toronto Press, 1972), pp. 1-12.

[10] PATRICIA TOBIN describes the *Bildungsroman* as the novel «performed» by time in *Time and the Novel: The Genealogical Imperative* (Princeton: Princeton University Press, 1978), p. 5.

[11] A. A. MENDILOW discusses the alteration of the sense of time by psychological perception in *Time and the Novel* (1952; rpt. New York: Humanities Press, 1972), pp. 118-26. Of the same subject Patricia Tobin says: «The elements of a novel, although fixed in temporal relation to each other, change their shape and fluctuate in their significance, because merely chronological succession becomes informed with the operations of cause and effect, and the novelistic character is seen as having assumed a unique destiny that was nevertheless inevitable» *(Time and the Novel,* p. 5).

the end of volume ten, *La Isabelina.* Similarly, Baroja places Aviraneta's account of the 1854 mob murder of the police chief Chico with other stories of vengeance that occur around 1834 in volume eleven, *El sabor de la venganza,* but naturally does not deal with that phase of Aviraneta's life until the final novel. In the first case, the author creates suspense by anticipating a future historical event while meeting his obligation to verisimilitude by explaining the origin of the material. In the second case, Baroja sacrifices chronological order for thematic unity by putting the murder of Chico with three other stories of revenge. He also continues the *in medias res* opening technique employed in *El aprendiz de conspirador* so that not only does he undermine the chronological order of historical events, but also that of the order of narration. At the beginning of *La veleta de Gastizar,* the reader witnesses the arrival in Ustáriz of three travelers from Bayonne. As the novel progresses, Baroja reveals their names —Ochoa, Lacy, and López Campillo— and something of their backgrounds as liberal émigrés, but not until the next novel, *Los caudillos de 1830,* does he tie these characters to Aviraneta and tell something of their activities in Bayonne. There is considerable chronological confusion in *La ruta del aventurero* and *Los contrastes de la vida* in which Baroja mixes the short narratives of the purely fictional character J. H. Thompson with those of Aviraneta. In Part One of *La ruta del aventurero,* «El convento de Monsant», Thompson appears with Aviraneta in Ondara (around 1825) and together they plot to reunite a pair of separated lovers, but not until Part Two, «El viaje sin objeto», does the reader learn Thompson's life history and his meeting with Aviraneta as prisoners in the Salón de Cortes of Sevilla in 1823. Aviraneta picks up his own life story of the years 1823-24 in the second through fourth stories of *Los contrastes de la vida* which relate experiences in Tangiers, Egypt, and Missolonghi with Lord Byron (the narration shared by both Thompson and Aviraneta) and chronologically lead up to his arrival at Ondara, with which the preceding novel begins. Such shifts create an overall impression of chronological disorder and subvert the reader's perception of historical time.

Other elements contribute to this impression. The variety of narrators and the high number of intercalated stories interrupt the linear development of Aviraneta's life. Aviraneta does not even appear in many episodes of the novels and in some novels he only appears marginally. The narrator (whoever it is at the time) must go back from time to time and pick up the loose thread of Aviraneta's experiences wherever he left it, which means a constant process of weaving backward and forward chronologically. Besides this, Baroja sometimes treats history as a circle. At times it takes shape in the overall structure of a novel, such as in *Con la pluma y con el sable,* which relates Aviraneta's experiences as chief councilman and organizer of the militia in Aranda del Duero. It chronicles the fall of the Liberals from power (1820-1823), from Aviraneta's role as «el tirano de Aranda» until he sneaks back to Aranda at night to bury his Liberal documents and papers. The novel opens with a description of the reforms initiated by Aviraneta and the parade of the militia in the town with the village idiot Tío Guillotina dressed in a gala uniform and wearing a three-cornered hat, a symbol of the Liberals and their ties with the French Revolution and Enlightenment, marching out in front. At the end of the novel Tío Guillotina reappears as if to confront Aviraneta. He is wounded and bleeding, his uniform is covered with mud, and the plumes have fallen from his hat. The same symbol returns, in a state of disgrace and defeat, yet Aviraneta's burying of the papers symbolizes that a more propitious historical moment for the Liberals will come. The circular movement seems without rhyme or reason. Like the eternal return or the wheel of Fortune, it is strictly a matter of fate. Baroja makes a reference to the eternal return in *Crónica escandalosa* when he tries to establish a circular structure for *Memorias de un hombre de acción* by adding epigraphs taken from previous novels in the series to the chapters in this novel and the final one, which indicates points of contact, of repetition within the series: «Las siluetas se desdoblan y se repiten. Todo se repite en la vida y en la literatura» (IV: 98).

Baroja treats the successive political conflicts in Spanish nineteenth-century history in a circular manner, too. The village eccentric and historian in Aranda, el señor Sorihuela, expresses this point of view in a discussion with Aviraneta: «'Porque la libertad no muere; todo deja un germen, y de esos gérmenes vendrán nuevas crisálidas y nuevas mariposas... Se eclipsa el absolutismo, y volverá; se eclipsará vuestra Constitución y volverá después. Todo vuelve...'» (*Con la pluma y con el sable,* III: 419). But Baroja illustrates the circularity of history simply by presenting the successive groups in power as beset by the same problems of division and self-interest. Despite the changing titles —*afrancesados* and *patriotas, liberales* and *absolutistas, carlistas* and *isabelinos,* or even factions within the same political group such as *comuneros* and *masones* or *cristinos* and *mendizabalistas*— the brutality of the wars, the demagoguery of the politicians, and the general anarchy of Spanish society remain the same. The conflict between those in favor of a constitutional monarchy and those in favor of an absolutist government, military and/or monarchical, runs throughout *Memorias de un hombre de acción* taking a number of forms and names and with power seesawing continuously back and forth between the two. There is no resolution of the struggle and no evolutionary progression of events, just an endless circle of change without change. Baroja also points out the circular movement of people who, like the weathervane in Gastizar, change political affiliations in accordance with the prevailing political current. Each ideology they assume may be radically opposed to the previous one, but they remain faithful to their own political and financial advancement. The change is superficial; the greed and self-interest stay constant. This dark vision of history annuls the importance of historical time because in a sense each moment is the same as the next, since it is undistinguished by an event that marks a genuine change, any kind of progress in the Enlightened-liberal sense. Baroja adds to this impression by putting in the background of the novels the concept of the Eternal Spain, removed from and untouched by historical events, a common theme of the Generation of '98. «A Aviraneta le vino a la imaginación el contraste de la España, tal como era, soñolienta, inmutable, con la agitación política de los últimos años, agitación que seguramente no había conmovido más que la superficie del país» (*Los recursos de la astucia,* III: 601). Baroja indicates that the eternal pattern of existence has no exit, it exists without the hope of transcendence or integration within a mythical world, a monotonous repetition: «Ya no pasaba nada en el pueblo. La rueda de la existencia oscura seguía girando constantemente: Nacer, vivir, morir. Nacer, vivir, morir...» (*Los caudillos de 1830,* III: 1009).[12]

Baroja seems preoccupied with only two aspects of time in *Memorias de un hombre de acción:* time as a marker of man's mortality and man's temporal response to that mortality. Baroja's works abound with *memento mori* and this series is no exception with wars, executions, numerous encounters with hangmen, and sudden deaths (many of them youthful).[13] The story «La canóniga» that forms part of *Los recursos de la astucia* is inscribed within the image of death. Damián, a coffin-maker, recounts the tale of the tragic lovers. His constant companions are a crow and a black cat, and he takes his *siesta* in a coffin. The focal point of his workshop is an ornate cloak decorated with skulls and crossbones, figures representing the ages of man, and images of Charon and Chronos. The clock bears the inscription which Baroja also uses as the epigraph of the novel and repeats at the end, «*Vulnerant omnes; todas hieren, la última mata*». The image of death dominates the tone of the work and foreshadows the violent deaths with which it ends and the historical events seem insignificant by comparison. Baroja ends the collection of narratives that comprise *El sabor de la venganza,* all of which involve violent deaths, with an epilogue bearing an epigraph from Ecclesiastes, «Todo es hecho del polvo y todo se tornará en el mismo polvo». The Spanish landscape that Alvarito Sánchez de Mendoza sees towards the end of the Carlist War in *La nave de los locos* is a visual monument to death, an almost surreal-

---

[12] LONGHURST refers to the presentation of man in *Memorias de un hombre de acción* as a prisoner of time on p. 257.

[13] On Baroja's concern with time and timepieces see D. HOWITT, «Baroja's Preoccupation with Clocks and his emphatic Treatment of Time in the Introduction to *La busca*», in *Hispanic Studies in Honour of Joseph Manson,* ed. Dorothy M. Atkinson and Anthony H. Clarke (Oxford: Dolphin, 1972), pp. 139-47.

istic impression of the destructive effects of the war. The most impressionable images of the battles and other historical events recounted by Baroja are the scenes of massive carnage and violent deaths. And death strikes suddenly, tragically and arbitrarily in the works of *Memorias de un hombre de acción.* The young Eusebio Lacy dies of tuberculosis after the disappointing attempt of the Liberals in 1830 to regain control of the Spanish government in *Los caudillos de 1830.* Max Labarthe, one of Aviraneta's agents sent into the camp of the Count de España, is killed as a Carlist soldier in combat while his friend Hugo Riversdale escapes the situation. The sudden appearance and disappearance of new characters in these works is typical of Baroja's novels, but the number of disappearances in death is exceptionally high. In fact, the consciousness that underlies this preoccupation with death resembles that of a seventeenth-century moralist, like Gracián, for whom death is not only the ultimate but the only reality. Political affiliations and conflicts, wars and petty acts of jealousy and vindictiveness fade into the background when compared with the affairs of this world that inevitably end in death.

Baroja opposes historical time and the reality of death with another concept of time professed by his hero. Although Aviraneta the historical figure lives and acts within the confines of historical time, he professes only to believe in a totally subjective temporal perception as an everlasting now. Accordingly, he acts only in response to his own internal impulses because historical circumstances have no reality for him and he cares little for the historical perspective that will examine his deeds:

> «No me ocupe, no me importa el pensar que dentro de cien años hay un buen señor que descubra mis andanzas. No me preocupa eso absolutamente nada... Ahora mismo mi preocupación es lo que tengo que hacer al salir de aquí, lo que haré esta noche, mañana, pasado. El año que viene ya tiene perspectivas muy lejanas, casi no existe para mí.» *(La Isabelina,* III: 1039)

Not only do Aviraneta's comments reveal an ironic attitude towards history and historical time, but also towards the chronicler of his deeds, «el buen señor» who wastes his time on such material, in other words Baroja himself. Baroja, who constantly denies his interest in history in critical writings and in the introduction to the series, places a self-deprecating comment in the mouth of the hero. Aviraneta's insistence on the here-and-now of experience characterizes his entire being: «Aviraneta era hombre poco propicio a vivir del pasado. Aviraneta era siempre actual» *(Con la pluma y con el sable,* III: 421). In a sense, Baroja explains his own subversive treatment of historical time in *Memorias de un hombre de acción* by pointing out its irrelevance in relation to temporal immediacy.

CAUSALITY

The imposition of laws of causality on historical events provides yet another method of ordering and contributing to the mythification of history. This is the essence of myth since primitive man felt compelled to read significance into the universe by abstracting patterns of meaning from repeated occurrences he observed in the world around him. He manages to incorporate unique incidents into the scheme of things by explaining them in terms of the general familiar patterns. A vestige of this impulse to explain the unknown in terms of the known remains in modern man's reference to accidents, especially calamitous ones, as «acts of God», implying the existence of some justifiable reason for their occurrence, but that it remains beyond human comprehension in the hands of an omniscient deity with a divine master plan. In Baroja's essays on history, discussed in the previous chapter, he rejects the association of the historian's task of presenting and explaining history with objectivity and scientific endeavor. Rather, he ties it with the subjective, intuitive impulses of the historian himself who interprets and endows history with order and meaning derived from his own prejudices and interests —a mythifying impulse. Baroja saw causality in history as a superimposed, artificial order and consistently denied its existence. The fictional editor of *Memorias de un hombre de acción*, Pedro Leguía, repeats almost verbatim one of Baroja's own comments about ordering history:

> La historia es siempre una fantasía sin base científica, y cuando se pretende levantar un tinglado invulnerable y colocar sobre él una consecuencia, se corre el peligro de que un dato cambie y se venga abajo toda la armazón histórica. Creyéndolo así, casi vale más afirmar las consecuencias sin los datos. *(El amor, el dandismo y la intriga, IV: 13)*

Leguía's statement reveals a rejection of history as an orderly construct, «tinglado» and «armazón», in which one action logically follows another. Aviraneta makes an even more pointed reference to the futility of ascribing logical order to events in general:

> Casi siempre el acontecimiento es traidor e inesperado. ¿Quién los puede prever? Aun contando con la casualidad, es difícil; sin contar con ella, es imposible. Se cree a veces dominar la situación, tener todos los hilos en la mano, conocer perfectamente los factores de un negocio, y, de repente, surge el hecho nuevo de la oscuridad, el hecho nuevo que no existía, o que existía y no lo veíamos, y en un instante el andamiaje entero levantado por nosotros se viene a tierra, y la ordenación, que nos parecía una obra maestra, se convierte en armazón inútil y enojoso. *(El escuadrón del «Brigante», III: 119)*

Aviraneta points out the false security of feeling that a plan, a cause-effect ordering of people, actions, and events is foolproof. The unforeseen may always intervene and disrupt what one felt was under control.

Caprice or chance *(casualidad),* to which Aviraneta alludes, a constant in Baroja's works, pervades *Memorias de un hombre de acción* instead of the order of causality. In fact, the unexpected has such a strong presence in the series that the reader anticipates the unexpected instead of the expected. In addition to creating suspense and maintaining reader interest, the pervasive element of chance illustrates Baroja's rejection of the mythifying impulse of causality. Rather, a demythified view of history emerges in which the arbitrary force of chance rules the universe. This approach to history stands in direct oppostion to the traditional concept of history as the presentation and explanation of historical events and may be considered by contrast an ironic, antihistorical approach. For Baroja, historical events exist without an explanation, as totally arbitrary phenomena without any ultimate significance —an attitude encompassed again within the notion of *historia humorística.*[14] In the series chance takes the form of hundreds of coincidences, surprise encounters, and illogical occurrences in which the influence of popular romance is visible as well as a view of the world as fundamentally disordered and chaotic. In *El escuadrón del «Brigante»,* Aviraneta escapes imprisonment by the French when caught while trying to rescue the Director of the Central Council of the Spanish patriots because it so happens that the French commander responds to a Masonic distress signal that he gives, and recognizing a brother Mason, sets the frightened Aviraneta free. One of the stories in the third novel of the series, *Los caminos del mundo,* relates the betrayal and brutal murder of Aviraneta's friend and business associate Volkonsky in Mexico around 1817 by his former beloved, a cruel and deranged young woman. Many years later during the first Carlist War, in the fourteenth volume, *Las figuras de cera,* Aviraneta bumps into the daughter of these unfortunate people at a costume party in Bayonne and vindicates his own role in the past events by recounting the story and presenting letters from Volkonsky and the treacherous Coral Miranda. The editor Leguía encounters by chance people who have known Aviraneta at different points in his career and manuscripts almost fall into his lap. *Los contrastes de la vida* is dedicated almost exclusively to sudden, ironic turns of events: an exemplary soldier who exhibits valor in the most ferocious battle permits himself to be gored to death in a bullfight because he suddenly sees his girlfriend flirting with someone else; a foolish, pretentious young Basque Aviraneta meets in Tangier vows never to enter the Egyptian army unless he is made a captain-general and can marry the viceroy's daughter —all of which comes to pass; Aviraneta's association with Byron at Missolonghi reveals this heroic event of the nineteenth century as a highly romanticized view of an anarchic and futile

---

[14] See LONGHURST, pp. 141-47, for more on Baroja's vision and presentation of history as deliberately chaotic and pointless.

undertaking. In all these accounts, Baroja's concern is with the illogical and capricious aspect of human nature and in the last instance the deflation of the popular concept of a historical event.

As with most elements of the Barojan fictional world, chance has both a positive and negative aspect. On the positive side, one can relate chance to surprise and spontaneity, highly valued qualities for Baroja. In a section of *La nave de los locos* in which the narrator compares old and modern inns, he links the character of the old inns with that of the *novela porosa*, both open to the unexpected: «¡Viva la fonda séptica y la novela séptica e infecciosa, donde se encuentran cosas inesperadas, y vaya al diablo la teoría microbiana!» (IV: 423). One of the protagonists of *Humano enigma,* and *La senda dolorosa,* Hugo Riversdale, regards surprise as the most important part of life: «'La vida corriente, sin aventuras, sin imprevistos, la verdad, no vale la pena» (*Humano enigma,* IV: 587). And of course the element of chance forms an integral part of the adventurer's life: «'Para mí, lo más simpático en la vida es la improvisación, maniobrando en lo imprevisto'» (*Los caminos del mundo,* III: 295). But chance also takes the form of disorder and bad fortune. Aviraneta associates it with war and opposes it to military strategy: «'Yo no he visto en la guerra más que desorden, brutalidad y estupidez. Casualidad, casualidad y casualidad'» (*Los caudillos de 1830,* III: 951). The most memorable symbol of chance in the series is the weathervane of Gastizar which «les parecía a todos un auxiliar del destino adverso, una de aquellas esfinges de una fauna desaparecida que no anunciaba más que calamidades» (*Los caudillos de 1830,* III: 1009).

These statements bring up the subject of fatality in *Memorias de un hombre de acción,* a significant force in its fictional world. Although causality does not form the basis for the movement from one episode to another, one senses that things could not have been other than they were. This feeling arises not from the historical events themselves, but from the retrospective perspective in examining them as a whole. Baroja clarifies his position through the words of J. H. Thompson:

> Esta idea de fatalidad es un poco confusa. Encerrando la idea de predestinación, es para mí falsa; pero significando sólo destinación, me parece exacta.
>
> No cabe duda que si uno marca en un papel una serie de puntos, se puede unir éstos con una línea; tampoco cabe duda que la tal línea tendrá un carácter: será recta o quebrada, y presentará una figura especial. A esta figura, después de hecha *a posteriori,* le llamaríamos necesidad, destinación, y si estuviera hecha *a priori,* le llamaríamos fatalidad, predestinación.
>
> En el punto de la línea no sabemos nada dónde va a caer el punto 2, ni en el punto 2 cuál va a ser el 3; pero trazados los puntos 2 y 3, podemos asegurar que de ninguna manera, aunque se deshiciera el Universo, podrían estar en otro sitio más que en el que están. (*La ruta del aventurera,* III: 711)

He rejects the mythifying approach, applying causality or any other pre-conceived pattern of thought or divine intervention to the events, which would provide some logic or order for proceeding from one to another. Instead he adopts a quasi-stoic attitude of «what has had to be», as Thompson interprets it, fate in the form of destiny, but unknown until it has already occurred. This «hands off» point of view takes the shape of fate as a blind, uncontrollable force that sweeps all in its path, best represented again by the Gastizar weathervane: «se hallaba desde hacía tiempo mohosa y no giraba con el viento; sin embargo, cuando los acontecimientos políticos eran grandes, sin duda la fuerza de la historia le hacía girar, quieras que no» (*La veleta de Gastizar,* III: 868). Baroja sees the force of history not as something that the senses perceive or the mind understands, but rather as something perceived only in terms of the effects it leaves on the human lives and world around us just as the weathervane's turning indicates the presence of the wind. Fate is also the natural environment for the adventurer: «Aquel pajarraco Aviraneta vivía en su centro, como los árbitros en los remolinos de la tempestad. Las convulsiones, los peligros, la guerra, las cárceles, eran su elemento...» (*Los recursos de la astucia,* III: 643). But by making it his element, the adventurer «es el que está más sujeto a la ley de la fatalidad, el que marcha más arrastrado por la fuerza de los acontecimientos» (*La veleta de Gastizar,* III: 907). He risks getting caught up in the forces that he must battle against to succeed at whatever he undertakes.

Fragmentation

The force of fate, chronological disorder, and multiple points of view create an overall impression of randomness and disjunction in *Memorias de un hombre de acción.* The novels seem to be only a collection of independent episodes and stories, self-contained units held together by the presence of a single central character or a single narrative voice:

> La constante que parece predominar en *Memorias de un hombre de acción* es su insubordinación a una trama unida: en cada volumen se nos ofrecen trozos de vidas, de paisajes, de conversaciones, tipos que entran y salen persiguiendo una aventura fugaz sin apenas producir una impresión, comentarios y generalizaciones del narrador. Interrumpe los relatos históricos, introduciendo anécdotas; interrumpe las tramas novelescas para hablar de la realidad; continuamente hace recordar al lector que no existe un solo mundo ni una sola perspectiva, y que sólo la suma puede permitir un acercamiento a la verdad: una verdad de la vida, no de la historia, según lo observa Matus.[15]

---

[15] Biruté Ciplijauskaité, *Los noventayochistas y la historia* (Madrid: Porrúa Turanzas, 1981), p. 167.

Baroja himself, in the voice of the narrator, ironically asks the reader's pardon for breaking the classical unities and refers to the loosely connected structure of the novels:

> El autor va a seguir su relato y a marchar a campo traviesa, haciendo una trenza, más o menos hábil, como un ramal histórico y otros novelescos. ¡Qué diablo! Está uno metido en las encrucijadas de una larga novela histórica y tiene uno que llevar del ramal a su narración hasta el fin.
> Iremos, pues, así mal que bien, unas veces tropezando en los matorrales de la fantasía y otras hundiéndonos en el pantano de Historia. *(Las figuras de cera,* IV: 213)

In this statement Baroja provides a glimpse of his work as weaving separate elements of history and fiction together to construct the novels. The bemused exclamation, the sense of commitment to the difficult task, and the image of the author stumbling over underbrush and sinking in the swamp attest to this awareness of the chaotic maze he is creating.

Some of the novels consist of several stories grouped together. The three narratives that comprise *Los caminos del mundo* cover several facets of Aviraneta's activities after the War of Independence. In *El sabor de la venganza,* Aviraneta's revenge on his political enemies and three other stories of vengeance make up the novel, the four united by a common theme. In addition to distinct narrative units within the novels, certain volumes cluster together to form separate units within the series. *La veleta de Gastizar* and *Los caudillos de 1830,* which share the same characters and historical moment, are companion novels, as are *Humano enigma* and *La senda dolorosa,* which tell about the Count de España. Volumes fourteen through sixteen, *Las figuras de cera, La nave de los locos,* and *Las mascaradas sangrientas,* present the life of Alvarito Sánchez de Mendoza, a fictional character residing in Bayonne during the last years of the Carlist War. Thus, while the novels tend to divide up into separate stories or episodes and *Memorias de un hombre de acción* into individual groups of novels, Baroja does unify the individual narratives by some means or other —common theme, historical moment, protagonist, characters. But still other elements contribute to the sense of fragmentation. The time shifts between moment of narration and moment of action, and multiple narratives, such as in *El escuadrón del «Brigante»,* cause abrupt breaks in the texts. The constant entrance and disappearance of characters disrupts the sense of continuity in the fictional world. Such spectacular leaps involved in picking up narrative threads as the continuation of Leguía's biography (started in the first volume) in the thirteenth volume of the series create an impression of truncated narratives and sudden starts and stops. Even the final farewell to the hero comes across as a summary dismissal by the narrator. The fact that the historical unity can only be seen in retrospect through the effort of a conscientious reader to outline dates, events, and narrative voices and organize them, also creates a sense of disjunction. The series contains an immense variety of materials (political cartoons, ghost stories, jokes, letters, excerpts from pamphlets, and history books) and draws on a wide range of literary genres (memoirs, epistolary novels, picaresque novels, farce, moral exempla, romance, serial novels, detective novels). The resultant combination of disparate fragments produces an artistic work and an image of the age that is at once a palimpsest, in that one reads each new approach to Aviraneta or the historical moment through the previous ones; a collage, in that one views the individual units as part of a whole; and a kaleidoscope, in that one derives seemingly infinite ways of seeing and assessing the fictional world from a finite number of parts.

This sense of fragmentary form corresponds to the divisions and rivalries within the social order. In fact, Baroja treats the reader to one panorama of disorder after another in *Memorias de un hombre de acción*. Splits exist in every political group of the period (the patriots of the War of Independence, the Masons, the Liberals, the Carlists, etc.) and among all classes of society. The officers of each military faction vie for supremacy just as their counterparts at Court compete for the monarch's favor. One of the most idealized battles of that age, the battle at Missolonghi, appears through Aviraneta's words as a nightmare of cultural misunderstandings, embattled egos, and rampant self-interest. The bloody scenes of war (mutilated bodies, ravaged lands, desolation), mass murders, political corruption, and the animalistic, brutal masses of Spain who cheerfully butcher their fellow countrymen in the name of one cause or another portray this historical period as a monstrous, disordered world that offers little hope for social cohesion or significance.[16] The sense of disorder created by the dense, varied, fragmented structure of *Memorias de un hombre de acción* offers the perfect artistic vehicle for Baroja to present the demythified chaos of nineteenth-century Spanish history. But beneath this disordered surface one senses something that gives structure and meaning to the whole.

---

[16] LONGHURST discusses the appropriateness of *La nave de los locos* as a title for the entire series on pp. 117-24.

IV

THE SEARCH FOR ORDER AND MEANING

> I walk among men as among the fragments of
> the future —the future which I envisage. And this
> is all my creating and striving, that I create and
> carry together into One what is fragment and
> riddle and dreadful accident.
>
> (NIETZSCHE, *Thus Spoke Zarathrustra*)

> For in both poetry and painting we demand a
> faithful mirror of life, of mankind, of the world,
> only rendered clear by the presentation, and made
> significant by arrangement.
>
> (SCHOPENHAUER, *The World as Will and
> Representation*)

ENTROPY AND AN AESTHETIC OF CHAOS

The preceding chapter seems to point to an underlying aesthetic of
chaos in the fictional world of *Memorias de un hombre de acción*. On
closer examination, however, certain fundamental structural and thematic
patterns emerge that organize and give meaning to the entire series.

The preoccupation with a disordered universe has been an especially
important focus of interest for philosophers and artists from the late nineteenth century to the present day. Baroja and his generation were writing
in the wake of the discovery of the Second Law of Thermodynamics, the
Entropy Law, that states that while the quantity of matter and energy
in the universe remains constant, the transformation of matter into energy
can only move in one direction and potential energy is inevitably reduced
and lost in the form of waste material. This physical law had a major
philosophical implication —recognition of the universe's irrevocable movement towards decay and disorder. A work such as Max Nordau's *Degeneration* (a very familiar book to Baroja and other members of the
Generation of '98 and the basis for Ossorio's existential malady in *Camino
de perfección*) illustrates the impact of entropy on the non-scientific world.
Recently, the art critic Rudolf Arnheim has applied the term «entropy»
to plastic art forms as part of a method of approach to minimalist and
disordered, abstract works of art. Arnheim sees a work of art as the

product of tension between two opposing forces: entropy, which he defines as a movement towards greater randomness, and the anabolic tendency or structural theme, which is a dynamic pattern of forces, not an arrangement of static shapes. The structural theme arises from profoundly human concerns and derives its values from the universal human condition. Without the anabolic tendency, according to Arnheim, art either slips into homogeneous insignificance or disintegrates into chaos. In either case, it becomes meaningless and is no longer art.[1] Arnheim's discussion provides an interesting theoretical framework for examining contemporary literature of disorder —ironic works, satire, farce. In terms of *Memorias de un hombre de acción,* a fundamentally ironic work, the demythifying elements I have just discussed and the demythified world of the texts can be identified with the force of entropy. Despite their process of demythification, however, Baroja's novels fall neither into meaningless chaos nor dull uniformity. The series is not nearly so disordered and Baroja is much more concerned with order than one might think. Furthermore, the underlying literary patterns offer the best clues to the personal philosophy that informs them.

At one point the narrator refers to the hero Aviraneta as «un coleccionista de empresas difíciles y peligrosas» (*Con la pluma y con el sable,* III: 424). The word «collector» concisely summarizes the protagonist's role as an adventurer. Aviraneta is an astute planner, a manipulator of people, situations, events, and objects. He gathers disparate materials together, and then *orders* the disordered particulars into a meaningful, unifed whole. He draws the different, opposing factions of the Liberals together to form a united political front in the secret society of La Isabelina. The forged papers of the Simancas represent a masterful organization of secret agents, double agents, government resources, and secret societies, to undermine the Carlist effort in the North. Even in his old age, Aviraneta's hobby of collecting shells and insects symbolizes the continuation of the ordering impulse within a more limited sphere of activity, the need to take unorganized forces or objects and impose one's own sense of order on them. Baroja's works abound with collectors (such as the junk dealer Chipiteguy of *Las figuras de cera*) and Baroja himself was an assiduous collector of books, engravings, political cartoons, etc.[2] But most significant is the image of Baroja «the collector» behind *Memorias de un hombre de acción,* as the organizer of the chaotic collection of documents, maps, folk tales, eyewitness accounts, serial novels, and other diverse materials. Baroja saw his task of writing the novels as

---

[1] RUDOLF ARNHEIM, *Entropy and Art: An Essay on Disorder* (Berkeley: University of California Press, 1971), and JEREMY RIFKIN, *Entropy: A New World View* (New York: Viking Press, 1980) are the sources of the information on entropy.
[2] E. H. TEMPLIN, «Pío Baroja: Three Pivotal Concepts», *Hispanic Review,* 12 (1944), 306-12.

detective work and as a chore of organization and transformation and Aviraneta's concern with order offers a fictional analogue to Baroja's preoccupation. Baroja's desire to order the series consists of more than simply the tendency of certain novels to cluster together or the fact that some novels focus on a specific protagonist. The anabolic tendency counteracting the force of entropy in *Memorias de un hombre de acción* takes the form of structural and philosophical patterns of forces, two complementary levels of textual order.

«MEMORIAS DE UN HOMBRE DE ACCIÓN» AS SATIRE

Part of the problem of understanding *Memorias de un hombre de acción* has been the failure to recognize its true literary form. In fact, the elements of disorder in *Memorias de un hombre de acción* discussed earlier can be accounted for in terms of the structural patterns of ironic literature, especially satire. The distance that Baroja and his narrative voices assume reveals the superior stance of the ironist, an attitude expressed by the narrator of *La nave de los locos:* «Dejamos en *Las figuras de cera* nuestros muñecos de carne y hueso, de carne y hueso literario, colocados como en un tablero de ajedrez antes de comenzar la partida y vamos a continuar ésta» (IV: 328). The characters are dolls that the author manipulates and leaves at will as if in a game. The removed position permits Baroja to see the characters as types of a moral, psychological, or physical nature and provides one more example of his activities as a *coleccionista*. Baroja's concern with presenting Aviraneta as a prototype of the adventurer is implicit in the title of the series, *Memorias de un hombre de acción*. For him, individualizing features represent only superficial, easily altered details. The junk dealer Chipiteguy's nephew Marcelino expresses this opinion during a discussion about wax figures:

> Tan cierto es que los hombres, en general, tienen tan poco carácter, que si a los más ilustres y mejor dibujados se les quitan los accesorios históricos, los bigotes y las patillas, los galones y los penachos, un par de frases y otro par de anécdotas, no les conocería ni su padre. *(Las figuras de cera,* IV: 232)

Baroja's interest in *tipos* identifies him with the satirist, who thinks of characterization in terms of stereotypes of a professional or psychological nature. Similarly, Baroja shares with the satirist the desire to strip away the surface illusions, in this case created by the trappings of glory, to reveal the underlying reality. In addition, the chronological jumble and lack of causality in the texts point to the indirection and lack of narrative progression inherent in satire. Neither the hero nor the political factions of his epoch move ahead socially or morally. Baroja raises Aviraneta to heroic stature in battle or espionage only to plunge him into pathos as the butt of a weak old man, a beautiful woman, or a powerful historical figure. The Liberals and Absolutists succeed one another in an endless circle of political change without change. The noble aspirations of the Liberals rapidly disintegrate into factions dominated by conflicting egos just as the Carlists, associated with God and the Church, disperse into bands of marauders who rape, steal, and destroy for personal satisfaction. Each movement in the novels generates an opposite movement, a process indicating the constant flux of a satiric text. The Count de España's snivelling cowardice shifts into a tragic sequence of Christlike martyrdom only to fall and disperse into the macabre farce of the phrenologist and his assistant. The rambling, episodic movement of the series with its impressions of loosely-tied independent narrative units shows yet another affinity with satire, with its predilection for journey or travel narratives. Baroja's own interest in travel books is well-known and many have noted a similarity between the episodic quality of his novels and the picaresque novel. The abrupt stops and starts in *Memorias de un hombre de acción,* the summary dismissal of characters and situations and the generally disjunct images that it generates recall satire's tendency to cut short its narratives, its unconcern with logical development, and its overall impression of incompletion.

The historical world in which Aviraneta moves is the underworld society of satire, the demonic world in romance. There are countless secret societies and organizations in the series: Masons, Comuneros, La Isabelina, the Simancas spy ring, etc. Aviraneta directs a number of the groups, which like the demonic underworld societies, are characterized by turbulence, conflict, and lack of cohesion, and use secret codes, exotic words, hand signals, disappearing ink, and other odd devices to communicate —the equivalent of a demonic language. Most of these societies have a subversive purpose. The «Conspiración del triángulo» of *Los caminos del mundo,* set up by Aviraneta, has the intention of murdering the despot Fernando VII. The purpose of *La Isabelina* is to insure that the then Infanta Isabel will succeed to the throne, an illegal activity, which goes against the wishes of the regent's relatives. When caught by the authorities, these groups disband and vanish rapidly and the members almost immediately start to denounce one another, showing the supremacy of self-interest and lack of genuine unity typical of the underworld. The members deal with each other harshly and at times cruelly. At one point, a group attempts to brand the informer on the forehead to avenge his betrayal of them. Aviraneta's role as master spy takes him in and out of the characteristic underworld dwellings, prisons and caves, and the state of exile. The guerrilla leader Merino, who doubts the protagonist's loyalty to the Spanish cause during the War of Independence, locks him into a haunted house. Aviraneta escapes only to have to spend the winter hiding in a cave. With the collapse of the Liberal government in 1823, the hero finds himself imprisoned again in the Cortes in Sevilla. He escapes to go into exile. In 1834 the authorities discover La Isabelina and Aviraneta spends a long time in the Cárcel de Corte in Madrid. For much of the latter part of his life, Aviraneta is in and out of jail and exile, often persecuted by the very people he has served most loyally. Through all of these experiences, the reader receives ample exposure to the immorality and barbarity of the prison world. But the brutality of the world outside the jail differs very little from that inside the prison world. Baroja spares the reader none of the horrors of war and Spain suffered internal warfare for much of the nineteenth century. The banquet of the birds of prey as they strip the battlefield, the hideous murders of the Carlist robber Bertache and his gang, a young woman's monstrous transformation when she blows out the brains of a helpless wounded soldier as he begs her for water, and the Count de España's terrorizing of his victims before executing them, attest to the fact that the underworld has engulfed all of the fictional historical world of *Memorias de un hombre de acción*:

> La nave de los locos era la alegoría de las estupideces de los hombres, el anfiteatro de las monstruosidades, el estanco de los vicios, en donde se exhibían la maldad, la perversidad, las manías diversas y todas las manifestaciones más o menos alegres de la mentecatez y de la gran tontería humana. Para Chipiteguy era indudable, como para su paisano Sebastián Brant, que la Dama Locura andaba suelta por el mundo. *(La nave de los locos,* IV: 328)

Baroja unquestionably possessed the satirist's desire to instruct his reader by «wounding» him through the exposure of evil and folly.[3] But many critics have missed Baroja's manipulation of style to achieve this effect. His description of soldiers executed by hanging gives some idea of his skill:

> Los guerrilleros, para completar la flora peninsular, junto al árbol adornado con españoles, ofrecían el engalanado por los soldados franceses. Uno y otro árbol en las noches calladas, debían de comunicarse sus quejas, arrancadas por el viento, y el perfume pestilente de sus frutos podridos. *(El escuadrón del «Brigante»,* III: 184-85)

The satirist's embittered, ironic sneer is visible with the mention of completing «la flora peninsular». At the same time, these words initiate

---

[3] The basis for the discussion on satire is derived from the following: EDWARD A. BLOOM and LILLIAN D. BLOOM, *Satire's Persuasive Voice* (Ithaca: Cornell University Press, 1979), ROBERT C. ELLIOT, *The Power of Satire: Magic, Ritual, Art* (Princeton: Princeton University Press, 1960), NORTHROP FRYE, *Anatomy of Criticism* (Princeton: Princeton University Press, 1971), GILBERT HIGHET, *The Anatomy of Satire* (Princeton: Princeton University Press, 1962), ALVIN B. KERNAN, *The Plot of Satire* (New Haven: Yale University Press. 1965), and ROBERT SCHOLES and ROBERT KELLOGG, *The Nature of Narrative* (New York: Oxford University Press, 1966).

an extended metaphor in which Baroja transforms the dangling bodies into the fragrant fruit of the trees. The traditional lyric and romantic image of trees sighing in the wind and as if in sympathetic correspondence to one another culminates with the jarring condensation of the disparate elements of the oxymoronic metaphor «perfume pestilente» in combination with the implied repugnance of «frutos podridos». The image follows a common pattern of development in sonnets with an initial comparison, expansion of this material, and a summary in the final line of the poem. Baroja employs poetic language here and the striking contrast between the lyric quality of the words and the revolting subject matter deflates its potential beauty and forces the grotesqueness and repulsiveness of the scene to stand out. Elsewhere Baroja uses other styles to produce a similar effect. In *La nave de los locos* Alvarito describes the aftermath of a struggle between Carlists and Liberals:

> En la casa reinaba el desorden. El portal se hallaba lleno de heridos, que los sanitarios iban trasladando; el suelo lo manchaban charcos de sangre. Se oían gritos desgarradores. Los cristianos establecieron un hospital en la iglesia y en la casa de baños, y los cirujanos empezaban a cortar piernas y brazos. (IV: 376)

In this passage, instead of poetic adornment, Baroja offers sparse, matter-of-fact reportage (which many people erroneously identify as his only style). The horrible scene culminates with the presentation of massive mutilation as if so many lumberjacks were going out to chop wood. But the fact that the style denies commentary or emotional involvement of any kind emphasizes all the more its brutality and implies a silent cry of outrage against the spectacle.

Baroja's vivid descriptions point to another pattern of forces that create order in *Memorias de un hombre de acción*, «imaginative centers», powerful visual images that coalesce and condense the disparate materials and disperse, fragmentary narrative threads and impressions of the texts.[4] Although critics have noticed the impact of painting on Baroja's writing, and especially that of impressionism, few have recognized the strong visual orientation of his art and its function as a unifying element.[5] In fact, while the reader must consciously work at reconstructing narrative

---

[4] The term is derived from HELEN GARDNER, *The Business of Criticism* (Oxford: Clarendon Press, 1959), pp. 23-24, as quoted in GEOFFREY HARTMAN, *Beyond Formalism: Literary Essays 1958-1970* (New Haven: Yale University Press, 1970), p. 33, and is developed by ALBAN K. FORCIONE in *Cervantes and the Mystery of Lawlessness: A Study of «El casamiento engañoso» y «El coloquio de los perros»* (Princeton: Princeton University Press, 1984), pp. 72-99.

[5] On Baroja and painting see FIDEL ROBLEDO, «Don Pío Baroja y la pintura», *Papeles de Son Armadans*, No. 175 (Oct. 1970), pp. 31-55. For more on the impact and importance of visual material on *Memorias de un hombre de acción* see BIRUTÉ CIPLIJAUSKAITÉ, *Los noventayochistas y la historia* (Madrid: Porrúa Turanzas, 1981), pp. 151-53.

and chronological sequences after finishing the series, pictorial images remain firmly in mind and create their own sense of order. The elaborate, detailed description of the weathervane with its monstrous, portentous whirling captures the spirit of disquiet and impending doom that accompanies the historical changes, political disillusionment, and changes in the personal lives of the major characters and their countrymen in *La veleta de Gastizar* and *Los caudillos de 1830* while also conveying the dizzying and monotonous circular movement of people switching political sides and of the daily human routine. In *Con la pluma y con el sable,* Baroja describes a political cartoon in which an enthroned Fernando VII holds court dressed in a clown outfit and carrying a sceptre in one hand and a skeleton (Spain) in the other. The devil sits next to him and in the background leaders of the Liberals hang from the gallows, while in the doorway of the Inquisitorial Office a demon burns a copy of the newspaper produced in London by the Liberal émigrés. In one pictorial image Baroja concentrates the basic historical conflicts of the age, problems that emerge during the War of Independence and continue into the present day. The conciseness of expression in political cartoons must have had a great appeal for Baroja, who valued clarity and precision in linguistic expression above all.

The trilogy *Las figuras de cera, La nave de los locos,* and *Las mascaradas sangrientas,* however, offers the most striking examples of the ordering effects of imaginative centers. In the course of the first novel, the wax figures initiate a discussion about human character (its general uniformity) and the superficiality of many great historical figures. Their malleability makes them a symbol of mankind, easily willing to remake itself to realize its own selfish purposes and to reshape itself in accordance with the dominant political and social forces of the time. And the people in the novel act like wax dolls playing out their roles —Alvarito and Manón as the budding young lovers, Chipiteguy using the wax figures to bring loot out of Spain to support the Liberal cause, and in the background, Aviraneta manipulating his political contacts and spy ring to make the Simancas plan succeed. The sinister appearance of the wax figures when they first arrive at Chipiteguy's horrifies Alvarito and stimulates his imagination to bring the figures to life in his nightmares. The novel spins out the implications of the discussion of the wax figures and imaginatively ties together all the different narrative threads in it. In *Las mascaradas sangrientas,* the description of the murder location provides the motif that unites the novel. The house first appears as a helpless being: «parecía dormir en la soledad, como un animal refugiado en su cubil o como un mendigo, sórdido y miserable» (IV: 502). By the end of the section, Baroja completes the personification by identifying the house with the murder victim: «Aquellas ventanas como pupilas apagadas, la cruz, el ruido del viento y el de la fuente; todo le hizo estremecerse de terror» (IV: 503). But the most imposing detail is the enormous blood stain: «Una hiedra espesa y verde subía por el muro de piedra y trepaba por la casa; pero sin duda cortada, había quedado seca y tenía un color pardo que cubría, como una mancha de sangre antigua, la pared del caserío» (IV: 502-03). The blood stain acts as the sign of the novel, generating and uniting the crimes and violence that fill its pages. The red ivy becomes the pool of blood stains on the murderers' shirts, which their sister struggles to wash out. This single murder announces the countless crimes and murders performed by Bertache and his gang in the last days of the Carlist War, which the novel includes, and the violent encounter between the robbers and Chipiteguy and Alvarito among the group of wax figures labeled the *Asesinos*. The crime has the effect of creating guilt, and the witness Paco Maluenda, while dying of tuberculosis, recounts the murder to Alvarito, as if confessing to a priest, just as at the end of the novel, Alvarito's father confesses to his son the truth about the family's humble origin, out of guilt for a lifetime of lying to him. The narrator confirms the intention of unifying *Las mascaradas sangrientas* under the blood-stained sign of crime as at the beginning of the novel, when, while looking around for a way to explore the spectacle of «la vieja España iba tropezando y desangrándose con las heridas al descubierto» (IV: 475), «apareció ante sus ojos un resplandor sangriento como una aurora boreal» (IV: 476).[6] At the center of the trilogy Baroja places *La nave de los locos,* which he initiates with the dominant image of the novel, an engraving of the *Ship of Fools* from Brant's satire:

> *La nave de los locos,* el carnaval o carro naval, símbolo de la gran locura de los mortales, era el barco de la Humanidad, que marcha por el mar proceloso de la vida, y en el cual se albergan los mayores disparates.
> ... ...
> Hermana en intención de *Las danzas de la Muerte,* así como éstas querían demostrar la igualdad de los hombres ante el sombrío esqueleto, con su guadaña y su reloj de arena, *La nave de los locos* quería probar la universalidad de la Dama Locura. (IV: 328)

As Alvarito and Manón travel through Spain searching for the kidnapped Chipiteguy they discover that madness reigns supreme in the war-torn countryside as the engraving comes to life. The Ship of Fools offers a

---

[6] Of this novel, one of the several genuine masterpieces in the series, interesting for its exploration of the darker side of human nature and its skillful manipulation of atmosphere and suspense, and strongly unified not only by the imaginative *desengaño* and stoicism, the following has been said: «si hubiera que juzgar esta novela aisladamente como válida en sí por su estructura y por haber creado un mundo auténtico, difícilmente cosecharía muchos elogios por parte de la crítica, pese a numerosos cambios a través de tres redacciones sucesivas» (CIPLIJAUSKAITÉ, *Los noventayochistas y la historia,* p. 167). Statements such as this one show to what extent the novels of *Memorias de un hombre de acción* have been misunderstood and not approached on their own artistic terms.

pictorial summary of its complementary novels, too. In *La nave de los locos,* the characters act like wax figures deprived of any signs of individuality or humanity, merely assuming roles that circumstances have assigned them or sinking into bestiality and violence as cruelty subsumes the whole fictional world. Alvarito and Manón's descent into the world of madness marks the beginning of their alienation from one another and shows that no human relationship can withstand the disintegrating pull of the underworld society. Just as the Ship of Fools lies at the heart of the trilogy, so does the trilogy provide an imaginative center for the entire series. The dark, fragmented, bloody vision of nineteenth-century Spain in the three novels offers a powerful visual summary of the demythified world that Baroja presents in *Memorias de un hombre de acción.* He shows man as monstrous in his moral debasement, a point of view very close in spirit to the *desengaño* literature of Gracián, whom he mentions at the opening of *La nave de los locos.* At this point, it becomes obvious that the demythified history of *Memorias de un hombre de acción* functions as a metaphor for a more universal statement about the disordered, amoral world of ordinary experience. In his exploration of Spain's recent history Baroja could not keep from presenting his ideas about the universal human condition, and because of that, could not escape moving back towards the world of myth.

THE PRESENTATION OF A METAPHYSICS

Elliott, following Frye, notes that satire follows a single intellectual pattern.[7] In the case of Baroja, the conventions of satire provide a literary vehicle for the expression and development of a personal metaphysics combining ideas gleaned and/or supported by the works of Nietzsche and Schopenhauer, a nascent existentialist perspective, and a strong moralistic attitude. This individual philosophy forms an intellectual foundation for the series.

Baroja shared with Nietzsche a primary concern with the people and things of this earth. For both men, there was no transcendent world or divine power, just the everyday world of the senses, but with man at the center of that reality. As Leguía states:

> El hombre es, como decía el filósofo griego, la medida de todas las cosas... Yo me contento con lo que abarca la medida humana; creo que hay en sus límites materia bastante con que llenar el corazón y la cabeza de un hombre, y no aspiro a más. *(El amor, el dandismo y la intriga,* IV: 79)

For Nietzsche, this concern takes the form of a search for what separates man from beast, man's values and his culture, in an effort to escape

---

[7] ELLIOTT, p. 187.

nihilism. For Baroja and in this series, it takes the form of an interrogation of Spanish national history as a product of the efforts of individuals to shape their destiny and an examination and evaluation of human responsibility in making that world. In his writings, Nietzsche stresses the individual man and consequently the superman, who achieves this position through self-overcoming, and is one of the central tenets of his philosophy. The large number of stories in *Memorias de un hombre de acción* that follow the *Bildungsroman* tradition shows Baroja's interest in self-development and reveals a similar «self»-centered tendency. Baroja's belief in the subjectivity of experience and the individual's determining of his reality complement this attitude:

> ¿Es que hay una realidad fuera de nosotros? Yo, lector de Kant y de Berkeley, no creo en más realidad que la de nuestro yo. Lo demás son disfraces de la madre Naturaleza, aspectos de la cosa en sí que no sabemos hasta qué punto existen, y si sus presentaciones ante nuestros sentidos son o no constantes. *(La ruta del aventurero,* III: 705)

As a result, he presents the reality of nineteenth-century Spanish history as filtered through the consciousness of a variety of «I's» and because of the subjective nature of the accounts, they sometimes contradict and/or add to each other, and this produces the ambivalence and subversion of different points of view:

> Las inteligencias y las conciencias son seguramente distintas unas de otras, no sólo por su contenido de impresiones venidas de fuera, sino por su esencia. Todo es individual en la Naturaleza, y como no hay dos hojas de árboles iguales, probablemente no hay tampoco dos conciencias iguales. *(El amor, el dandismo y la intriga,* IV: 14)

Similarly, Nietzsche warned against «pure» or «absolute» concepts, realizing that only subjective, limited, and relative views exist:

> There is *only* a perspective seeing, *only* a perspective «knowing»; and the *more* affects we allow to speak about one thing, the *more* eyes, different eyes, we can use to observe one thing, the more complete will our «concept» of this thing, our «objectivity», be.[8]

Even in his preparation of the series Baroja felt an obligation to consult a variety of often-contradictory sources. The emphasis on the exceptional individual, the superman, in Nietzsche's philosophy explains his dislike for the government and any other institution that has a leveling effect on human nature. Baroja despised political parties, official doctrines, and generic terms of any kind, and, significantly, he stresses Aviraneta's independence and marginality and often contrasts him in a positive light

---

[8] FRIEDRICH NIETZSCHE, *On the Genealogy of Morals* and *Ecce Homo,* ed. and trans. Walter Kaufmann (New York: Vintage Books, 1969), p. 119.

with the masses. The author's rejection of classical aesthetics and his preference for an open and seemingly disordered fictional world correspond to Nietzsche's rejection of a formal system in his philosophy as an untruthful approach. Yet as in the philosopher's case, if Baroja's works are examined as a whole and on their own terms, certain consistent patterns emerge. The speech of Señor Sorihuela and the examples of circular time in the series indicate the impact of Nietzsche's concept of the eternal return on Baroja. Both men oppose Christian historical time and prepare the way for a return to mythical time in their works.[9] The Nietzschean eternal recurrence implies that life has no meaning or purpose and the absurdity, disorder, and general pointlessness of human endeavor in *Memorias de un hombre de acción* provide evidence of Baroja's agreement with this attitude. Thompson cannot finish the narrative in «El viaje sin objeto» in *La ruta del aventurero* because «él creía que en el segmento de nuestra limitada vida nada tiene objeto ni fin» (III: 697). The fragmentary, episodic quality of the series attests to Baroja's skepticism about logical development and completion in human activities. Nietzsche's denunciation of causality and his statement in *Twilight of the Idols* that man's essence is fatefulness, has its fictional counterpart in the lack of causality and strong sense of fate in *Memorias de un hombre de acción*.[10] Finally, Nietzsche and Baroja share the ironist's view that an emphasis on the negative aspects of life can bring about positive change; they hope to heal by wounding. Just as Zarathustra strives to create new values by destroying the old concepts of good and evil, Baroja wishes to stimulate the moral reform of the individual by subverting the ordinarily mythified and heroic vision of Spanish national history.[11]

Baroja, like Schopenhauer, has an extremely pessimistic attitude towards life and man. Schopenhauer describes life in the world as a combination of will and representation, yet will almost inevitably triumphs over man's rational powers and emerges in struggles and desires, products of egoism. Thus life is unending strife and affliction, a battle of wills that transforms the world into a vast panorama of war: «This world is the battleground of tormented and agonized beings who continue to exist

[9] For Baroja, Heraclitus, and the eternal return see CARMEN IGLESIAS, «El 'devenir' y la acción en la obra de Pío Baroja», *Cuadernos Americanos*, 21, No. 3 (May-June 1962), 263, and by the same author, *El pensamiento de Pío Baroja: Ideas centrales*, Clásicos y Modernos, No. 12 (México: Antigua Librería Robredo, 1963), pp. 41-43.

[10] WALTER KAUFMANN, ed. and trans., *The Portable Nietzsche* (New York: Penguin Books, 1976), pp. 492-501.

[11] I here follow WALTER KAUFMANN, *Nietzsche: Philosopher, Psychologist, Antichrist* (Princeton: Princeton University Press, 1964). On the impact of Nietzsche in Spain see PAUL ILIE, «Nietzsche in Spain: 1890-1910», *PMLA*, 79 (1964), 80-96, and GONZALO SOBEJANO, *Nietzsche en España* (Madrid: Gredos, 1967). On the influence of Nietzsche on Baroja see especially SOBEJANO, pp. 347-95, and IGLESIAS, «La filosofía», in *El pensamiento*, pp. 25-70.

only by each devouring the other».[12] The historical scenario of the series portrays man as a perpetually embattled and cannibalistic creature. One of Baroja's favorite observations about man, derived from Plautus, is repeated throughout *The World as Will and Representation: Homo homini lupus* (Man is a wolf for man). The spectacle of civil war, betrayal, murder, and the actions of such figures as Merino and Cabrera provide a historical-fictional dramatization of this negative view of man.

Schopenhauer also viewed the world as disordered and chaotic. Only the intellect can give it order and significance. He esteemed art and history (a form of fiction for him and Baroja) as examples of reason's ability to see through the confusion of everyday existence and get at the essence of life:

> The true philosophy of history thus consists in the insight that, in spite of all these endless changes and their chaos and confusion, we yet always have before us only the same, identical, unchangeable essence, acting in the same way today as it did yesterday and always.[13]

This is precisely the display of endless flux, change without change, that Baroja presents in *Memorias de un hombre de acción*. Undoubtedly he derived much of his pessimism as well as his concepts about history and art from the philosopher. Yet whereas Schopenhauer's pessimism pushes him towards denial of the will in asceticism, Baroja moves towards Nietzschean vitalism and a philosophy that closely resembles existentialism.

According to Northrop Frye, each literary mode has its own existential projection. He links existentialism with the ironic mode:

> The existential projection of irony is, perhaps, existentialism itself; and the return of irony to myth is accompanied, not only by the cyclical theories of history mentioned above, but, in a later stage by a widespread interest in sacramental philosophy and dogmatic theology.[14]

Baroja himself wrote about the influence of such ironic philosophers as Heraclitus, Schopenhauer, and Nietzsche on his ideas and writing, but he had little regard for existentialism as a philosophical movement:

> Ya la denominación de este sistema existencialista nos parece a la mayoría una vacuidad o una fantasía... Pero ¿qué quiere decir existencialismo? Yo creo que no quiere decir nada: casi parece un camelo. *(Galería de tipos de la época*, VII: 815)

Baroja's peevish tone develops into one of outright annoyance and denunciation:

---

[12] ARTHUR SCHOPENHAUER, *The World as Will and Representation*, trans. E. F. J. Payne, II (New York: Dover Publications, 1966), p. 581.
[13] SCHOPENHAUER, II, pp. 444-45.
[14] FRYE, *Anatomy of Criticism*, pp. 64-65.

> Yo no veo en lo que he leído sobre el existencialismo nada nuevo que
> no se haya dicho en filosofía.
>   Sobre la relatividad de la vida y del pensamiento del hombre, Protá-
> goras y Heráclito dijeron todo lo que se puede decir; respecto a la angustia,
> al temor a perder la vida, todas las religiones se han ocupado de ello. Tam-
> poco hay aquí nada de una gran novedad. *(Bagatelas de otoño,* VII: 1307)

There are few who would disagree with Baroja's assessment of existentialism being nothing new. William Barrett has described existentialist
philosophy as an outgrowth of major social changes that occurred in the
eighteenth and nineteenth centuries, including increased mechanization,
bureaucratization, and alienation. Existentialism emerges as a response
to the indifference and limitation of personal freedom imposed by the
mass society.[15] Baroja greatly admired two novelists who have been associated with existentialist thought, Stendhal and Dostoyevsky. In addition,
two of his contemporaries, Machado and Unamuno, have been linked to
existentialism.

Despite Baroja's refusal to recognize existentialism as a philosophical
system, there are still numerous points of contact, especially in terms of
his general philosophical position as revealed through his novels. All of
his works present existence as a problem and his heroes' quests can easily
be reduced to the most fundamental philosophical issue facing modern
man —the ontological quest, the search for self. Baroja's heroes search
for a viable form of existence, which translates as an impossible (therefore, it is always the «failed» hero we see) reconciliation of uncompromising truth to self and pursuit of a project that is an outward expression of that self on the one hand, with all of the contingencies and chaos
of the society, the Others, he encounters. In *Memorias de un hombre de
acción,* Baroja explores this existential problem on a grand scale as Aviraneta, the embodiment of Spanish liberalism (a combination of the liberalism of the French Revolution and the Romantic movement), the adventurer ideal, and the existential hero, faces the mediocrity, chaos, and
ironclad conservatism of Spanish society. But once again, the historical-
fictional world conjured up by the author is a metaphor for the challenge
facing all modern men to create order out of chaos and meaning out
senselessness. Aviraneta's record of failure, his victimization by powerful
men, and his death as an unknown historical figure attest to the anxiety
facing the sincere man as he confronts doubt, meaninglessness, and fate.
The cruel world that Baroja portrays in *Memorias de un hombre de
acción* is the same as Dostoyevsky's criminal universe in *Crime and
Punishment,* Kafka's dehumanized, mechanistic world in *The Trial,* or
the hopelessly alienated society of Sartre's *No Exit.* But Aviraneta has

---

[15] WILLIAM BARRETT, *Irrational Man: A Study in Existential Philosophy* (Garden City, New York: Doubleday, 1958), pp. 30-31.

neither the «bad faith» of the nameless, petty bureaucrat in *Notes from the Underground* nor the escapist «adventures» of *Nausea*'s Roquentin to defend his sense of selfhood from the void. He has only his own philosophy of integrity and action to generate and maintain that self. And like a true existential hero, he always *chooses* to act in accordance with his own beliefs and to accept responsibility for those actions, risking ignominy and death, and sacrificing personal ties in the process of self-creation.

Baroja has in common with the existentialists (as with Schopenhauer and Nietzsche) the focus on the subjectivity of experience and the primary concern with man's existence in the world, as his portrayal of nineteenth-century Spanish history as a combination of different subjective experiences —Leguía's, Aviraneta's, Alvarito's, etc.— reveals. Furthermore, Baroja's use of first person narratives in the form of memoirs also links him to the fictional techniques of existential literature. From Kierkegaard on, the existentialist author insists on his imprisonment within his own subjectivity and the unavoidable identification with his fictional characters, but by projecting himself into the texts as a fictional author or editor dealing with «found» manuscripts, the author distances himself ironically from the fictional world.[16] This attitude recalls Baroja's identification of himself with Aviraneta and Leguía at the beginning of *El aprendiz de conspirador* and his constant shifts in tone and point of view to avoid univocal consistency and to create distance between himself and his characters.

Baroja's treatment of time also shows an affinity with the existentialist temporal perception. Kierkegaard and Heidegger stress that death is the inexorable human fate and that man's response to this fact determines the significance of his life. Time is no longer an external logical phenomenon, but rather a subjective temporal perception with ruptures and discontinuities, a way of orienting oneself in the universe. Existential time involves freeing oneself from historical time and plunging oneself into a permanent «now» through ceaseless striving and activity. Such activity has no purpose, but rather is self-fulfilling. Existential time blends easily with the cyclical time of the cosmos.[17] Baroja also regards death as the most important temporal phenomenon. In his treatment of time in *Memorias de un hombre de acción,* he constantly subverts the linear progression of historical time and replaces it with cyclical time and Avira-

[16] EDITH KERN, *Existential Thought and Fictional Technique: Kierkegaard, Sartre, Beckett* (New Haven: Yale University Press, 1970).
[17] On existential time see HANS MEYERHOFF, *Time in Literature* (Berkeley: University of California Press, 1966), pp. 63-79, and JOHN HENRY RALEIGH, «The English Novel and the Three Kinds of Time», in *Time, Place, and Idea: Essays on the Novel* (Carbondale: Southern Illinois University Press, 1968), 43-55, at pp. 45, 54-55.

neta's everlasting now. And for the adventurer, action is everything. Even when Aviraneta thinks, he immediately begins to transform thought into action: «Su pensamiento era siempre dinámico; no podía discurrir sin unir al discurso una idea de acción, y cuando llegaba a ésta comenzaba a poner los medios para realizarla» (*Con la pluma y con el sable*, III: 422). «Action for action's sake» constitutes his entire existence. The replacement of historical time with the permanent now subverts the basis for causality, the relationship between past and future. Time no longer moves in a specific direction and events no longer mark its flow in a logical or meaningful fashion. The only core of meaning resides in the self. In existentialism, the significance of life lies in authenticity or in the integrity of the self —acting in full awareness of one's freedom and responsibility. Because of this, man is constantly alone and alienated from his fellow man.[18]

The fragmentation and alienation of man in *Memorias de un hombre de acción* shows that Baroja has a similar notion of the fundamental human condition. His characters act like molecules bouncing around in a glass, always in motion, occasionally colliding with one another, rarely having genuine sympathy or rarely in harmony with one another, and they stop moving only to die or to enter a solipsistic state. As Baroja illustrates in *Humano enigma*, the Other always remains a mystery to the individual. Yet he, too, insists on the positive value of human integrity, truth to self: «Si Aviraneta hubiera sido filósofo y hubiera intentado postular su ley moral, la hubiera formulado así: 'Obra de modo que tus actos concuerden y parezcan dimanar lógicamente de la figura ideal que te has formado de ti mismo'» (*Con la pluma y con el sable*, III: 423). Baroja also suggests that this core of authenticity endows life with meaning and compensates for what otherwise might seem a lifetime of difficulties and failures, as Aviraneta states: «'Lo único que me queda para vivir es la idea de haber obrado siempre con arreglo a mi conciencia'» (*Crónica escandalosa*, IV: 1032).

A central philosophical pattern that underlies and orders the fictional world of *Memorias de un hombre de acción* emerges from the preceding comparisons. Baroja may have begun the series as an interrogation of Spanish national history, but it ends up simply as a pretext for a more

---

[18] In my observations on existentialism I follow HAZEL E. BARNES, *The Literature of Possibility: A Study in Humanistic Existentialism* (Lincoln: University of Nebraska Press, 1959), WILLIAM BARRETT, *Irrational Man*, MARJORIE GRENE, *Introduction to Existentialism* (Chicago: University of Chicago Press, 1959), EDITH KERN, *Existential Thought*, EVERETT W. KNIGHT, *Literature Considered as Philosophy: The French Example* (London: Routledge and Kegan Paul, 1957), DAVID DUNBAR McELROY, *Existentialism and Modern Literature: An Essay in Existential Criticism* (New York: Greenwood Press, 1968), and JEAN WAHL, «The Roots of Existentialism», in *Essays in Existentialism*, by JEAN-PAUL SARTRE, ed. Wade Baskin (Secaucus, New Jersey: Citadel Press, 1979), pp. 3-28.

universal comment on the fundamental human condition, and thus, as Baroja's most ambitious and most thorough examination of man's existential problem. Baroja has a skeptical, ironic attitude towards the world and feels that it is absurd, meaningless, and directionless in and of itself. Yet since he denies the existence of any divine order or power, Baroja feels that one must stoically and resolutely face the world as it is and meet it on its own terms. Man lies at the core of Baroja's universe. While the author has no faith in collective reform or rapid and large-scale change, he does feel that both the cause and the cure of man's existential illness lie in the individual. He insists again and again on the individual's responsibility for his actions and the importance of integrity to self. If man maintains that central core of integrity, then life acquires meaning whether it accrues material awards or not. Authentic existence endows man with essence in Baroja's universe, and for him, the existential problem of endowing life with meaning is a moral issue. The demythified world of *Memorias de un hombre de acción* is a morally debased world where bestiality and self-interest rule and a metaphor for Baroja's dark vision of the ordinary world of human experience. The demythifying, destructive, disordering process to which he subjects that world in the novels to strip away the surface illusions, however, only forms half of the process in the series. He reintegrates the fragments into a meaningful whole on another plane, within the ordering patterns of his man-centered, skeptical philosophy and its aesthetic projection, ironic fictional form, and a consistently moral point of view.

BAROJA THE MORALIST

Baroja's moralistic perception of the universe is everpresent in *Memorias de un hombre de acción*. He often assumes a moralistic stance in judging the men and the actions of the age through the voice of the narrator. Although the author clearly shares Aviraneta's sympathy with the Spanish national cause during the War of Independence, he also denounces the debased life of the *guerrillero* through his hero's words:

> El ser guerrillero es, moralmente, una ganga; es como ser bandido con permiso, como ser libertino a sueldo y con la bula del Papa.
> Guerrear, robar, dedicarse a la rapiña y al pillaje; preparar emboscadas y sorpresas, tomar un pueblo, saquearlo, no es seguramente una ocupación muy moral, pero sí muy divertida. *(El escuadrón del «Brigante», III: 153)*

Baroja's use of words that imply religious sanction and enjoyment of these activities heightens the reader's sense of their moral debasement. He likewise denounces prison, society's institution for punishing injustice, through Aviraneta's observations:

> La cárcel es la universidad de lo perverso... Los monstruos físicos vagan
> por el mundo; los monstruos morales tienden a reunirse en la cárcel. Aquí
> se completan, se complican, se hacen más perfectos en su monstruosidad.
> *(El sabor de la venganza,* III: 1126)

Often Aviraneta's criticism of the major political figures of the epoch has
a moral rather than a socio-political focus. He emphasizes Fernando VII's
cruelty rather than his Absolutism and political ineptitude: «'era senci-
llamente un miserable, un hombre cruel y sanguinario que llenó de horcas
España, donde mandó colgar a los que le defendieron con su sangre'»
(La Isabelina, III: 1047). Even the regent María Cristina, whom Aviraneta supports for most of the series, receives criticism for her rather
coarse and common character as indicated by her over-indulgence in
eating and free sexual activity.

Those who identify Baroja's emphasis on man's lack of morality with
a celebration of the darker side of human nature miss the fact that Baroja the ironist assumes a critical attitude towards such immorality. In
addition to the observation just mentioned, he often incorporates poetic
justice in *Memorias de un hombre de acción,* which at times he applies
with rigor comparable to the divine vengeance of the Old Testament. In
a number of episodes, characters pay for their moral flaws by acquiring
a physical appearance that corresponds to their internal ugliness. Paca
Dávalos, the unprincipled beauty in an episode of *El sabor de la venganza,* manipulates the two men who love her, Castelo and Chico, to
satisfy her whims. Eventually she and Castelo become leaders of an underworld society that thrives on drinking, gambling, and prostitution, and
they arrange the mob murder of the police chief Chico in 1854. But the
murder and a long life of debauchery take their toll. Paca ends her days
screaming obscenities as a charity case in a hospital. She has become a
monstrous, repulsive old woman —obese, alcoholic, and with her flesh
eaten up by venereal disease. Only the visit of her daughter, who has
become a nun to pay for her mother's sins, eases her final days. Castelo,
also aged and physically deformed, hangs himself to escape the ghost of
Chico that pursues him during his drunken delirium. La Tiburcia and
Bertache, the evil pair implicated in the murder of *Las mascaradas sangrientas,* have a similar fate. In other cases, Baroja pays back the culprits
in kind. In another tale of *El sabor de la venganza,* a jealous husband,
Don Tomás, arranges a violent death for his young nephew Miguel, who
has fallen in love with his wife. The uncle digs a deep hole in his ware-
house and covers it so that when the young man enters the room in the
dark he plunges to his death. Don Tomás and his accomplice cover the
hole with the stored goods and the wife dies shortly after the murder
from heartache. Many years later, Don Tomás enters a bizarre cult of
penitents, la Escuela de Cristo, whose members perform self-castigation
using the most primitive methods. One night, two friends of the long-dead

Miguel Rocaforte disguise themselves as ghosts and appear in front of Don Tomás's window, claiming to be Miguel's ghost. Don Tomás dies of fright, as planned by the victim's friends, just as he and a friend had plotted Miguel's death. In the tale of vengeance «La canóniga» in *Los recursos de la astucia,* the penitentiary Sansirgue avenges himself for an imagined affront by Miguelito Torralba by delivering the young man into an ambush by the Liberals. Years later, when Sansirgue's responsibility is revealed, the terrorist Absolutist organization known as El Angel Exterminador catches him alone and hangs him. All of these examples of poetic justice reveal Baroja's belief in man's moral responsibility. For Baroja, sometimes retribution involves a noble sacrifice from innocent people, like the daughter of Paca Dávalos or the sister of the murderers in *Las mascaradas sangrientas* who complements the physical action of washing the bloodstains from her brothers' shirts with the spiritual action of washing away their sins by devoting her life to God. To show the devastating consequences of man's low moral character Baroja represents violence as generating more violence and/or exacting sacrifice and suffering from innocent victims. He insists that this moral disease infects even the highest levels of society, as Aviraneta observes in retrospect:

> Cuando veo ahora desde lejos mi época, comprendo que nuestro carácter, al mismo tiempo cuco e insensato, ha sido la causa de muchas desdichas. En España no es íntegramente el pueblo difícil de dirigir, sino el cabecilla, el letrado, que es casi siempre egoísta, petulante y orgulloso. *(Desde el principio hasta el fin,* IV: 1128)

Baroja's preoccupation with the lack of leaders who embody superior guiding spiritual values, a concern he shares with the other members of the Generation of '98, becomes apparent in this statement. He appeals for nothing short of a major moral reform, not on an unrealistic scale of massive social change, but rather in terms of individual transformation and integrity.

His presentation of characters whose moral exemplarity stands out like an island of integrity in a sea of demythification and debasement proves that he believes in the possibility of such reform. The Liberal guerrilla leader El Empecinado marches to his death at the end of *Los contrastes de la vida* with great nobility and courage. After his capture, the Absolutists exhibit him publicly in a cage for scorn and abuse. On the day of his execution, however, Don Juan Martín manages to untie the rope around his wrists on the way to the hangman and grabbing a sword from one of the guards, he tries to slash his way through the crowd. A group of soldiers immediately bayonets him to death. The police chief Chico submits stoically to his murder by the mob in *El sabor de la venganza*. Among the life stories of Aviraneta's *guerrillero* companions in *El escuadrón del «Brigante»,* Baroja places the tale of Antonio García, El

122

Tobalos, once the magistrate of a village. In the narrative El Tobalos insists on prosecuting the son of a wealthy neighbor for murder (which the young man did not commit). Two men had previously been hanged for the crime, and El Tobalos pursues and achieves justice at enormous personal expense —the powerful family and the town turn against him, his daughter, in love with the murderer, and his wife die, and he loses all of his personal property. Significantly, Baroja presents each of these cases as a truly tragic and heroic occurrence without any ironic undercutting. Although the vision is a bleak one and the bleakness increases as the series progresses, Baroja's sympathy undoubtedly lies with the man who maintains his core of moral integrity regardless of the cost: «'mi simpatía va hacia el hombre templado que marcha al suplicio con la sonrisa en los labios más que a la turba aulladora y cobarde'» (Aviraneta in *El sabor de la venganza,* III: 1156). It is only natural that in a world devoid of values, the worth of men of true moral fibre would not be recognized and they would be punished rather than rewarded. Baroja shows special admiration for men who show courage and integrity in facing death. Here, too, his attitude is reminiscent of the existentialists, who feel that a man shows his true worth in the manner in which he meets his fate. Aviraneta offers the most consistent thread of moral integrity in the work. The narrator qualifies his integrity as «su ley moral» and despite the hero's Machiavellian tendencies Baroja obviously intended for him to have a strong moral character: «La moral de Aviraneta era moral de cómico, moral de teatro, moral un tanto inmoral; pero moral fuerte, al menos para él» (*Con la pluma y con el sable,* III: 423). Towards the end of the series, an observer insists on Aviraneta's moral probity:

> «El infame Aviraneta, el malvado Aviraneta, es un personaje calderoniano o un tipo del Romancero; en cambio, muchos que son espías y logreros en la realidad, pasan ante la multitud por hombres probos, de una moral intachable. Usted prefiere serlo que parecerlo.» (*Crónica escandalosa,* IV: 1033)

Despite Aviraneta's constant exposure to the underworld, he emerges morally sound and unscathed by its debasement.

The adventurer's achievement of moral superiority in *Memorias de un hombre de acción* indicates that even within the context of a demythified world some form of transcendence is possible. For Baroja, transcendence into an idyllic society or a divine world no longer exists as a real or fictional possibility and so the potential for transcendence becomes internalized and limited to the individual, as an endeavor of self-realization manifested in moral integrity in which a perfect correspondence exists between inner moral strength and outer appearance through action. It must be realized, however, that this vision of transcendence has its basis in the moral universe of Baroja's earlier works. In a sense, it is simply a reformulation of the conflict of good and evil in those novels. Baroja described himself as a moralist:

> Así como la parte estética de la vida no me ha preocupado mucho, la parte moral sí. En la literatura me ha pasado lo mismo... La moral, no sólo en la vida, sino en la literatura, es la que tiene más trascendencia. *(Galería de tipos de la época, VII: 810-11)*

His moralistic stance accounts for the seemingly paradoxical forms of literary expression he employs —romance and satire. The protagonists of his novels, men of dedication and lofty ideals, constantly come face to face with the real, morally inferior world. The confrontation between real and ideal worlds generates much of the tension in his works. The utopian community in *Paradox, rey* must inevitably yield to the invading forces of contemporary Europe. Fernando Ossorio works his way through the barren landscape and debased towns of Castile before integrating himself into the superior, apotheosized bourgeois life he discovers in Valencia, only to find it threatened by his mother-in-law's superstitions. The tormented protagonist of *El árbol de la ciencia* thinks he has established a perfect island of tranquility in the chaos of everyday life, but the real world intrudes with the birth of the baby and the death of his wife. When the real world appears in his fiction, Baroja almost always dons his ironic mask, distances himself from his characters and their activities, and plunges into the conventions of satire. His entire literary production is based on this pendulum movement between mythification and demythification.

Through the author's preoccupation in *Memorias de un hombre de acción*, one sees a submerged world of romance and myth poking through the chaos of demythified history to offer man some form of transcendence and meaning within this world. For if on one level, that of the particular, Baroja *de*mythifies, disorders, and fragments, on another more universal level he unifies, re-orders, and *re*mythifies. Behind his hero's adventures and the moral vision of *Memorias de un hombre de acción*, one catches a glimpse of Baroja winding his way through the labyrinth of experience, back to the world of myth.

V

THROUGH THE LABYRINTH: THE UNDERWORLD
SOCIETY

> But Heraclitus will remain eternally right with
> his assertion that being is an empty fiction. The
> «apparent» world is the only one: the «true» world
> is merely added by a lie.
>
> (NIETZSCHE, *Twilight of the Idols*)

> For this reason the result of every purely objec-
> tive and so of every artistic, apprehension of things
> is an expression more of the true nature of life
> and existence, more an answer to the question,
> «What is life?»
>
> (SCHOPENHAUER, *The World as Will and
> Representation*)

MORAL INVERSION, CRIMINALITY, AND THE DEMONIC

Baroja initiates the reader into an underworld society in *El aprendiz
de conspirador* when the fictional editor of the series Leguía finds himself
caught up in a whirlwind of political conflicts and cloak-and-dagger
activities. The underworld society can best be described as the opposite
of the transcendent world of romance, associated with perfect order,
harmony, absolute good, beauty, and fulfillment. The demonic society is
associated with evil, death, decay, disorder, egotism, truncation, and dis-
memberment.[1] In *Memorias de un hombre de acción,* the author identifies
the darker side of life —destruction and death, secrets and deceit, cruelty
and alienation, as manifested by personal incidents and large-scale events
in a historical context— with archetypal imagery of the underworld. This
identification consists of a presentation of disorder, egotism, fragmentation, perverted values, and criminality as normal human behavior. Baroja
dwells especially on the element of illusion, on the ironic discontinuity

---

[1] For more on the underworld and demonic imagery see NORTHROP FRYE,
Anatomy of Criticism (Princeton: Princeton University Press, 1971), pp. 147-50
and 223-39, and chapter four, «The Bottomless Dream: Themes of Descent», in
his *The Secular Scripture* (Cambridge, Mass.: Harvard University Press, 1976),
pp. 95-126.

between surface appearance and underlying reality, deceit and truth, what things seem to be and what they really are. Such contrasts offer a specific example of José Maravall's observation that the author tends to intellectualize his material and replace intuitive, spontaneous views of life with an intellectualized concept of the observations.[2] This simultaneous exploration of particular/general, demythification/remythification, and illusion/truth reveals that paradox and discontinuity lie at the heart of *Memorias de un hombre de acción* and characterize Baroja's attitude towards life.

The underworld society of *Memorias de un hombre de acción,* unlike that of such earlier novels as *El mayorazgo de Labraz* and *Las inquietudes de Shanti Andía,* does not exist in tandem with an idyllic, orderly, transcendent world. As a result, Baroja poses in the novels the existential problem of how to manipulate that world in order to establish one's own margin of authenticity, truth to self, and creation of one's self through outward expression in activity. Man only achieves some measure of peace and escape from the tumult of daily life through withdrawal and inner solace or ceaseless strife and action. Alvarito Sánchez de Mendoza of the *Las figuras de cera* trilogy, Miguel Aristy of *La veleta de Gastizar,* and Pello Leguía all achieve this sort of transcendence through solitude, while Aviraneta remains faithful at least in spirit to the philosophy of action all his life.[3] The hero is the most successful character of the series in terms of finding a margin of authenticity while still remaining in the underworld. Thus, Aviraneta acts as a ball of thread to lead the reader through the labyrinth of intrigue and illusion. Baroja does not project an entirely negative attitude towards the underworld, however. As with any aspect of his world view, his treatment of the underworld society is complex, contradictory, and rich in its philosophical and artistic implications. Despite his apparent dislike for the brutality of that world, he obviously feels drawn by its protean nature and the creativity and ingenuity it inspires.

The underworld of *Memorias de un hombre de acción* is morally a world-turned-upside-down, a world of inverted values inhabited by human beings whose barbarity transforms them into grotesque creatures. With the observant eye of a doctor, Baroja shows a keen awareness of the sickness of the world and the pathology of the human condition.[4] In the series the illness takes the form of a pervasive *desequilibrio,* a kind of social madness, as Aviraneta indicates:

---

[2] JOSÉ ANTONIO MARAVALL, «Historia y novela», in Vol. I of *Baroja y su mundo,* ed. Fernando Baeza (Madrid: Arión, 1961), 162-82, at. p. 170.

[3] JEAN WAHL discusses the existentialist concept of transcendence in immanence on p. 14 of his Introduction to *Essays in Existentialism,* by JEAN-PAUL SARTRE, ed. Wade Baskin (Secaucus, N. J.: Citadel Press, 1979).

[4] E. H. TEMPLIN, «Pío Baroja and Science», *Hispanic Review,* 15 (1947), 165-92. On p. 168 TEMPLIN refers to Baroja's «roving clinic» and describes him as a doctor prescribing an ascetic regime, the vital lie, and the action remedy.

«Mientras la sociedad viva como un organismo en perpetuo desequilibrio..., el gobierno será bárbaro y depravado; tendrá el político algo de
las atribuciones del cirujano: cortará la carne enferma y la sana, gozará
de una verdadera dictadura para el bien y para el mal.» *(Los recursos de
la astucia,* III: 613)

Of course, the forceful and painful healing powers that the hero associates
with the surgeon resemble those of Baroja the satirist who directly
attacks the evils of society and imposes a strong moralistic vision of good
and evil on the fictional world. Baroja has no faith in a possible large-
scale cure for social disequilibrium, mostly because he has no faith in
mankind in general. Aviraneta expresses this pessimistic attitude towards
human nature: «'No hay pueblo que pueda tener un gobierno de hombres
justos. Tendría que haber un medio social sano, cuerdo, en perfecto equi-
librio. Es decir, que para sostener una utopía habría que inventar otra'»
(Los recursos de la astucia, III: 613). One senses a Nietzschean pessimism
behind both of these statements, a fundamental mistrust of man as a
social animal.

Baroja's pessimism goes even further though, in his portrayal of the
nineteenth-century Spanish historical world as an essentially criminal
society. Through his hero he denounces a wide range of historical figures,
from Carlos IV, Fernando VII, and Godoy —«Los padres, el hijo, el fa-
vorito, todos rivalizaron en abyección y vileza» *(El escuadrón del «Brigante»,* III: 125); to national heroes like Palafox —«me pareció un hombre inepto, ambicioso y de poca integridad moral» *(El escuadrón del «Brigante»,* III: 124); and Merino —«soez, egoísta y brutal» *(El escuadrón
del «Brigante»,* III: 150). These figures, regardless of their affiliations
with Absolutists or Patriots, share the same criminal character. Carlos IV
and Godoy sell out the Spanish people to the French. Fernando VII betrays his country and the faith of the people by becoming a tyrant. Palafox denies any association with La Isabelina in 1834 and makes little
effort to get Aviraneta out of prison. Merino and his *guerrilleros* use the
popular political cause to legitimize their fanaticism and cruelty. In each
case, the individual seizes an opportunity given to him by historical circumstances to realize his own selfish desires at the expense and suffering
of a number of people who placed their faith in him. Baroja unmasks their
criminal behavior to show that they have no right to their historical
labels as leaders or heroes. He subverts the traditional attitudes towards
these figures presented in formal histories. Leguía's comments about the
lives of the famous historical figures he reads in the *Biografía Universal*
reveal this attitude:

... casi todos ellos habían sido de una perfecta inmoralidad: ladrones incon-
secuentes y traidores. Además, no sólo ocurría esto, sino que casi todos
los traidores habían sido premiados, y casi todos los hombres fieles a
una causa acababan en la miseria, en la prisión o en el patíbulo.

Era un ejemplo verdaderamente inmoral. *(El amor, el dandismo y la intriga,* IV: 33)

Baroja also presents a literary criminal world in *Memorias de un hombre de acción* as a truly demonic society. In «Una intriga tenebrosa» of *Los caminos de mundo* the Barón de Oiquina relates his and Aviraneta's involvement in «la Conspiración del Triángulo», the attempted assassination of Fernando VII in 1816. Baroja uses archetypal demonic motifs to describe the criminal society of a historical epoch in this tale. Most of the action occurs at night and is characterized by confusion, confinement, secrecy, and disguise. Death hovers over all the occurrences. The societies themselves are loosely tied together to withstand the stresses of betrayal and internal dissension, which eventually lead to their rapid dissolution and disappearance. Aviraneta assumes the role of the double agent in the world of espionage. The conflict between two demonic societies forms the basis for the plot in which the Masonic lodges set up a group of conspirators who under Aviraneta's direction plan to murder Fernando VII and reestablish Carlos IV on the throne as a constitutional monarch. As in any demonic society, the conspirators have their own secret methods and language —a brotherhood arranged in a triangular chain in which each member knows only his initiator and the two new members whom he initiates and who communicate by using special cutout chessboard designs that when superimposed on letters isolate the key words. They also use sympathetic ink and Solomon's seal as an indicator of special correspondence. The headquarters of the society is in a small attic in an old house in a back street near the Royal Palace in Madrid, accessible only by a rope ladder from the top floor —all in accord with the dark, confined space demonic societies occupy. As usual, traitors within the organization threaten to destroy it, although the hero finds out in time to denounce them to the police and save the group initially. Another demonic society, the Sociedad de Santa Fe, headed by one of the King's favorites, Corpas, wishes to promote the more stringent Absolutism of Fernando's brother Don Carlos. Aviraneta, disguised as a hunched-over old man, infiltrates this group to attend its meetings in a secret place. The hero arrives in a dark, closed coach and at the meeting finds an assorted group of grotesque, threatening priests and clerics with their own secret signs and countersigns. The narrative culminates in an encounter between Aviraneta and his companions (whose true affiliation has been revealed to the fanatical brotherhood) and the Santa Fe Society in another secret meeting place. The scene ends in a mad scramble in the dark (after the hero eliminates the only light source), an almost surrealistic escape across the rooftops of Madrid, and a chilling encounter between the hero and a symbol of death, a corpse surrounded by lights for a wake. Eventually Aviraneta turns in Corpas and the Santa Fe group to the police before they can denounce his group of conspirators. The story ends with the disbanding of both societies, lack of success on both sides, and the hero's refuge with a handful of associates in the house of the hangman of Madrid.

Baroja resorts to the archetypal demonic society to describe the criminal world of *Memorias de un hombre de acción* on more than one occasion. The atrocities of Bertache and his band in *Las mascaradas sangrientas,* their demonic revelries, perversion, and barbarity, the predominance of disorder and self-interest among the gang, and Bertache's nightmarish, feverish death after robbing the ornaments from figures of saints at a hermit's hut, ally them with the devil and the forces of darkness. The trail of the marauders across a barren landscape strewn with ruins, the wreckage of war, and maimed and starving people, reinforces the impression. Aviraneta's account of the Cárcel de Corte in *El sabor de la venganza* during his imprisonment as director of La Isabelina is the description of a descent into hell: «La cárcel es como la imagen negativa de la vida moral. Allí la bajeza, la fealdad, la maldad, el odio, todo lo más horrendamente humano, se muestra a lo vivo» (III: 1126). Baroja's touching the bottom of the underworld with the criminal societies permits ironic comparisons that emphasize the world-turned-upside-down aspect of the series. Since perversion and inverted values reign supreme, very often the marginal characters of this world show the greatest amount of humanity and compassion. The hangman who hides Aviraneta and his friends in *Los caminos del mundo* shows great philosophical composure. He takes pride in his profession and stays aloof and indifferent to the conflicts of the world he keeps at a distance, as indicated by the narrator's ironic comment: «daba la impresión de que habitaba un mundo sin gente», III: 364). In *La nave de los locos,* Alvarito meets a strange gentleman who treats everyone he meets with kindness, including a hangman and a leper, speaks of fraternity among men as more important than equality and liberty. He finds out shortly afterward that this man simply referred to as «El Caballero» is a homosexual. In this case Baroja's ironic view goes so far that it threatens to undermine such Christian values as charity and kindness to one's fellow man by associating them with what society regarded as sexual perversion. After witnessing the murder in *Las mascaradas sangrientas,* Paco Maluenda is taken in by an aged, half-crazed marquis who lives with his family in an isolated mountain home after years of suffering persecution for his Liberal affiliations. His kindness forms a sharp contrast with the bloody murder Maluenda has just witnessed. These ironic visions of the alienated man as the upholder of true brotherhood indicates how far Baroja feels society is from an ideal fraternal state in its uncompromising rejection of the genuine spirit of compassion and fraternity.

THE PROBLEM OF SELF AND SOCIETY

But while the criminal societies he presents in *Memorias de un hombre de acción* offer an extreme example of man's fallen condition, the secret societies and political parties of the epoch offer an equally disturbing image of the lack of social equilibrium and prove to be mere distortions of what ideal fraternities should be. Much of the Spanish history of the first half of the nineteenth century is inscribed within the efforts and conflicts of the secret societies. As an adolescent Aviraneta belongs to El Aventino, an organization that has its roots in the French Enlightenment. He later joins the Masons, who play a crucial role in Spanish politics of the period. In *El escuadrón del «Brigante»*, his Masonic distress signal to the French officer when caught while trying to free the director of Spanish patriotic forces reveals a spirit of brotherhood that transcends political and national differences, but the enormous political range among the Spanish lodges of the epoch, from Absolutist to Liberal inclinations, indicates that ideological contrasts undermine any attempt at a united political front. Aviraneta points out the importance of the lodges as the basis for the political developments of the time: «En ellas se inició la política de los partidos españoles de la primera mitad del siglo XIX» (*El escuadrón del «Brigante»*, III: 232). Aviraneta soon finds the hopes for Liberal reform that he places first in the Masons and subsequently in the *comuneros* and *carbonarios* disappointed. He becomes disgusted with the mumbo-jumbo, secret signals, and self-conscious names of the organizations and infuriated with their inefficacious methods. The failure of the *carbonarios* to free four of their own from a public execution in Paris illustrates the disorganization and impotence of the group in *Con la pluma y con el sable*. In addition, the rivalry among the Masons, *carbonarios*, and *comuneros* demoralizes and weakens the political efforts of the Liberals, making them easy prey for the Absolutists (*Con la pluma y con el sable*, III, 509-11). In Aviraneta's description of the political situation during 1820-23 (*Con la pluma y con el sable*, «Confusión», III: 462-65), he points out the elements of confusion and lack of cohesion that typify the moment: numerous half-secret, half-public societies of Liberal and Absolutist persuasions, members who place self-interest above the public good, promotion of political ideas that lack general public support, militaristic leanings of all groups, politicians more interested in rhetoric than ideas, divisions and accusations through the press of the respective political parties among groups of the same political persuasion, and general demagoguery and fanaticism of all parties concerned. The same divisons and problems with unity recur throughout the historical period of *Memorias de un hombre de acción* within both the secret societies and the recognized political parties. Internal conflicts and personal competition defeat the Liberal attempt of 1830 to enter the country. Personal interest and intrigue destroy the efficacy of María Cristina's regency and the subsequent reign of Isabel II. The secret society that Aviraneta founds, La Isabelina, stands in opposition to this pattern of internal dissension: «'¿No le hablé a usted en Ustáriz... de un plan que tenía, ... de constituir una sociedad secreta en que se fundieran masones, comuneros y carbonarios para defender la libertad?'» (La Isabelina, III: 1033). Aviraneta wishes precisely to form a cohesive, effective brotherhood that would overlook minor differences in the face of a common, unifying cause. He combines political moderation with the desire to consolidate the Liberal forces: «'Respecto a mi orientación general, era llegar al máximo de liberalismo compatible con el orden, exterminio del carlismo por todos los medios posibles y Constitución del año doce, modificable en parte si se consideraba necesario'» (La Isabelina, III: 1033). But the ideal society soon succumbs to the forces of social disintegration. Fernando VII's death splits the group between the isabelinos and cristinos and a denunciation by certain government officials leads to the arrest of the leaders of the society and its disbandment. Baroja's presentation of the fragmentation and rivalry among the secret societies and political parties of the epoch, however, represents more than just astute political analysis and criticism. It underscores the generally pessimistic attitude present throughout the series towards man as a social animal capable of feeling genuine fraternity towards other human beings and of organizing and uniting with others in a common cause. In the underworld society of Memorias de un hombre de acción, confusion, division and unrestrained egos undermine any attempt at cohesion and although the characteristics may not seem as extreme as those of the criminal societies, the difference is strictly one of degree and the effects are equally disastrous for Spanish society. Through his unique vision of Spanish society Baroja condemns the contemporary world as a diseased, underworld society.

Baroja's presentation of society in such a negative light raises the issue of the problematic relationship between the individual and society. E. H. Templin has identified the essential problem of Barojan characters as the search for a margin of individuality and independence within the limitations of the world and within their own limitations.[5] As Paul Ilie has pointed out, the isolation of the Spanish hero in the literature of the Generation of '98 is an outgrowth of their frustration with the lack of national social development filtered through the Nietzschean preoccupation with the relationship between the individual and the group and Nietzsche's skepticism towards social movements.[6] In the underworld of

---

[5] E. H. TEMPLIN, «Pío Baroja: Three Pivotal Concepts», Hispanic Review, 12 (1944), p. 312.
[6] PAUL ILIE, «Nietzsche in Spain: 1890-1910», PMLA, 79 (1964), pp. 89-90.

Memorias de un hombre de acción, however, the individual who maintains his core of integrity must isolate himself from society. Alienation is the price of integrity. Aviraneta's relative and mentor Etchepare retires into near-isolation after taking part in the French Revolution. He dies alone after spending years in communion only with Nature: «No tenía relaciones sociales. Sus amigos eran los árboles, las rosas, una nube que sonreía en el cielo, un faro que guiñaba a lo lejos su roja pupila...» (*Con la pluma y con el sable,* III: 493). Miguel Aristy of *La veleta de Gastizar* and *Los caudillos de 1830* remains untouched by the political upheavals of the time. He maintains the stance of the tranquil observer and thinker, outside the line of fire: «Aquella vida del campo, inmóvil sin estímulo para la ambición, que a muchos embrutece, a él le había convertido en un filósofo» (*La veleta de Gastizar,* III: 884). In both cases, the individual exchanges human fraternity, which Baroja has shown as impossible in a genuine form in the underworld society, for a more intellectualized, internalized form of existence that promises to uplift spiritually. In the character El Tío Juan, the gamekeeper of the Aristy property, the author gives some idea of the human price paid for maintaining one's integrity. At the end of *Los caudillos de 1830,* the gamekeeper's true identity is revealed. He is the husband of Madame Aristy cast out of his home on account of his wife's fear that his freethinking ideas might injure the children. As a result, El Tío Juan spends most of his life alienated from his family and unknown to his children. Aviraneta, the one character who seems to be the great exception to the inseparability of isolation and integrity, really offers the strongest proof of the rule. Despite a lifetime devoted to unselfish activity on behalf of Liberal ideals, he remains on the margin of the mainstream of political activity and ignored by the historians of the epoch. Instead of recognizing his patriotism and valor, people denounce him as a traitor and associate him with some of the bloodiest deeds of the period —the murders of monks in Madrid of 1834 and the riots of Barcelona of 1835. Aviraneta creates and carries out one of the most successful conspiracies of the time, the Simancas papers that split the camp of Don Carlos and precipitate the end of the first Carlist War. After the death of Fernando VII, he alone has the courage to speak out in favor of immediate action on the part of his fellow Liberals to consolidate their power: «Era un Robespierre sin sostén social, sin partidarios, amargado, ácido, después de haber conocido la miseria y la inquietud en todas las formas. Era un Robespierre de España, de un país pobre, áspero, desabrido, frío y sin efusión social» (*La Isabelina,* III: 1046). Time and time again the hero finds himself alone in a cell, blamed for things he did not do or betrayed by self-serving spies and intriguers. He is the last of the leaders to leave jail after the denunciation of La Isabelina, the vast majority of his companions simply forgetting about him. Towards the end of his active life María Cristina and her followers abandon Aviraneta and persecute him by exiling him from Spain and France. «Abandoned», «alienated», «alone» —words that sum up his life as an adventurer also describe his old age, in which his activity is reduced to the confines of his own home and his life as a conspirator is all but forgotten. The solitude and alienation of the man of integrity from the underworld society in *Memorias de un hombre de acción* reveals another affinity with Nietzsche, for whom solitude is man's essential and tragic condition, and with existentialist philosophy, which envisions man as forlorn and abandoned in an absurd world which he must endow with meaning by asserting his freedom to make himself.[7] Man's isolation from his fellow man, not only from society as a collective group, increases the sense of alienation of the individual in *Memorias de un hombre de acción*. The Count de España points out that each man is an enigma for his fellow man in *Humano enigma*. Alvarito meditates on the same subject while observing his companions in a stagecoach bound for France: «pensaba en ese gran misterio que somos unos para otros, y a veces uno para sí mismo. '¿Quién sabe lo que pensará ese hombre, lo que preocupará a esta mujer, lo que soñará esta jovencita, si es que sueña con algo?', se decía» (*La nave de los locos*, IV: 472). Baroja stresses, as do existentialist writers, the individual's incapability of understanding the Other.[8] The abundance of first-person narratives in *Memorias de un hombre de acción* emphasizes the individual's imprisonment within himself and his need to impress himself on and explain himself to the Other. Aviraneta's life story represents, among other things, a cry for recognition from the Others of his existence and being as a man of action, a search for escape from a solipsistic state.

In *Being and Nothingness* Sartre explores at some length the problem of the Other. Being-in-the world, the ultimate existential project of all human beings, is examined as a highly complex ontological problem.[9] Sartre addresses the issue of the existence of the Other, not as an object, but as another subject of being. For him as well, the Other remains an enigma and man must constantly struggle to overcome the alienation and anxiety he feels in the face of the Other. This is just one example of how Baroja and his contemporaries dealt with existential problems in a fictional context that would later be presented as more formal philosophical issues in existentialist philosophy.

[7] See EUGENE GOODHEART, «Nietzsche and the Aristocracy of Passion», in his *The Cult of the Ego: The Self in Modern Literature* (Chicago: University of Chicago Press, 1968), 114-32, at p. 128, and JEAN WAHL, Introd., *Essays in Existentialism*, p. 19.

[8] EDITH KERN, *Existential Thought and Fictional Technique: Kiekegaard, Sartre, Beckett* (New Haven: Yale University Press, 1970), p. 241.

[9] JEAN-PAUL SARTRE, *Being and Nothingness*, trans. Hazel E. Barnes (New York: Washington Square Press, 1966), p. 596. See especially «Being-for-Others», pp. 299-556. Subsequent references to this edition of *Being and Nothingness* will be cited parenthetically in the text by page number.

A World of Illusion

The underworld society of *Memorias de un hombre de acción* is also primarily a world of illusion. And if the underworld society is the true reality of the apparently orderly society of the bourgeoisie, within the underworld things are again not what they seem to be. Baroja constantly contrasts surface appearance and underlying reality in the series. Written correspondence between supposed relatives is actually communication of political information and secret plans conveyed by sympathetic ink or hidden key words. The papers discovered by a Carlist that reveal Maroto's affiliation with a Masonic society are actually forgeries arranged by Aviraneta and planted in the Carlist camp by his agents. The Duchess of Vejer and her niece, who rent a home from Madame Aristy in Ustáriz, turn out to be two French prostitutes working as spies for Calomarde and the Absolutists. The murders of monks in Madrid in 1834, seemingly a vicious act by *cristinos* and *isabelinos,* were probably instigated by *realistas* as a provocation. The wax figures that Chipiteguy and his workman transport across the border into Spain, ostensibly to display at the Pamplona fair, actually serve as hollow receptacles to carry treasures back into France to finance the Liberal cause. The Spanish leaders' ideological inclinations shift so often and to such extremes that it is impossible to tell what their real beliefs are, if they have any. As Baroja describes in «Cambio de máscaras» in *Desde el principio hasta el fin,* political quick changes of appearance characterize the entire period:

> Ni por las ideas ni por el temperamento se podía saber con claridad quiénes eran los liberales y quiénes los reaccionarios... Narváez, al principio muy liberal, se hizo reaccionario. González Bravo, de carbonario y enemigo furioso de la reina Cristina, se convirtió en conservador, clerical y carlista. (IV: 1122)

This vision of the world as a universe of deceitful appearance extends to the concept of mankind itself: «La civilización, en último término, es como una piel muy fina sobre la animalidad humana; el menor movimiento rompe la piel y sale a flote la barbarie nativa» (*Las mascaradas sangrientas,* IV: 515-16). The violent occurrences in the series strip off the surface illusion of culture and refinement. This pessimistic and suspicious attitude also emerges in relation to language as a vehicle of communication. Leguía mentions language in this context while recalling his days as a spy in Bayonne: «La frase de Talleyrand, o de quien sea, de que la palabra es un medio de ocultar el pensamiento, era uno de mis dogmas» (*El amor, el dandismo y la intriga,* IV: 83). Language functions as a means of dissimulation, as a mask to hide the truth rather than to express it. Hugo Riversdale, one of the major characters in *Humano enigma* and

La senda dolorosa, shows a similar lack of confidence in language by commenting on its inadequacy to convey deep emotions:

> «Yo, cuando quiero a una persona, no me gusta decírselo; me parece algo cínico y sin gracia; lo mismo me pasa si me quieren; me gusta sentir el afecto en los detalles y en los hechos, no en las palabras. Una de las cosas más bellas de la vida es callar.»
>
> ... ...
>
> «La palabra es siempre algo cínico y vulgar», añadió él. «Los pueblos que aman las frases son pueblos mentirosos y fanfarrones.» *(La senda dolorosa,* IV: 724)

This scorn of the world recalls the seventeenth-century attitude towards language as deceitful illusion, an aspect of the vanity of this world.[10] This is one of the few instances in which Baroja makes even an indirect comment about language, and it is significant that the attitude revealed is one of a negative moral judgement in which language is seen as an instrument of deceit. Many characters in the novel undergo the experience of *desengaño,* disillusionment and unmasking that leads to greater self-awareness and the attainment of authenticity, another similarity with seventeenth-century literature. As the Liberals' attempt to regain power in Spain in 1830 sinks more and more into disorganization and conflicts between egotistical leaders, young Lacy's romantic visions of war and his idealistic ideological inclinations, fed by tales about Napoleon and memories of his father, dissolve into a deeply pessimistic attitude towards war, the Liberal cause, and mankind in general. His *desengaño* ends with the breaking of his spirit and death, but not before he established a truly Romantic reciprocity of emotions with the natural surroundings at Gastizar. Leguía tries to become an adventurer, but after a few serious brushes with death as a spy he realizes his future lies elsewhere: «Yo, al conocer a don Eugenio, intenté imitarle, y quise ser como él; pero la corriente de la vida me fue llevando por otros caminos y terminé convirtiéndome en un señor tranquilo y burgués» *(El amor, el dandismo y la intriga,* IV: 14). A fever that Leguía suffers, symbolic of the feverish life he has led as a spy, removes all illusions about becoming an adventurer and makes him aspire to the tranquil existence that corresponds to his true character: «Mi impulso por la acción había desaparecido. Aquella fiebre, que me había durado cerca de dos meses, arrastró mis ambiciones, mis preocupaciones y mi erotismo» *(El amor, el dandismo y la intriga,* IV: 167). Towards the end of *Las mascaradas sangrientas* Alvarito's father, in a deathbed scene similar to that of Don Quijote, confesses that all of his hidalguesque pretensions are nothing but lies,

---

[10] In a similar vein, JACQUES DERRIDA describes style in Nietzsche's works as a protective veil related to the female's love to dissimulate and seduce: *Spurs: Nietzsche's Styles,* trans. Barbara Harlow (Chicago: University of Chicago Press, 1979), pp. 51-71.

«'una mascarada carnavalesca de mi alma'» (IV: 562). Alvarito reacts by leaving behind the illusions of his youth: «Los conceptos hidalguescos, con los cuales había vivido, tuvo que olvidarlos y abandonarlos, como la serpiente deja su piel en el camino» (IV: 653). He loses one identity to gain another more authentic one, consonant with his new self-awareness and set of values: «tendió a pensar que la única superioridad posible era la del espíritu y la de la virtud, y él creía poseerla en proporciones modestas» (IV: 564). In each of these cases, the process of becoming undeceived culminates in a conversion in which the individual achieves a new and heightened awareness of himself and tries to pursue a new life that corresponds to that concept, the essence of authenticity, of becoming and making one's self. The entire series of the *Memorias de un hombre de acción* is, in a sense, described by this process of *desengaño*. By unmasking the illusions and myths about Spanish history of that epoch, the heroes and famous occurrences, Baroja creates a new perspective on and awareness of the Spanish national consciousness that shaped the present disjunct, petty, and mediocre society of his generation, based not on heroic deeds and national unity, but rather on bloody and brutal wars, self-interest, and social fragmentation. He wishes to undeceive his reader on a more universal level, too, to make him aware of his responsibility to shake free of the lower animal structure that lies beneath the illusion of humanity and forge a new, more humanistic self.

Understandably, the motifs of masks, disguise, and role-playing figure prominently in the underworld society of *Memorias de un hombre de acción* and they have a variety of functions. On a more literal level, numerous scenes in the series take place at masked balls or costume parties and in many incidents some of the participants wear masks or disguises. In *Los caminos del mundo* at a masked ball Aviraneta meets María Visconti, a young woman who, disguised as a boy, works with the conspirators plotting the assassination of Fernando VII in order to avenge her brother's death by murdering the man who betrayed him. Alvarito's beloved Manón appears at a costume party dressed as a hussar shortly before the kidnapping of Chipiteguy in *Las figuras de cera;* this foreshadows her disguise as a boy and another appearance dressed as a hussar in *La nave de los locos* when she and Alvarito scour northern Spain in search of Chipiteguy. As Aviraneta indicates, «Un baile entonces era un lugar de enredos y de maquinaciones» (*Los caminos del mundo,* III: 323). David Challis points out that a masked ball in Baroja's novels often provides a point of departure for episodes of intrigue, aggression, and self-assertion, and that the mask or disguise represents a visual correlative to the subversive nature of the conversations. He also associates the cloaked figures in Baroja's works with an established sequence of events:

> The routine established for cloaked figures as early in Baroja's novels as *El mayorazgo de Labraz* (1903), that is, the steps, beginning with the pre-

arrangement of a meeting to be held after dark, the donning of the cloak, the travel to another environment, the intrigue and the rapid dissolution of the group afterward, is retained in both the longer and the shorter versions of the Aviraneta text. The pattern is repeated in *Los Caudillos de 1830* (1918) where Aviraneta appears as a more experienced figure of intrigue.[11]

The narrative pattern corresponds quite clearly to the descent motifs of romance and, in fact, the masks and disguises often signal a descent into an underworld society, as confirmed by several episodes from *Memorias de un hombre de acción*. The murderers of the two women in *Las mascaradas sangrientas* leave the city to commit the crime disguised in capes and masks on a Carnival Sunday. The action initiates the whole sequence of nightmarish events observed by Paco Maluenda and prepares the atmosphere of suspense and horror that finally dissolves in the bright sunshine the following day. The scene in *Con la pluma y con el sable* conforms even more closely to the archetypal patterns of descent in romance. The members gather after dark, all masked and with three of them sitting as judges at a table lit by candelabra. Guards drag in Regato and after a round of accusations, a black curtain is drawn to reveal two masked men carrying a brazier. At that precise moment a policeman's whistle breaks the chain of events and as the officers raid the room the prisoner flees and the *carbonarios* disband rapidly into the night. Baroja almost inevitably associates masks and disguises with the darker side of human nature, even in the cases of María Visconti and Manón. María's disguise transforms her into a self-willed instrument of revenge who stabs to death her brother's denouncer. While at the initial party Manón's hussar costume seems merely a harmless expression of the impulsiveness and audacity of her character, her donning of the hussar costume in the home of her great-uncle Papa Lacour in *La nave de los locos* marks the high point of her increasingly wild and careless behavior as she travels through Spain with Alvarito. In his eyes, she begins to fit into the crazed savagery and disintegration that surrounds them in the war-torn countryside.

To extend Challis' discussion of disguise as self-expression a little further: despite the close association I see between role-playing and the underworld in his novels, Baroja undoubtedly considers disguise a visual manifestation of the will to become another and an indication of the human ability to remake oneself creatively.[12] María Visconti and Manón

---

[11] DAVID J. CHALLIS, «Pío Baroja and Disguise as Self-Expression», Diss. University of Pittsburgh, 1973, p. 101. On the cloak see pp. 72-120 and on the masked ball see pp. 33-41.

[12] Challis summarizes and describes his findings on disguise on p. 202: «In his appreciation of the annual variety of Carnival disguises he escapes the crushing conformity of social institutions; secure in the protection of the cloak,

deliberately transform themselves to assume roles in other societies. Their disguises afford them a freedom they have not experienced before, although Manón's wild self-indulgence points out the dangers of giving in to one's impulses without thinking of the consequences. Baroja has a highly critical attitude towards individuals who assume new identities not by literally disguising themselves, but rather by constantly shifting their political and ideological affiliations. In a satirical passage from *La veleta de Gastizar* Baroja compares the local celebrity Domingo José Garat, whose political activities date from the French Revolution, to the famous weathervane: «Entre Garat y la veleta de Gastizar había grande semejanza. Los dos eran ornamentales, los dos versátiles; pero Garat había cambiado con los vientos reinantes mejor que la veleta de Gastizar, que se hallaba desde hacía tiempo enmohecida» (III: 871). Garat's friend Choribide is an even more repulsive opportunist who assumes new identities and manipulates socio-political situations for his own benefit: «;Fue moda ser filósofo, fuimos filósofos; luego republicanos, fuimos republicanos; después terroristas, luego thermidorianos, después bonapartistas; hemos sido realistas y ultramontanos; ahora aparecemos como liberales. Garat y yo hemos sido todo'» (III: 895-96). Baroja objects to such role-playing not only on account of its hypocrisy and immorality (the narrator comments on Choribide: «Para él no había moral, ni derecho, ni nada; sólo había necesidades que engendraban ambiciones en que se salía ganando o perdiendo»; III: 894), but also on account of the lack of authenticity it represents. The ideological costumes these men put on and the actions they perform do not correspond to genuine internal feelings and attitudes. Their constant changes destroy any sense of the expression of a coherent self; their actions indicate a fragmented contradictory being or no being at all. Sartre has stated that, «a man is nothing else than a series of undertakings, that he is the sum, the organization, the ensemble of the relationships which make up these undertakings» and that the only way to determine the value of a feeling or belief is by confirming it and giving it shape in an act.[13] Role-playing becomes a philosophical and psychological issue of deceit and authenticity, Self and Other in *Memorias de un hombre de acción.*

René Girard's, *Deceit, Desire, and the Novel* offers the best guideline for examining this aspect of Baroja's works. Girard has labeled «triangular» that desire which is borrowed from another's desire or acquired through a mediating agent. The individual who has such a desire, the *vaniteux*, finds himself caught up in a world of imitation and dissimul-

he aspires to daring deeds; in the antics and witticisms of the fool he achieves physical and verbal agility.»

[13] JEAN-PAUL SARTRE, «The Humanism of Existentialism», in *Essays in Existentialism*, ed. Wade Baskin (Secaucus, N. J.: Citadel Press, 1979), 31-62, at pp. 48-49 and 44.

ation (an inauthentic world), surrenders his ability to choose his own desire, and can end up fragmenting or destroying his self. Girard contrasts the *vaniteux* with the passionate man who, unconcerned with the desires of the Other, has an intense and spontaneous desire that comes from within.[14] In some cases, Baroja points out the consequences of role-playing as an expression of triangular desire. In a reference to the Count de Montijo, leader of one of the Masonic lodges, Aviraneta indicates that, «Como muchas personas del tiempo, Montijo aparecía con dos caras; ahora que él mismo no sabía cuál era la suya propia» (*El escuadrón del «Brigante»*, III: 230). In addition to the obvious bemused irony of the statement, Baroja also indicates the total lack of identity of Montijo, whose being is reduced to two disguises with no way to distinguish which, if either, corresponds to the underlying reality. In other cases, the development of a character's life indicates the emptiness of triangular desire. Manón chooses to imitate the actions of the barbaric Ollarra and the anarchic ways of her great-uncle in Spain, and this drives her away from Alvarito. Later she chooses to marry into and adopt the ways of the French nobility, partly out of anger at Alvarito for not writing to her while he was in prison (his letters were intercepted by a jealous young man). By assuming a role that denies her heritage and does not correspond to her true feelings, she severs herself forever from Alvarito, Chipiteguy, and what they represent —the solid, honest, hard-working values of the middle class. Yet Baroja by no means condemns everyone who changes his identity or assumes a new role. He condemns only those who do so out of immorality, deceit, meanness of character, and inauthenticity —triangular desire, and not those who experience a genuine conversion. Jesús López del Castillo, the spy called El Rostro Pálido of *Los confidentes audaces,* has three major identities in the course of his life, as he himself describes: «'primero, holgazán; luego, confidente, y ahora, trabajador'» (IV: 893). Each one of them corresponds to his being at the time, but the third phase is clearly valued above the others because it arises from a conversion scene in which López del Castillo feels genuine emotions for the first time while helping a young woman care for her sick child. This spontaneous awakening of love transforms him and makes him another, and as a natural consequence he leaves the cynical, self-serving identities of «holgazán» and «confidente» behind. Baroja also distinguishes morally between types of disguised individuals on the basis of the motivating factor behind the assumed identity. El Tío Juan, the

---

[14] RENÉ GIRARD, *Deceit, Desire and the Novel: Self and Other in Literary Structure,* trans. Yvonne Freccero (Baltimore: The Johns Hopkins University Press, 1976). The basic concepts of the book are presented in chapter one, «'Triangular' Desire», pp. 1-52. GIRARD discusses the darkest side of triangular desire in chapter ten, «Technical Problems in Proust and Dostoyevsky», pp. 229-44, and chapter eleven, «The Dostoyevskian Apocalyse», pp. 256-89.

husband of Madame Aristy, maintains his disguise as a gamekeeper to maintain his radical liberal ideas without injuring or endangering the lives of his family. Baroja clearly sympathizes with this man who has led «una vida íntegra, de fanático por sus ideas» (*Los caudillos de 1830,* III: 994). He heightens the reader's appreciation for the character's authenticity by contrasting it with the deceit of Choribide, who shrugs off El Tío Juan's integrity: «'La vida es cambiar. Yo no creo que ser esclavo de sus prejuicios sea una superioridad'» (III: 994). Aviraneta responds with a sneering put-down that reveals the author's high regard for the disguised Liberal.

Of all the characters who disguise themselves in the series, Aviraneta appears in by far the greatest variety of costumes and roles. And it is a supreme irony of Baroja that the individual who seems the most deceitful is actually the man of greatest integrity. In *Los caminos del mundo* he assumes the identity of a priest to free his friend Arteaga from jail in France and during the assassination attempt against the King enters Spain as a pedlar, poses as a barber and Absolutist, and flees the imbroglio with the Sociedad de Santa Fe dressed as a friar. His disguise as a poor merchant saves him from execution as a Liberal officer in *Los recursos de la astucia* and the role of the Italian perfume seller Aviranetti permits him to spy on the court in *Con la pluma y con el sable.* He assumes the role of the dead British officer Mac Clair in *La ruta del aventurero* so he can land safely and stay in his country for a while despite his exile status. Aviraneta moves freely in and out of tertulias of all political persuasions and social standings. Yet despite the hero's mastery of the art of illusion and disguise, he remains the man of integrity, of authenticity, aloof from the deceit of the *vaniteux.* In fact, he is the man of spontaneous desire, the very opposite of the *vaniteux.* Spontaneity plays an important part in his activities: «'Para mí, lo más simpático en la vida es la improvisación, maniobrando en lo imprevisto'» (*Los caminos del mundo,* III: 295). His personal integrity contrasts with the fragmented being of the *vaniteux* (Girard, p. 91): «Si cada individuo, como suponen algunos observadores, en vez de ser un yo, es un conjunto de yos oscuros y embrionarios, lo que hacía Aviraneta lo hacía con todos los Aviranetas de su alma» (*Con la pluma y con el sable,* III: 400). As in any underworld society dominated by illusion and deceit, Aviraneta must often use the weapons and adopt the postures of the very society he opposes and dissimulate in order to hide the true purpose of his actions.[15] In *Los confidentes audaces* the narrator muses about the hero's response if any of his companions in a stagecoach were to ask his profession: «él hubiera

---

[15] GIRARD talks about how revealing one's desire can create new obstacles in the world of triangular desire and how the key to success is dissimulation (p. 107). He develops these ideas further in chapter seven, «The Hero's Askesis», pp. 153-75.

podido contestar que su especialidad consistía en preparar conspiraciones e intrigas, construir sociedades secretas y en otros menesteres extraños y misteriosos, más o menos prácticos y necesarios en una sociedad mal organizada» (IV: 811). Antonio Zaro, a friend of the hero's, when asked about Aviraneta's method of operation, responds: «'maneja los recursos del desorden y de la anarquía como medio de dividir a los adversarios cuando se propone desorientarlos y arruinarlos'» (*Los confidentes audaces*, IV: 814). Baroja insists on the purity of the purpose behind the disguises and deceitful methods of Aviraneta. Often deceit is the only protective device he possesses. When a traitor denounces La Isabelina to the government the hero resorts to his skillful manipulation of language to save his own hide: «Me batí con el juez y con el fiscal y les mareé con declaraciones contradictorias. Hice como el calamar, que enturbia el agua para escaparse» (*El sabor de la venganza*, III: 1117-18).

Aviraneta's role-playing however, has greater significance than just as a means of surviving in and combating the underworld society. E. H. Templin has related the private moral nature and the outward amorality of Baroja's adventurers with their imaginative abilities and capacity for sustaining illusion, which keep them from suffering psychological emptiness. He then associates this with the adventurer's potential to transform action into adventure.[16] This statement recalls Nietzsche's view of reality as nothing but illusion and doubtless the adventurer's somewhat cynical view of the world and his mastery of the art of illusion reinforce this viewpoint. Actually, rather than merely an escape from ontological emptiness, Aviraneta's disguises and role-playing function as an ontological affirmation, *self*-expression in a much wider sense than Challis has used the term. His disguises represent an expansion, a moving outward of the hero's being, an externalized, creative manifestation of his desire to exercise his will: «Aviraneta sentía cierto amor por la farsa. El representar una pequeña comedia le gustaba; le daba la impresión de la elasticidad de su espíritu, la utilizaba para sus fines y era como la literatura de un hombre iliterato» (*Con la pluma y con el sable*, III: 395). Aviraneta's self always appears in terms of outward activity, assumed roles of one sort or another. Sartre has written in similar terms about the relationship between existentialism and humanism:

> But there is another meaning of humanism. Fundamentally it is this: man is constantly outside of himself; in projecting himself, in losing himself outside of himself, he makes for man's existing; and, on the other hand, it is by pursuing transcendent goals that he is able to exist; man, being this state of passing-beyond, and seizing upon things only as they bear upon this passing beyond, is at the heart at the center of this passing-beyond.[17]

[16] TEMPLIN, «Three Pivotal Concepts», p. 321.
[17] SARTRE, «Humanism of Existentialism», p. 61.

The hero of *Memorias de un hombre de acción* has such an outward projection of self, a perpetual transcendence in immanence, moving out of his self and into the world in roles and disguises that ultimately are simply one more way of authentically representing his being-in-the-world.

Girard undoubtedly uses Sartre's discussion in *Being and Nothingness* as the basis for his explanation of triangular desire. By turning to the same work, one can derive a greater understanding of Baroja's seemingly dualistic vision of role-playing as both deceitful, hypocritical, and negative and yet positive, creative, and part of the imaginative aspect of the human spirit. According to Sartre, man has a non-determined being (page 71). The very essence of his nature is freedom, manifested in his ability and obligation to remake himself constantly (p. 72). But the man of bad faith abuses his freedom through deceit. He consciously chooses to mislead those around him by projecting a false image of his self. Inevitably he betrays himself as well because he reaches a point at which he no longer recognizes his own true nature. The result is an ontological vacuum; he loses his being (p. 89). The man of bad faith corresponds to Garat, Choribide, and most of the political and historical figures Aviraneta encounters in his adventures. No man wears the mask; only the mask remains. Sartre contrasts bad faith with sincerity (authenticity). The sincere man consciously dissociates himself from himself. He can see and analyze himself as an object. On the basis of what he sees, he projects that self into the world in the form of action. The moment that action is realized, the authentic man consciously submits himself to analysis again as the basis for more action (pp. 109-10). Thus, such a man exercises his will creatively, freely, energetically, and in accordance with the most profoundly human characteristics of man's being. He escapes the void of non-being by consciously creating himself. Aviraneta is the sincere man, constantly making and re-making himself in a variety of roles, but the sum total of his actions offer a record of his unwavering truth to the core of his own being.

THE WORLD AND THE NOVEL AS CARNIVAL

Baroja's treatment of Carnival, a recurrent motif in his novels as well as a subject that has psychological and sociological interest for him, reveals a similarly complex attitude towards the underworld society. He explains his own feelings about the festival and what he thinks it represents in two essays. Baroja has always felt that there was something «transcendental» about Carnival and, «De chico me producía una mezcla de atracción y de miedo» («Las raíces del Carnaval», V: 1057). The child's sentiment of simultaneous fascination and horror reappears in the writings of the adult who seem to wallow in the darker, bestial side of man —the brutal murder in *Las mascaradas sangrientas* and the bloody scenes of violence, mutilation, and death— while still feeling outrage and fear. Carnival had a strong impact on his youthful imagination:

> Eran también para mí los Carnavales un motivo de excitación a la mitomanía. Recuerdo haber inoculado para mi uso en la niñez una historia en que unas máscaras me amenazaban, historia que tuve durante algún tiempo por verídica, hasta que la sometí al libre examen, la destruí y me libré de ella. (V: 1057)

At the end of Chapter II I refer to one aspect of Baroja's motivation in writing *Memorias de un hombre de acción* as exorcising the demons of his own historical past. The child who finds himself obsessed (note the use of the word «inocular» that has connotations of being «pervertido» or «contaminated» by something in addition to the literal «innoculated» or «infused») by a nightmarish story of pursuit by masked figures, and who subsequently examines the tale critically and logically to the point of destroying it and freeing himself from its spell, becomes the artist who critically and ironically examines the myths about Spanish history, contemporary society, and mankind in general to subvert and destroy them and to free himself from their hold. It is the same impulse that any ironist or satirist possesses and that of an ironic philosopher such as Nietzsche, whose *Twilight of the Idols* and *On the Genealogy of Morals* demolish the foundations of traditional morals and values. The image of freeing oneself from an obsession appears again at the end of the series when Baroja the narrator abruptly and almost brutally takes leave of his hero and his adventures:

> Ya no sólo termino la obra, sino que liquido lo que tengo de género de comercio que lleva por nombre novela histórica.
>
> ... ...
>
> Hace tiempo que el autor va haciendo esta liquidación, y como el barco desarbolado, va echando parte de la obra muerta al mar. (*Desde el principio hasta el fin*, IV: 1170)

The use of words like «liquidación» and «echando» conveys the idea of discarding and eliminating useless or used up material. One has an image of Baroja the author emerging and freeing himself of the underworld that his own historical and philosophical concerns, critical nature, and interest in Aviraneta have dragged him into. Although Baroja as a child may have freed himself of that frightening pursuit by the masked figures, the fascination with Carnival and the underworld definitely persists in the adult. He celebrates certain characteristics of Carnival, above all its variety: «El Carnaval es, o por lo menos ha sido, la fiesta más completa de los hombres. Lo tiene todo: la risa, la barbarie, el disimulo, el miedo, la inquietud y la perfidia humana» («El demonio del Carnaval», in *Vitrina pintoresca*, V: 819). Its combination of opposites, the darkest and lightest aspects of life, appeals to Baroja: «se toca por un extremo con la Danza de la Muerte y la Nave de los locos, con la hechicería y los aquelarres, por otro, con el culto del Sol y de la Naturaleza» (V: 820). He insists on its fundamentally human quality: «no es una ficción ridícula y sin valor, sino una tremenda realidad henchida de sustancia humana» (V: 820). And finally, Baroja makes an eloquent defense of the festival on the basis of its vitality:

> Al enterrarlo y hundirlo en la oscuridad, no se hunde para siempre en el olvido a Baco y a Momo, cuya mitología no había llegado a los pueblos actuales, no se pierden sólo las siluetas de Arlequín o de Pierrot, ni se acaba con el grotesco entierro de la sardina, celebrado en Madrid e ilustrado por Goya, lo que se hunde en el fondo de la Historia y del silencio es una de las fantasías más irracionales y absurdas, pero más vitales, de la Humanidad. («Las raíces del Carnaval», V: 1061)

As Mikhail Bakhtin has pointed out, the original spirit of Carnival combines parody, travesty, humiliation, and degradation with revival, renewal, and regeneration. Baroja's attitude towards Carnival reveals that he is much closer to the authentic festival spirit than to the strictly negative satire of many of his contemporaries.[18] Baroja, who recognized the positive and negative aspects of role-playing, also appreciated the inherently dual nature of Carnival. That same duality is apparent in his combination of passive/active heroes, satire/romance, and demythification/remythification.

Baroja also points out the variety of demons represented and unleashed in Carnival, demons of evil, sadism, cynicism, the macabre, fear and terror, and the disquieting effect of the masks. He mentions that the Greeks and Romans limited the days of Carnival in fear of the destructive powers it unleashed and that the good, celebrative qualities it embodied could become evil, violent ones:

> Cuando se leen *Las bacantes,* de Eurípides, se queda uno asombrado al ver a un dios borrachón, tranquilo e inofensivo convertido en un dios trágico y feroz, y a sus sacerdotisas furiosas y homicidas manejando sus tirsos como flechas y desgarrando las carnes sangrientas. («El demonio del Carnaval», V: 820)

Most often in *Memorias de un hombre de acción,* Baroja presents this darker vision of the holiday, a travesty of Carnival, a frenzied festival of evil and deceit. He reveals his awareness that this is a perversion of Carnival's original spirit. Alvarito invokes this view of Carnival in summarizing the individuals he sees during his search for Chipiteguy: «daban a Alvarito la impresión de que seguía viviendo en pleno carnaval grotesco

---

[18] MIKHAIL BAKHTIN, *Rabelais and his World,* trans. Hélène Iswolksy (Cambridge: Mass.: The M.I.T. Press, 1965). See especially the Introduction, pp. 1-58, and chapter three, «Popular-Festive Forms and Images in Rabelais», pp. 196-277.

y zarrapastroso, cuyas figuras eran dignas de ocupar un lugar dentro de *La nave de los locos»* (IV: 371). The Carnival that Baroja identifies as a profoundly human celebration becomes a wild expression of brutality and subhuman behavior. Madness has engulfed the entire world, at least according to Aquiles Ronchi, a friend of Aviraneta: «Para Ronchi la vida no había sido más que un eterno Carnaval. Todo era locura en el mundo, de arriba abajo» (*La nave de los locos,* IV: 472). In both of his essays Baroja mentions the magical power of the mask in primitive cultures, how it symbolizes the acquisition of a new spirit and how one literally becomes the animal or figure it represents by donning the mask. The ritual appears in *Las mascaradas sangrientas,* in which Maluenda purchases a mask exactly like those of the Iturmendi brothers, all three masks described as «feas y bastas» (IV: 499), in order to follow them with greater ease. The disguise makes it much easier to pass the Carlist guards at the city gates and to go through the streets unrecognized on the Carnival Sunday. But the masks and the holiday also signal the unleashing of negative energy as the Iturmendi leave the city to murder La Veremunda and her mother. The brothers become as «ugly and coarse» as their masks, as if the disguise transformed them into animals or complemented their animal natures. Maluenda's donning of the mask indicates his complicity in the murder, which he watches and does nothing to prevent. He enters the underworld of the Iturmendi and all three men find themselves tied to the demonic society of Bertache and his gang and committed to a life of violence. In a less dark context, Padre Chamizo, one of the narrators of *La Isabelina,* associates Carnival with the figurative disguises that politicians of the epoch assume in Madrid:

> ... toda aquella gente, la que más bullía tenía su misterio en la política y algo que ocultar... Aquello era un carnaval. En ningún sitio podía aplicarse mejor la frase de Goya, un pintor sordo que conocí aquí en Burdeos, que hizo una estampa de gente con careta, y puso al pie la leyenda: «Nadie se conoce.» (III: 1018)

One sees only a disguise, an illusion of his fellow man, but no one really knows the Other. Baroja seems to imply that Spanish society of that time and that society in general is a grotesque imitation, a travesty of what human society should be since it lacks the intimate knowledge of one another needed as the basis for a genuine cohesive brotherhood. In contrast to the limited and controlled madness of Carnival, Baroja's underworld offers a grim spectacle of perverted humanity in wild pursuit of material gains or insubstantial goals —power and prestige.

In *La nave de los locos* Baroja presents the most direct contrast between the genuine vitality and exuberance of Carnival and its grotesque parody in the surrounding society. Alvarito travels to Spain after Chipiteguy's return in order to check on the inheritance left by his recently deceased grandfather. On his way to visit the villages of his mother and father he spends a Carnival Sunday in Vitoria. For the first time in months Alvarito shakes off the depression caused by Manón's departure and his frustrated love for her by joining in the festivities. He flirts with young women and feels lighthearted again. The people of the city are celebrating in an especially animated manner in reaction to the end of the unhappy war years. Baroja inserts a paraphrase of some stanzas celebrating Carnival from the poem *La nave de los locos:*

> ¡Carnaval! ¡Carnaval! Los pintados y los teñidos y los encorsetados, los graves puritanos y los sesudos moralistas temen tus gritos y tus actitudes pánicas. Tus farsas desenmascaran las farsas solemnes que ellos quieren conservar; tus risas descomponen la sociedad estólida del funcionario lógico y petulante.
>   ¡Carnaval! ¡Carnaval! A tu lado, las religiones y sus templos son de ayer, los títulos son de ayer, la ciencia y el arte son de ayer, y en cambio tú, en una forma o en otra, eres eterno. (IV: 394-95)

For Baroja, the revelry of Carnival represents freedom and release from the false, limiting structures of society. He has little respect for traditional social order and the conventional mentalities behind it. In a typical Baroja inversion, social institutions become the illusion and the deceit of the world while the masks and disguises of Carnival are the reality. Carnival permits the genuinely human side of man, his passions and his impulses, to express themselves without disrupting into violence or destruction. Alvarito ends his day by attending a melodrama, that in its sentimental representation of life seems even more grotesque than the masks of Carnival:

> Al melodrama, terrible y de sentimentalismo absurdo y enfático, la manera de representarlo le hacía más grotesco. El jugador, héroe del melodrama, hombre bajito, disimulaba la pequeñez de su estatura con zapatos de tacón muy alto; estaba pintarrajeado como una careta, llevaba barba rubia postiza, que le temblaba al hablar con su voz de falsete, y miraba con una insistencia cómica al apuntador. La mujer del primer galán, legítima, al parecer, en la realidad y en el drama, embarazada de ocho meses, declamaba lloriqueando con hipo angustioso. El padre del jugador parecía un energúmeno, daba miedo y hacía reír al mismo tiempo, y únicamente el traidor era gracioso y resultaba simpático, a pesar de su maldad melodramática. (IV: 395)

In contrast to the vitality, creativity, and spontaneity of Carnival, everything about the melodrama is contrived, false, and unnatural: a pint-sized hero wearing high-heeled shoes, masklike make-up, and a false beard, and who has trouble remembering his lines while concentrating on maintaining his falsetto; an eight-months pregnant whining woman playing the sweet, innocent heroine; a man in the father role whose acting makes people laugh at him as well as fear him; and an actor who portrays the

146

arch-enemy in the play in such a way that the audience likes him rather than hates him. The fact that Baroja uses vocabulary and phrases easily associated with Carnival —«disimulaba», «careta», «barba postiza», «energúmeno», and «daba miedo y hacía reír al mismo tiempo»— heightens the contrast. As a result, the juxtaposition of the two experiences has an almost a bathetic effect on Alvarito and the reader. The play is only the beginning of a series of experiences in a trip of *desengaño* for Alvarito, after he touches the very core of life in the Carnival in Vitoria, in which illusions about his country, its institutions, and his family background are stripped away. At the performance that night he meets Señor Blas, the older businessman who assumes the role of *desengañador* in Alvarito's journey by accompanying him and initiating his encounters with the harsh realities of Spanish society. The older man's appearance corresponds to the part he plays: «con ojos claros y expresión un poco ruda, de ingenuidad y de franqueza» and «respiraba lealtad y buena fe» (IV: 395). Alvarito returns from his trip convinced that his country and mankind in general are yet another Ship of Fools, a world in which the negative side of Carnival has gone wild.

A final significant aspect of Baroja's fascination with Carnival is that he associates it with literature: «El Carnaval es una fiesta anárquica de masas desorganizadas, de individualismo, que puede ser fino y amable o rajado y violento. En esto se parece a la literatura, que tampoco puede ser de masas» («El demonio del Carnaval», V: 820). Rarely does Baroja give a more accurate and concise description of his own writing even in an essay on that subject. Baroja's novels resemble a controlled anarchy in which elements are constantly threatening to, and sometimes do, get out of hand. They are obviously products of a highly individualistic author whose characters reflect his individualism and his iconoclastic nature. His tone and style range from the lyrical and the poetic to the abrupt and brutal. One might also apply to his works the following observation about Carnival: «El Carnaval viene de una corriente subversiva, demoníaca, antisocial, humana, demasiado humana, diría Nietzsche» (V: 820). Notice that Baroja, following Nietzsche, opposes humanity and society. For him, society has ceased to reflect genuine human nature whereas Carnival frees this true human nature. His literature, and especially this series, springs from the subversive, demonic impulse of the ironist. Nietzsche's breaker of the table of values, unmasking illusion and hurling verbal abuse at accepted traditions and institutions in an attempt to reach that which is most profoundly human. And he views this irony as creative in its destruction, human in its antisocial quality, and regenerative in its death-dealing blows. Baroja the ironist possesses the genuine Carnival spirit of returning to what is authentically human by attacking the oppressive, false values of society. He wishes to unleash the human spirit and free men to make and be themselves. In such a world, Aviraneta would be recognized as a superior, heroic figure. Baroja also associates subversion with *humorismo*:

> La broma, el humorismo, es casi siempre una alusión, una exposición indirecta, incompleta, a veces enteramente deformada, de una idea escondida del autor y en relación con una tendencia afectiva que busca el manifestarse y el realizarse de una manera íntegra o fragmentaria. Debajo de toda manifestación de humorismo hay un instinto de injuria, de venganza o de erotismo dormido, como enterrado en lo inconsciente. (*La senda dolorosa*, IV: 739)

Humorismo has some of the characteristics of the underworld society. The narrator describes it as a verbal disguise, an indirect and deformed illusion that masks an underlying and possibly subconscious desire to wound or shock —again the impulse of the satirist. Baroja values this kind of illusion as an efficacious method of expression and it is wise to remember that one can regard *Memorias de un hombre de acción,* among other things, as an *historia humorística.* Baroja turns traditional concepts of history and historical novel *(Episodios nacionales)* upside down in the series. He deforms, fragments, and demythifies any attempt to unify and explain in a rational manner the historical events of the period, and he presents as the hero of *Memorias de un hombre de acción* a subversive Liberal spy, all but forgotten by historical texts. The values and the vision that remain after the attack reflect the author's own attitudes and beliefs —stoicism, individualism, iconoclasm, and a firm commitment to integrity, creativity, and spontaneity. These are values that one can find in the underworld society only by establishing one's own margin of authenticity.

Despite the pessimism of such a vision, Baroja maintains his faith in these values, like a soldier who refuses to surrender even in the face of overwhelming odds. In *La veleta de Gastizar,* Baroja the narrator expresses these sentiments in one of the most beautiful, lyrical, and melancholy passages from the entire series, «Las estelas sentimentales»:

> Las generaciones han ido moldeando nuestros instintos, lo consciente y lo inconsciente, les han dado una forma, un sentido; pero en este conglomerado de nuestra personalidad, la inteligencia se ha separado de sus viejos compañeros y ha comenzado a marchar sola.
>
> Así, nuestra época ha dado, más que ninguna otra, santos sin ideas religiosas, ateos místicos, mujeres honradas con alma de cortesanas y cortesanas con aspiraciones de monja.
>
> Ante esta disociación de su personalidad, el hombre, que antes que nada quiere creer y poner un pie firme sobre la tierra, mira a su alrededor, y cuando encuentra una ruta la va siguiendo.
> ... ...
> Y cuando se deciden van, como los demás, a ciegas y siguen la estela que dejaron las grandes corrientes sentimentales pasadas.
> ... ...

En todas las esferas de la actividad humana, en la religión y en la política, en la literatura y en el arte quedan estas estelas sentimentales. Todos los grandes hechos de la Historia, todas las grandes corrientes han pasado por la inteligencia y por la sensibilidad de los pueblos dejando una estela.

Ahora, al notar esa estela que queda en el mar de las ideas, que es la nuestra, la que hemos escogido, quisiéramos avanzar por ella rápidamente y llegar a su más puro origen. Ya es tarde, el barco ha pasado para siempre y ya no volveremos a divisar sus velas.

Los astrónomos nos han hablado de que la distancia de algunos astros es tan grande que su luz tarda en llegar a la Tierra cincuenta, sesenta, ochenta años. Así puede muy bien suceder que una estrella haya desaparecido o se haya desplazado y, sin embargo, nosotros la sigamos viendo en el cielo de las noches espléndidas.

¡Qué triste, qué melancólico resulta pensar que una de esas estrellas que parece que nos guía y nos contempla puede no existir ya y, sin embargo, estarla viendo!

Así, en la vida moral y en la vida sentimental cabe sospechar el carácter místico de las ideas y de los dioses, y seguir en la corriente que produjeron ellos cuando todavía eran dioses e ideas. (III: 907-08)

Baroja laments the dissociation of mind and soul that has caused the rupture of the correspondence between illusion and reality, surface appearance and underlying substance. Now he would agree with Nietzsche that illusion is the only reality and that only traces or vestiges of what were once effective ideas and beliefs remain. Man finds himself caught between reason and impulse, thought and will. But Baroja does not react to the situation with despair. He rather insists that while man must act in the full realization that his ideals may be nothing but illusions, like the starlight that shines although its source may have disappeared, he must act nonetheless as if his beliefs still had their original force and meaning behind them. Baroja's hero Aviraneta wanders through the illusion, disguise, and deceit of the underworld society of *Memorias de un hombre de acción* with unwavering faith in the value of fraternity, freedom, and personal integrity —following his *estelas sentimentales* despite almost certain defeat.

VI

THE EMERGENT HERO

> Para comprender algo humano, personal o co-
> lectivo, es preciso contar una historia. Este hombre,
> esta nación, hace tal cosa y es así *porque* antes hizo
> tal otra y fue de tal otro modo. La vida sólo
> se vuelve un poco transparente ante la razón his-
> tórica.
>
> (ORTEGA Y GASSET, *Historia como sistema*)

> For one thing is needful: that a human being
> attain his satisfaction with himself —whether it be
> by this or by that poetry and art; only then is
> a human being at all tolerable to behold.
>
> (NIETZSCHE, *The Gay Science*)

APPROACHING THE BAROJAN HERO

Aviraneta, the man of action, stands at the center of the turbulent world of *Memorias de un hombre de acción*. Without understanding the nature of his heroism and what he represents in Baroja's search for a solution to the fundamental existential problem, how to endow life with meaning in an absurd world, the overall meaning of the series is lost. Yet on account of their seemingly simple and yet paradoxical natures, Aviraneta and all of Baroja's heroes resist the attempt of critics to describe them in more general schematic terms. Luis Granjel divides Baroja's characters into three groups, each of which expresses a certain attitude the author has towards life at some point during his career: Passive figures, associated with Baroja's years of maturity and the withdrawn, often stoic and ironic view of the spectator; active figures, associated with Baroja's youth and comprised of both individuals who seek to escape life and those who seek to dominate it by the assertion of a strong will; and the adventurers, whose imaginative experiences represent a fulfillment of the author's own desires. Dwight Bolinger divides Baroja's characters into two major categories, those viewed from without and those viewed from within. Although most of the characters fall into the former group, the most important ones fall into the latter, which he subdivides into the proxies, who serve as the author's mouthpiece, and the inventions, who appear in the form of Baroja's imagination projected into a different environment. Bolinger splits the inventions into heroes, figures of courage, adventurousness, and action, and Hamlets, characters whose desires lead to non-active futility and disillusionment. He also sees an intermediate semi-hero whose active life starts out well, but ends in failure.[1] Granjel's classification system provides no insight into the author's method of characterization, how the characters function in the novels, and what they represent. Obviously, there is always some correspondence between an author's attitudes and personal life and the fictional world he creates, and Baroja's novels may show a closer relationship than most, but to split the author's life in sections, correlate certain personality characteristics labeled «active» and «passive» with these divisions, and account in this manner for tendencies one sees in fictional characters is inadequate and misleading. Passive and active characters coexist in almost all of Baroja's novels and not necessarily in opposition to one another. Miguel Aristy and Aviraneta share the same fictional space in *La veleta de Gastizar* and *Los Caudillos de 1830,* and while their respectively active and passive natures contrast with one another, nothing indicates Baroja's preference for one life style over another, and, as a matter of fact, the tranquil observer and the man of action share the same disillusioned viewpoint at this fictional moment. Aviraneta leads an active life, but from time to time he steps back from the action spatially or temporally to become a passive, critical spectator. Furthermore, such important characters as Shanti Andía and Leguía make the transition from an active to a passive life in Baroja's novels. Granjel's system does not allow for this recurrent pattern. Although Granjel correctly links the adventurer with the imagination and flights of fancy, this definition unfortunately continues the tradition in Baroja scholarship of erroneously identifying the adventurer with an escapist, vacuous hero who arises from Baroja's own childish desires to realize his dreams and evade reality. Bolinger's basic premise of distinguishing characters viewed from without from those viewed from within shows a major misconception regarding characterization in Baroja's novels. He separates characters that receive more extensive treatment and have evidence of some sort of internal life of ideas, impulses, and opinions from those who offer only a rapidly glimpsed external appearance, and he thus really only makes an initial distinction between characters of greater and lesser importance. In regard to the term «proxies», rarely does any figure in Baroja's novels function consistently and exclusively as the author's mouthpiece. Baroja often divides his ideas among characters in order to develop and refine them in the course of a discussion. The central conversation between

[1] LUIS GRANJEL, «Autor y personaje en la obra barojiana», *Cuadernos Hispano-americanos,* Nos. 265-67 (July-Sept. 1972), pp. 3-10, and DWIGHT L. BOLINGER, «Heroes and Hamlets: The Protagonists of Baroja's novels», *Hispania,* 24 (1941), 91-94.

Hurtado and Iturrioz in *El árbol de la ciencia* provides an example of this technique as does that among Aviraneta, Ochoa, and a young painter in *Las figuras de cera.* As for the «heroes and Hamlets», here Bolinger makes the mistake of equating traditional concepts of success and failure with Baroja's own attitudes towards his protagonists. Aviraneta's reputation as a historical figure hardly creates the impression of an outstandingly successful person, yet Baroja unquestionably considered the man he labeled «hombre valiente, patriota atrevido, liberal entusiasta» (*El aprendiz de conspirador,* III: 12) a hero. The limitations of these systems reveal their inadequacy as a means of approaching and understanding Aviraneta's role in the series.

Carlos Longhurst's discussion of the hero and characterization in *Memorias de un hombre de acción* shows the greatest sensitivity and depth of understanding of the complexity and nuances of the topic to date. He correctly suggests that the creation of the characters is the major factor in the writing of Baroja's novels and in a section devoted to Aviraneta states that the protagonist has, above all, an ideological function. Longhurst rightly takes issue with the interpretation of the hero as merely a representative of «action for action's sake», pointing out in support of this view Baroja's insistent contrast between the superiority of Aviraneta's integrity, courage, and devotion (apparent from the beginning —*El aprendiz de conspirador,* III: 11-12) and the mediocrity of the times and the similarity between Aviraneta's ideological preoccupations and those of a twentieth-century dissident. He wisely rejects the more traditional identification of the hero with the Nietzschean superman within the realm of action for a similarity between the two based on a common moral ground of man rising above his lower animal nature through the assertion of a strong will.[2]

From the standpoint of many of his critics, Baroja's characters are the weak point of his artistry. Ortega y Gasset criticizes the large number of figures that appear in his novels and the lack of development of the characters, and accuses Baroja of asserting his opinion of them instead of allowing them to create their own reality within the fictional works. Furthermore, Ortega states that Baroja should show (he uses «mostrar») his characters to the readers through their external and internal actions and criticizes the author for not establishing a correspondence between their actions and their souls.[3] Since Ortega's time, many critics have either supported his viewpoint or tacitly ignored these statements and permitted them to go unchallenged. As a result, a number of the accusations have

[2] CARLOS LONGHURST, «La creación de los personajes», chapter five of *Las novelas históricas de Pío Baroja* (Madrid: Guadarrama, 1974), 200-36, at pp. 200-09.
[3] JOSÉ ORTEGA Y GASSET, «Ideas sobre Pío Baroja», in *El Espectador (1916-1934),* Vol. II of his *Obras completas,* 4th ed. (Madrid: Revista de Occidente, 1957), 69-102, at pp. 93-101.

become commonplaces of Baroja criticism. The author himself responds to a number of the comments in the «Prólogo casi doctrinal sobre la novela» at the beginning of *La nave de los locos* (IV: 308-27). Concerning the large number of characters in his novels, Baroja defends his practice in the name of openness and variety:

> Un poco como consecuencia del gusto por la unidad estrecha del asunto y por la novela cerrada es el presentar en ella pocas figuras. Todo lo que sea poner muchas figuras es, naturalmente, abrir el horizonte, ensancharlo, quitar unidad a la obra. En esto se nota, creo yo, la influencia de la cultura clásica y de la medieval. Lo clásico tiende a la unidad; lo romántico, a la variedad.[4] (IV: 318)

He places himself within a tradition by asserting that precedents exist for this practice. As to the lack of development in his characters, Baroja points out that some of the figures exist only in a vague, schematic form and cannot be further developed: «Hay personajes que no tienen más que silueta y no hay manera de llenarla. De algunos a veces no se pueden escribir más que muy pocas líneas, y lo que se añade parece siempre vano y superfluo» (IV: 32). Baroja always advocates linguistic economy, using the fewest number of words necessary to capture adequately the personality of the individual or the spirit of the moment:

> Para un espíritu impresionable, muchas veces el insinuar, el apuntar, le basta y le sobra: en cambio, el perfilar, el redondear, le fastidia y le aburre. Cada cosa tiene un punto en su extensión y en su perfección muy difícil de saber cuál es. (IV: 321)

He launches into a rather lengthy explanation of why his characters lack a well-developed psychology. He asks who, of the greatest novelists of the nineteenth century, presents characters with a thoroughly-developed psychology as the basis for clear motivation? He points out that Stendhal's characters have contradictory, imperfect psychology and that while Dostoyevsky's characters do possess a clear psychology, it is derived from their subconscious or pathological natures (IV: 315-18). Baroja thinks that the author who has the ability to explore psychology in literature «se hunde poco a poco en la ciénaga de la patología» (IV: 318). He has never intended to do so:

> Yo no he pretendido nunca marchar por esos derroteros, y Aviraneta presenta, como mis demás personajes, el tipo mal determinado del hombre que es esencialmente racional; por tanto, reflexivo y tranquilo. No tiene, ni pretende tener, el fatalismo de lo inconsciente. (IV: 318)

---

[4] LONGHURST (pp. 230-36) accounts for the large number of characters in Baroja's novels as a response to the variety of people encountered in life and as a desire to create diversity and authenticity in the fictional world.

As for the author's non-intervention in the text, Baroja mentions a number of fine authors who have established a precedent for the introduction of his own opinions and attitudes into his novels:

> También se asegura que el autor no debe hablar nunca por su voz, sino por la de sus personajes.
> Esto se da como indiscutible; pero ¿no hablaron con su propia voz, interrumpiendo sus textos, Cervantes y Fielding, Dickens y Dostoievski? ¿No interrumpía Carlyle la historia con sus magníficos sermones? ¿Por qué no ha de haber un género en que el autor hable al público como el voceador de las figuras de cera en su barraca? (IV: 324-25)

According to Baroja, an author cannot remain impassive to his creations: «Se podrá fingir la indiferencia, pero nada más» (IV: 324). He insists that at the root of a writer's works lies his own personality and all the experiences that have contributed to the shaping of an author's «fondo sentimental»: «Todos los novelistas, aun los más humildes, tienen ese sedimento aprovechable, que es en parte como la arcilla con la que construyen sus muñecos, y en parte como la tela con la que hacen las bambalinas de sus escenarios» (IV: 325).

The point is not which of the two writers «won» the debate over characterization and the nature of the novel in general, but what I wish to emphasize is that Ortega y Gasset in his two articles on Baroja and in *Ideas sobre la novela* expresses an attitude towards art and the novel completely different from Baroja's, whether in the prologue of *La nave de los locos* or in his numerous essays on the novel and art.[5] As Baroja himself suggests, the difference of opinion boils down to a conflict between a Classical, more normative approach to the novel complete with a prescriptive attitude towards achieving unity and clarity, plot construction and characterization, and a Romantic approach with an organic, anarchic concept of unity that respects multiplicity of form and the right of the individual artist to create characters and construct plots in accordance with his own desires and artistic beliefs. Baroja, ever the opponent of opinions or dogma that threaten to limit and close off that which should be open and full of possibilities, assumes the role of the defender of artistic freedom and the novel as a protean form that includes an enormous variety of characters, scenes, and events:

> Pensar que para tan inmensa variedad puede haber un molde único me parece dar una prueba de doctrinarismo, de dogmatismo. Si la novela fuera un género bien definido, como es un soneto, tendría una técnica también bien definida (IV: 323)

---

[5] For more on the debate between Ortega y Gasset and Baroja over the novel see DONALD L. SHAW, «A Reply to *Deshumanización* —Baroja on the Art of the Novel», *Hispanic Review*, 25 (1957), 105-11 and CARMEN IGLESIAS, «La controversia entre Baroja y Ortega acerca de la novela», *Hispanófila*, No. 7 (September, 1959), pp. 41-50.

> En bueno o en malo, yo me figuro tener algo de ese goticismo del autor medieval que necesita para sus obras un horizonte abierto, muchas figuras y mucha libertad para satisfacer su aspiración vaga hacia lo ilimitado. (IV: 323)

More importantly, though, Ortega's comments on Baroja's characters reveal a general misunderstanding of the author's approach to characterization. Baroja sees human beings in terms of types, *tipos,* categories determined by observing individuals, dividing them up into groups with similar characteristics, and in the process, determining exactly what those characteristics are and reserving them as the basis for fictional characters. Baroja writes about *tipos nacionales* (*Nuevo tablado de arlequín,* V: 133) with geographical and anthropological bases (terms such as *el latino* and *el germano* abound in his works). One of the volumes of his memoirs bears the title *Galería de tipos de la época.* He writes down *tipos literarios* in the prologue to *La nave de los locos.* And the title of the series is *Memorias de un hombre de acción,* not *Memorias de Eugenio Aviraneta,* one of the clearest indications that Baroja conceives of his hero not only in ideological terms as Longhurst has indicated, but also as a psychological and philosophical prototype, instead of an individual whose idiosyncracies and personal development he wishes to dwell on. Baroja has mentioned his tendency to view men in terms of types:

> Yo creo que el tipo visto o entrevisto con cierta claridad, en un medio ambiente conocido, tiene su vitola y su trayectoria, que se imponen al autor. Un hombre se parece, en general, a una serie de hombres. Cierto es que puede llevar una ruta diferente a tipos parecidos; pero no es muy probable, a no ser que haya en él un elemento psicológico que se desconozca por completo y que dé una sorpresa. Evidentemente, las sorpresas no son grandes, y si se dan algunas veces, tienen su causa en observaciones incompletas y en teorías falsas.
>
> Los tipos accesorios, todos los que he visto, si podía utilizarlos, los he utilizado; ahora creo que cada personaje tiene capacidad de amplificación especial que no se puede exagerar. (*La intuición y el estilo,* V: 1075-76)

Baroja offers a glimpse of himself as a collector of human types, choosing and categorizing men, just as he does political cartoons, newspaper clippings, and engravings —akin to Aviraneta, the collector of adventures, and Chipiteguy, the junk dealer who classifies his material as either objects to sell or museum pieces. Baroja, reviewing his types, decides which ones possess a character he can expand and which remain limited in character. He fashions his characters from classes of individuals, psychological conglomerates, that while they admit variety and nuances have their origin in a more abstract, generalized view of mankind. Baroja's concept of the *tipo* suggests that all of his principal characters have such an ideological basis. His adventurers, skeptics, representatives of *abulia,* dissidents, and artists are, as many have pointed out, amazingly articulate and they often discuss the most crucial philosophical, political, and scientific issues of the day —determinism, Nietzschean philosophy, the «problem» of Spain, war, changes in the social structure— in an educated layman's terms. But more significantly, those issues seem to drive them, direct and redirect their lives in the course of the novel.

Yet another important aspect of Baroja's characterization has escaped Ortega y Gasset. Ortega's feeling that psychologically-complex characters are a necessity in a good novel smacks of the old argument for «well-rounded» characters as opposed to «flat» ones. But since Baroja is primarily a writer of romance and ironic literature or satire the apparent simplicity of his characters should come as no surprise. The heroes and heroines of romance have never been noted for psychological complexity. They, their helpers, and enemies are part of the drama of the conflict between good and evil in which their «personalities» can be reduced to a few set qualities that establish them as symbols of good and evil and have remained unchanged over the centuries. Nor do satirical figures possess psychological complexity. They fall into a set pattern of railers, cynics, symbols of professions, and caricatures of individuals, professions, and ideologies. In short, the writers of romance and satire tend to reduce the personalities of their characters to the essential qualities necessary to create a desired effect. Baroja sees himself within the tradition of the realistic novel, whose origins he traces back to the *Satyricon,* the *Golden Ass* and the *History of Theagenes and Chariclea* through Cervantes, Quevedo, *Lazarillo de Tormes* to Defoe, Fielding, and Smollett up into the nineteenth-century realistic novel (*La intuición y el estilo,* V: 1076-78). It is not especially important that Baroja knew something of the evolution of the modern novel, but it is significant that he was aware that the realistic novel had its origins in works of romance and satire and he wished to place himself within that evolving tradition. As a writer of romance and satire, Baroja takes a moralistic and judgmental attitude towards his characters, although with varying degrees of distance, both conditions accounting for what Ortega considers the author's habit of giving his opinion of the characters rather than developing them as independent entities. Ortega's statement that Baroja should «show» his characters through their actions recalls the «showing vs. telling» argument, but as Wayne Booth has indicated in *The Rhetoric of Fiction* there is always some «telling» in a text and it is simply a question of how much.[6] Baroja's ideological and moralistic approach to characterization is the major force shaping the nature of the hero Aviraneta.

Scattered comments among Baroja's writings provide insight into his

[6] See chapter one, «Telling and Showing», in WAYNE C. BOOTH, *The Rhetoric of Fiction* (Chicago: University of Chicago Press, 1961), pp. 3-20.

perception of heroism. He emphasizes that the quality of the hero's ideas does not make him heroic:

> Si puede haber un héroe de la religión y un héroe de la Monarquía y otro de la República, es evidente que la calidad de las ideas no es lo que hace al héroe, sino una exaltación espiritual, de origen desconocido, que se puede poner en una cosa o en otra. («Prólogo» to *La nave de los locos,* IV: 316)

The stress that the author places on a mysterious spiritual exaltation reveals a Romantic attitude towards the hero. Aviraneta displays such zest and vitality in *Memorias de un hombre de acción.* Baroja mentions that he had no need to go back to a more heroic period of Spanish national history to discover figures worthy of admiration.

> Para sentir el patriotismo, yo al menos no he necesitado enterarme bien de las épocas brillantes de la historia de España. Me ha bastado conocer los primeros tiempos del siglo XIX, de alteraciones y de dolores, porque en las acciones históricas me ha entusiasmado más el ímpetu que el éxito y más el merecimiento que la fortuna.
> ... ...
> Los esfuerzos de los que no tuvieron éxito y conservaron la energía y el valor dan todavía una impresión más efusiva que los que llegaron al éxito y a la fama. *(Rapsodias,* V: 895)

In an obvious reference to Aviraneta, Baroja points to several of his major qualities: integrity, a strong will, and devotion to a cause. He rejects material and political success as prerequisites for heroism and, instead, upholds the stoic attitude of the man who remains faithful to himself and to his cause in an epoch that encourages mediocrity and charlatanism. The hero appears as a socio-political underdog who never gives in despite certain defeat. For Baroja, the hero requires the mysterious, dark underworld I discussed in the last chapter:

> Para que haya novela sugestiva tiene que haber penumbra en el hombre o en el ambiente. El héroe y el aventurero necesitan, como las quimeras góticas, la bruma, la confusión y el misterio. No resisten la luz demasiado clara. *(Vitrina pintoresca,* V: 779)

The hero and/or his environment lack clarity and definition; they remain separate from the modern, fixed, and well-defined social environment: «la sociedad moderna no produce el héroe literario ni el aventurero» (V: 779). Aviraneta's historical world does provide the necessary atmosphere for an adventurer to emerge and become a hero:

> El medio social del comienzo del siglo XIX daba el misterio, permitía la existencia del aventurero y la posibilidad de convertirlo en héroe. Había, o parecía haber, flexibilidad individual y social, que el escritor aprovechó a su modo. (V: 779)

AVIRANETA: THE ACTIVE HERO

Several basic qualities characterize the hero Aviraneta. Despite the assertion of the royalist Ignacio Arteaga in *Los caminos del mundo* that, «las ideas, en el fondo, creo que le preocupaban menos de lo que él se figuraba» (III: 296), Aviraneta maintains his loyalty to liberal ideals throughout *Memorias de un hombre de acción*. Baroja makes a point of providing the protagonist in his formative years with a spiritual mentor (Etchepare) whose background embraces the most radical liberals of the French Revolution. Although Aviraneta fights with the patriots against the French during the War of Independence he does feel an ideological rift between his own political attitudes, which coincide mostly with views of the Englightenment, and those of Merino and other religious zealots of the time. He joins the Liberal secret societies, the Masons and the Carbonari, and supports unfailingly through the years the Constitution of 1812. On several occasions he is expelled from Spain on account of his loyalty to the Liberal cause. When Aviraneta wishes to seize an opportunity to *impose* his views on the Spanish people it is always in the name of freedom, as the tyrant of Aranda during the Liberal triennium or inciting the Liberals to rise up in the name of the Constitution after the death of Fernando VII. Baroja portrays his hero as a supporter of universal liberal ideals, as in a discussion between the Consul in Bayonne, Gamboa, and Aviraneta:

> —¿Qué es para usted el liberalismo? —preguntó Aviraneta.
> —Yo veo el liberalismo en el régimen constitucional y en el reinado de Isabel II.
> —Bien. Ese es el liberalismo español actual, práctico; pero fuera de ése, hay otro liberalismo universal, más importante: la filosofía, la razón, el libre examen.
> —Ese no se debate ahora.
> —Ese se debate siempre. ¿Qué me importaría a mí de Isabel II si con su reinado no hubiera posibilidad de vivir con más libertad que con el reinado de ese estúpido Carlos? Mi liberalismo es libertad de pensar, libertad de movimientos, lucha contra la tradición que nos sofoca, lucha contra la iglesia... *(Las mascaradas sangrientas,* IV: 539)

Aviraneta predicts the hollowness of social reform not accompanied by spiritual reform:

> —¿Qué pasará? Que se pondrán todos a defender con entusiasmo las formas, lo que es accidental, lo que es accesorio; el Parlamento, la democracia, técnicas y técnicas para que pueda farolear la clase media... Lo que es esencial, el espíritu, el humanismo, eso no lo defenderá nadie. *(Las mascaradas sangrientas,* IV: 539)

Longhurst cites at greater length the conversation between Gamboa and Aviraneta as evidence of the hero's ideological function, but I want to stress the complexity of Aviraneta in comparison to Zalacaín and Shanti Andía. Baroja goes to considerable effort to emphasize the hero's devotion to a more universal liberalism. Aviraneta's articulate manner suggests an intellectual dimension to his character missing in the other two adventurers. Moreover, Baroja juztaposes Aviraneta's idealism with the opportunism of the time. In *El amor, el dandismo y la intriga* Leguía mentally contrasts the aloof, superior indifference of the cynic Stratford Grain to Aviraneta's willful engagement in the affairs of the world (IV: 56-57). Leguía feels repugnance towards the man who declares himself incapable of ever taking up arms to fight for a cause and who wants to keep himself clear of the stain of contact with the world. Aviraneta, on the other hand, «aceptaba el tiznado suyo para mejorar la sociedad» (IV: 57). This position recalls on the one hand Nietzsche's celebration of man and this world as the domain of life and the strong-willed supporters of the everlasting yea, and on the other hand the existentialist commitment to action and involvement in the world as a humanistic endeavor and one that leads to creation of self. Baroja endows his hero with moral and spiritual superiority as well as with a firm, consistent ideological make-up.

Aviraneta possesses a strong will that drives him to realize his ideals:

> Aviraneta no era de los turbulentos que languidecen en tiempo de paz. Llevaba la turbulencia allí por donde iba; la paz era también para él la guerra, porque constantemente estaba intrigando, conspirando, ejerciendo sus facultades de dominación y de lucha. *(Con la pluma y con el sable,* III: 421)

He manifests his will in a perpetual dynamism that seems to animate the world around him. More conservative and sedentary types like Leguía, Arteaga, and even Father Chamizo of *La Isabelina* find themselves caught up in his world of subterfuge. His strong will makes him an anachronism in a world of complacency: «había nacido demasiado temprano o demasiado tarde, probablemente demasiado tarde... Tenía la base del gran aventurero, del gran conquistador, la fe en sí mismo, la voluntad tensa y fuerte» (*El amor, el dandismo y la intriga,* IV: 15). While he lacks the egotism of other heroes of the age like Espartero, Mendizábal, and Palafox, who use their fame as a springboard to political power, Aviraneta has the astuteness to realize that one must exercise an opportunity to achieve a goal; one must exert one's will when fortune smiles in one's direction. He learns this very early in his career when he engineers the elopement of Paquita and Frassac: «Aquel incidente me hizo afirmarme en la idea de que hay que tener más ímpetu que respeto, porque, como dice Maquiavelo, la fortuna es *donna*» (*El aprendiz de conspirador,* III: 111). On occasion after occasion, Aviraneta acts in accordance with that early determination. He sees the division between Maroto and the traditionalists in the Carlist camp and he devises the Simancas documents to split the enemy camp apart even further. He surveys the court of Fernando VII to find where the weak spots lie so he can plant himself or colleagues in the Absolutist organizations. Everywhere he goes, he attends the teas and soirées of fashionable salons and visits the town taverns so he will know where the sympathies of that social group lie and what the power structure of that particular town or village is. All of Aviraneta's reconnoitering prepares him to recognize the proper moment for action when it arrives. Obstacles provide a unique attraction for the strong-willed hero. For Aviraneta, according to Arteaga, «la única vida estribaba en hallarse metido en un infierno de dificultades, en un torbellino ciego, al cual pretendía dominar» (*Los caminos del mundo*, III: 295-96). In confronting blocking elements Aviraneta exercises and strengthens his will and sharpens his wits and his ability to act effectively:

> Uno de los entusiasmos de Aviraneta era lo difícil. Lo difícil es la gran atracción de todos los aventureros; lo difícil exige inteligencia, tesón, frialdad, nervios duros, espíritu ecuánime. Intentar lo difícil, imponerse una tarea ardua y superior a las fuerzas de la generalidad, trabajar como un condenado. Este era su orgullo. (*Con la pluma y con el sable*, III: 423)

> Es indudable que los obstáculos enriquecen nuestra vida y la van moldeando. (*El amor, el dandismo y la intriga*, IV: 14-15)

Aviraneta combines a strong will with an unending resourcefulness that enables him to extricate himself from any difficult situation:

> Para un hombre tan fértil en recursos como él, de un valor y de una serenidad rara, la dificultad era el mayor atractivo. (*Con la pluma y con el sable*, III: 423)

> Su espíritu, fértil en recursos, encontraba remedio para todos los males. (*El amor, el dandismo y la intriga*, IV: 14)

Sartre has written that obstacles and adversity are essential to man's ability to exercise his freedom.[7] Barriers and limits challenge man to use his will in overcoming them, thereby realizing his fullest and most creative potential as a human being. In this context, Aviraneta's enthusiasm for the difficult can be appreciated as a manifestation of the superior vitality of the sincere man. Aviraneta can face up to the chaos that surrounds him and mold its contingencies into effective and meaningful activity.

When the hero does face defeat, his remarkably resilient spirit enables him to recover. When Aviraneta confronts resignation and withdrawal as a result of betrayal or disappointing and dangerous political circumstances he invariably ends up returning to fight again. The moment Aviraneta

---

[7] JEAN-PAUL SARTRE, *Being and Nothingness*, trans. Hazel E. Barnes (New York: Washington Square Press, 1966), p. 622. Subsequent references to this edition of *Being and Nothingness* will be cited parenthetically in the text by page number.

finds himself safe and sound in Gibraltar in 1823 after fleeing the Absolutists and the invading French (at the end of *Los recursos de la astucia*), he renounces his decision to give up his turbulent existence and vows to return to fight for freedom. At bleak moments he recognizes that the tide will eventually turn again in his favor: «Sin embargo, pensando en su vida, no tenía más remedio que reconocer que cuando se cerraba un camino ante él inmediatamente se abría otro nuevo» (*Con la pluma y con el sable*, III: 460). Shortly after his angry withdrawal from the Liberals in 1830 in disgust over the poor organization and internal divisions among the troops planning to re-enter Spain in *Los caudillos de 1830* Aviraneta finds himself at the head of an important secret Liberal organization, La Isabelina. Even in his later years Aviraneta cannot completely withdraw from an active life:

> Al llegar a la corte pasé una temporada desilusionado, resignado, creyendo que ya, como hombre de aventuras y energía, había concluido. Pensé que era el epílogo, el final definitivo; pero al cabo de algún tiempo noté que todavía era capaz de tomar parte en cualquier empresa difícil. (*Desde el principio hasta el fin*, IV: 1126)

As a last resort he falls back on the stoic, ironic side of his nature to overcome difficulties: «Me sostenía el estoicismo y la falta de necesidades» (*Desde el principio hasta el fin*, IV: 1117). Aviraneta possesses not only resilience, but also an elasticity of spirit that he exercises to remake himself and his situation constantly in accordance with his own set of values:

> Del fondo el espíritu suyo brotaba un manantial de energía que le permitía elasticidad suficiente para no dejarse laminar por la reglamentación estrecha de un público; estaba rompiendo constantemente el tejido de preocupaciones que forma la vida estacada alrededor del hombre. (*Con la pluma y con el sable*, III: 422)

Aviraneta has been described as «the fulfillment and sum of all his (Baroja's) partial 'embryonic' egos», but he also represents an existentialist Self constantly born and reborn out of that Self's projection onto the world of what that Self means to make it.[8] Aviraneta constantly breaks the bounds of tradition within himself: «Aviraneta no podía, seguramente, deshacer la tradición en el espíritu de los demás, ni en el espíritu del pueblo; pero la rompía en sí mismo constantemente» (*Con la pluma y con el sable*, III: 422). His vision of the future and his ideals inspire him to undertake any deed, no matter how daring and no matter how it breaks with tradition: «La ilusión, la eterna esperanza, fingiéndole para el día

---

[8] E. H. TEMPLIN, «Pío Baroja: Three Pivotal Concepts», *Hispanic Review*, 12 (1944), 322, and Marjorie Grene, *Introduction to Existentialism* (Chicago: University of Chicago Press, 1959), pp. 49-50.

siguiente oasis espléndidos, le hacía en el instante decidirse a algo ligero y fuerte como un pájaro de presa» (III: 422). Aviraneta's reality is his own, forged out of his self and what he subjectively projects on to the world. While Baroja does not consistently show his hero as a man consciously aware of his decisions and responsibilities to choose and channel his freedom into certain directions, the comments made by the narrators (whether characters or not) indicate that he is a man who has elected the loneliness and responsibility of self-realization, of making oneself —an ethic suggested by Nietzsche's writings and incorporated into existentialist thought.[9] Aviraneta often appears in *Memorias de un hombre de acción* in association with imagery of breaking and rupture, of piercing boundaries —whether physical (walls, prisons, windows) or more abstract (social conventions, traditional morality, mediocre politics). He transcends obstacles in a literal or figurative way, often destroying the limiting factor, even if it is an element of his own character —a moment of sentimental attachment that threatens his freedom, for example. In many ways, he is a destroyer, a manipulator of chaos and disorder who fragments that which has been whole. This is nothing unusual for satirical works and underworld societies, but it also associates him with the peculiar negativism that pervades Nietzsche's works. It by no means, however, should be misconstrued as nihilism, for Aviraneta like Zarathustra breaks the table of values to prepare the way for positive reconstruction:

> Nietzsche's insistence that the negative may not be evil from a long-range point of view, but a necessary stage in the development toward something positive, is not a casual point in his thought but one of the characteristic motifs that recur throughout: one must negate, one must renounce conformity, one must break the ancient tables of values —in order to prepare for the creation of something positive.[10]

In order for man to make himself, he must have the resilience of Aviraneta, who re-makes himself in accordance with the obstacles he encounters, but who also can re-shape his spirit with an act of the will —he is a man who can overcome himself.

Baroja valued highly sincerity and integrity in men and in art. In one of his essays in which he contrasts classical and anarchic forms of writing, he states:

> Yo creo que en literatura y en arte todo es posible para el hombre sincero.
>
> Es posible que este libro sea íntegramente bueno o íntegramente malo, que tenga algo que esté bien y algo que esté mal, que sea mediocre en su totalidad... Como digo, para mí, en arte y en literatura todo es posible. *(Las horas solitarias*, V: 233)

---

[9] WALTER KAUFMANN, *Nietzsche: Philosopher, Psychologist, Antichrist* (Princeton: Princeton University Press, 1974), p. 158 and GRENE, pp. 51-53.
[10] KAUFMANN, pp. 170-71.

He writes in defense of his own «anarchic» style and also in defense of each artist's right to create in accordance with his own artistic principles and point of view. Some will regard a work of art as bad, others as good, still others as mediocre, but as long as that work is a sincere representation of what the artist wishes to express then it has some value for Baroja. The author transforms this same view of sincerity into the moral code of his hero:

> Si Aviraneta hubiera sido filósofo y hubiera intentado postular su ley moral, la hubiera formulado así: «Obra de modo que tus actos concuerden y parezcan dimanar lógicamente de la figura ideal que te has formado de tí mismo.» *(Con la pluma y con el sable, III: 423)*

Throughout the series Aviraneta proves to be the man of sincerity and integrity that Baroja admires: «'Don Eugenio ha muerto tranquilo, como lo que era, como un hombre de verdad... Siempre ha sido igual, de joven y de viejo. Desde el principio hasta el fin'» *(Desde el principio hasta el fin, IV: 1166)*. Baroja clearly appreciates the man who aspires to go beyond himself to attain his ideal Self. In a conversation with the historian of Aranda, Sorihuela, Aviraneta's reference to himself and his fellow Liberals as «nosotros los filósofos» elicits a sneering reply from the pedantic gentleman, but the author's voice interrupts the narrative to comment:

> Pero siempre resultará que los que dicen: «Nosotros los filósofos», aspiran a ser filósofos, y los que dicen: «Nosotros los brutos», aspiran a ser más brutos de lo que son. Y entre una aspiración y otra, no cabe duda que la primera es mejor... *(Con la pluma y con el sable, III: 420)*

Notice that the statement has moralistic implications, that rising above oneself is better than wallowing in one's animal nature —yet another echo of Nietzsche's attitude towards overcoming oneself. Baroja's emphasis on his hero's integrity ties Aviraneta even more closely to existentialist thought which values integrity of character and action, and has been referred to as «an ethic of integrity».[11] Aviraneta, despite his modifications and adaptations to overcome obstacles in his path, remains true to his principles. At the end of the series, he may seem older and more disillusioned by experience, but he does not renounce his ideals of freedom and justice nor give up his way of life spent in service to them. In fact, *Memorias de un hombre de acción* stands as an artistic monument to both these things and as an appeal for individuals to recognize and uphold the values embodied in the hero, above all integrity, in a world of confusion and deceit:

[11] GRENE, p. 144.

163

> Aviraneta fue siempre hombre de una pieza. Desde su juventud hasta la vejez siguió siendo el mismo, sin variar en nada. Para él no había posibilidad de cambio.
>
> Le sucedía como a algunos tipos de animales, como, por ejemplo, al gato, que son demasiado perfectos para evolucionar.
>
> Aviraneta era también demasiado perfecto en su género para cambiar. *(El amor, el dandismo y la intriga,* IV: 15)

At the end of his life, he refers to the core of integrity that sets him apart as a hero and links him to the modern existentialist hero as the essence and justification of his existence: «Lo único que me queda para vivir es la idea de haber obrado siempre con arreglo a mi conciencia» *(Crónica escandalosa,* IV: 1032). It is the credo of the authentic man.

As the title of the series indicates, Aviraneta is above all a man of action. Yet the notion of action in Baroja's heroes has proved to be a problematic issue for many of the author's critics. Ortega y Gasset praises Baroja's capture of a new European sensibility that seeks something greater in life than mere utility and wishes to channel its desires into some all-absorbing enterprise. But he criticizes Baroja for reducing action to mere adventure and the true man of action into an adventurer driven by turbulent impulses. Ortega defines action as «la vida entera de nuestra conciencia cuando está ocupada en la transformación de la realidad», and he sees the key point as the *alteration* of reality rather than just its reflection.[12] Alberich gives an incomplete and somewhat erroneous analysis of the Barojan man of action:

> El «hombre de acción» barojiano, aparte de ser un resultado de la fe de Baroja en el individuo como último y único valor, es también el último destilado de una larga tradición de la literatura aventurera, a la que se ha despojado de todo elemento extraño a la «acción» misma, incluso de su finalidad.[13]

Ortega bases his argument concerning Baroja's portrayal of Aviraneta as the man of action on the following statement:

> En apariencia, la vida de un hombre de acción es un juego de azar, una lotería en la que se emplea mucho dinero, y sólo de tarde en tarde toca un premio pequeño; en realidad, la vida de un hombre de acción, si es una lotería, es una lotería que toca siempre, porque el jugador lleva el mayor premio en el máximo esfuerzo. La acción por la acción es el ideal del hombre sano y fuerte; lo demás es parálisis que nos ha producido la vida sedentaria. *(Los recursos de la astucia,* III: 578)

He especially objects to the phrase «la acción por la acción», which he interprets (and Alberich and others seem to concur with his opinion) as

---

[12] ORTEGA Y GASSET, p. 90. Comments are summarized from pp. 72-93.

[13] JOSÉ ALBERICH, «Baroja y la novela de aventuras inglesa», in his *Los ingleses y otros temas de Pío Baroja* (Madrid: Alfaguara, 1966), 103-20, at p. 116.

an endorsement of meaningless, pointless activity as a means to shape one's life. In reality, the context of the phrase points to quite another meaning. With the lottery image, Baroja indicates that the man of action does not win or lose on the basis of realizing his intentions or plans in activity, but rather that action is its own reward and that the man of action pursues action for its own sake because the effort and will that it represents is what makes that man what he is. It is yet another example of how Baroja's hero coincides with the existentialist man who makes himself and literally wills himself to be.[14] While in action, man is a non-reflective being. He loses the anguish derived from the consciousness of freedom, choice, and his own responsibility for self-creation. And as he acts, man creates his own set of values (*Being and Nothingness*, pp. 74-77). Aviraneta's activities reveal a consistent ideological pattern exhibiting the ontological worth outlined by Sartre. Baroja makes his hero non-reflective because Aviraneta's self-generation through activity must never become stymied by meditation. His years of intellectual growth and decision come early, but once the commitment to freedom and liberalism has been made, he devotes himself entirely to action.

Furthermore, Aviraneta engages in anything but pointless activity. I have already shown that he possesses a consistent, firm ideological basis throughout the series. He directs his activity towards establishing freedom and justice in Spain. But all of his actions have very specific goals, as well: to split the enemy camp, to undermine the authority of enemy leaders, to introduce Liberal ideas into Spanish society. On one of the few occasions in which he chooses not to act, during the attempted Liberal invasion of 1830, he does so for ethical and practical reasons —he does not want to serve in such a hopelessly disorganized group and deal with such selfish, self-important leaders. Zalacaín fits most closely with the view of the man of action as a mere adventurer. Yet even in his case, Baroja feels the need to tie him, no matter how superficially, to the Liberal cause, and elsewhere in the novel he makes a quasi-Romantic association between Zalacaín and Nature. In addition, Aviraneta exercises precisely that ability to transform reality that Ortega sees as the heart of action. Alberich correctly indicates that the man of action represents, among other things, Baroja's faith in the individual as the only and ultimate thing of value in the world. But Baroja also indicates in the course of the novels that adventure emanates from the man of action's subjective perception and transformation of reality and that it has precisely that spiritual quality that Ortega identifies with *acción:*

---

[14] See JEAN-PAUL SARTRE, «The Humanism of Existentialism», in *Essays in Existentialism*, introd. Jean Wahl, ed. Wade Baskin (Secaucus, N. J.: Citadel Press, 1979), 31-62, at pp. 35-36.

No cabe duda que los mismos hechos, los mismos acontecimientos recogidos por espíritus diferentes, son absolutamente distintos, en forma tal que lo que para uno es una aventura rara y casi absurda, para otros es un accidente vulgar y corriente de la vida cotidiana.

Las inteligencias y las conciencias son seguramente distintas unas de las otras, no sólo por su contenido de impresiones venidas de fuera, sino por su esencia. Todo es individual en la Naturaleza, y como no hay dos hojas de árboles iguales, probablemente no haya tampoco dos conciencias iguales.

... ...

El espíritu del aventurero es el que crea la aventura, más que las contingencias de la vida exterior. *(El amor, el dandismo y la intriga,* IV: 14)

The individual's imagination creates adventure more than external circumstances.[15] Sartre has defined adventure as a moving outward into the world in which the possibilities of self are realized. Outward form corresponds to an inner awareness and desire to realize certain ontological possibilities (*Being and Nothingness,* pp. 277-83). The central conversation between Anny and Roquentin in *Nausea* illustrates this concept of adventure. For them, adventure emerges from a heightened sense of awareness of self, time, and existence. One selects a «special moment» and the feelings experienced in living that moment create the sense of adventure. In Roquentin's opinion, no one can encounter true adventure any more in the course of everyday life. By the end of the novel, however, he discovers that art can transform life into adventure. Roquentin decides to pursue adventure, art, by becoming a writer. Before the end of the series, Aviraneta also discovers the connection between adventure, art, and life and chooses to create adventure and art through his own creative medium, action.

Most importantly, though, Baroja identifies action as a form of transcendence, not a traditional vertical movement, but rather the horizontal transcendence of existentialism, of moving beyond oneself by engaging with the world and in the process forging one's being. Transcendence is projection of self toward and through the world (*Being and Nothingness,* pages 249-51). Sartre has described existentialism as an «ethics of action and involvement» in which a man is the sum of his acts.[16] This is the type of action Baroja refers to in labeling Aviraneta a man of action. He does not appear as a traditional, larger-than-life hero who embodies certain elements in the social structure. Baroja presents him as a hero rather because he maintains a willful, rebellious, nonconformist spirit and a commitment to an unpopular, idealistic cause. Aviraneta and Baroja's other men of action have high aspirations, but they always seek goals that they can realize in this world. Baroja conveys faith in the fact that heroes of this kind will never completely disappear:

[15] E. H. TEMPLIN, «Pío Baroja and Science», *Hispanic Review,* 15 (1947), 170.
[16] SARTRE, «Humanism», p. 50.

«Hay demócratas... que creen que el mundo puede hacer desaparecer con el tiempo a los héroes y a los aventureros.

Esta idea me parece una idea falsa y ridícula. Siempre habrá un desequilibrio entre la realidad y la utopía que permita una aventura al que tenga fondo de aventurero.

Además, ¿es apetecible que desaparezca todo lo que sea esfuerzo, improvisación y energía?; no veo por qué el ideal de la vida haya de ser llegar a una existencia mecanizada y ordenada como una oficina de comercio. No creo que se pueda alcanzar esto. ¿Cuándo se han hecho cosas admirables sin esfuerzo y sin heroísmo?¿Se harán alguna vez? Yo creo que nunca.

Por más que quieran cerrar, alambrar, el recinto social, siempre habrá boquetes libres para escaparse; por más que los Gobiernos decreten que los hombres deben ser unos buenos cerdos tranquilos cuyo ideal sea el pesar muchas arrobas, siempre habrá jabalíes entre ellos.» (*El sabor de la venganza*, III: 1119-20)

In this quotation Aviraneta associates idealism and projection of the imagination in action, «desequilibrio entre la realidad y la utopía», with the adventurer's impulse to act. He reveals that the man of action aspires to transcend reality through his actions. The adventurer is also an embattled spirit fighting against bureaucracy and complacency and Baroja celebrates him as a heroic figure who escapes or breaks through the limits imposed on man by modern societies.

Certain ambiguities in Baroja's presentation of the hero complicate his characterization. As I mentioned earlier, the issue of fate frequentlv arises in *Memorias de un hombre de acción* in relation to the hero. In fact, Aviraneta has been referred to as «a modern restatement of the ancient dilemma of free will».[17] Baroja stresses the hero's strong will and resourcefulness, yet often Aviraneta suffers frustration and humiliation in his activities because of situations beyond his control:

Se sentía él también una rueda de un reloj de otra clase o de otro tamaño; rueda inútil y que, sin embargo, era perfecto en su género.

La rabia de pensar que sólo en una esfera alta de actividades hubiese podido desarrollar sus condiciones, y que la suerte y el ambiente le impedían escalar este puesto, empujándole automáticamente hacia abajo, a un medio para el cual no tenía condición alguna, le irritaba y le conducía a una profunda desesperación. (*Los caudillos de 1830*, III: 954)

In addition to his victimization by fate, the hero also carries within him an element of fatalism: «Aviraneta no se sentía fatalista, y, sin embargo, lo era. Tenía demasiada confianza en sí mismo para no creer un poco en su estrella» (*Con la pluma y con el sable*, III: 424). Later Leguía reiterates on a more general level: «Indudablemente, hay algo fatal en el aventurero» (*El amor, el dandismo y la intriga*, IV: 14). But are fate and fatalism totally irreconcilable with the free will of Baroja's hero? In the «Estelas

[17] TEMPLIN, «Three Pivotal Concepts», p. 325.

sentimentales» passage quoted at the end of Chapter V, Baroja suggests that the combination of the two is an essential part of the human condition. By exercising one's will in choice man automatically engages with the world around him and circumstances he cannot determine (yet another similarity with existentialism). Man leaves himself open to fate, victimization by forces around him, and subjugation by the Other. For Baroja, fate has meaning only as a man-made entity and not as divine intervention. To exercise one's freedom and will man must run the risks of frustration and disappointment imposed from the outside because only by those acts, those of a true man of action, can man realize himself and escape spiritual paralysis. Baroja addresses the apparent paradox just before the «Estelas sentimentales» segment:

> El hombre de acción es el que cree que obra casi exclusivamente por sus propias inspiraciones, el que afirma más su albedrío, el que escoge lo que debe hacer y no debe hacer y, sin embargo, es el que está más sujeto a la ley de la fatalidad, el que marcha más arrastrado por la fuerza de los acontecimientos. *(La veleta de Gastizar, III: 907)*

In these lines, the author makes explicit the challenge of the man of action as he engages with the world. His assertion of himself, his movement out of himself and into the world, means getting caught up in and at times pitted against the people and events within it. Instead of rejecting free will, however, Baroja pays tribute to the man of action's courage and integrity in his loyalty to Self and commitment to his ideals.

Aviraneta's morality offers another example of his complex nature. In the course of the novels, Baroja refers to the hero's ability to sacrifice many people for the sake of an even greater number or for the sake of a cause. There are repeated references to his disregard of traditional morality:

> Inconscientemente, la moral era para él una cuestión de pulcritud, como la buena ropa o la buena caligrafía. *(Con la pluma y con el sable, III: 423)*
>
> Aviraneta era maquiavelista en la teoría y en la práctica. La gran fraseología masónica del tiempo, que giraba alrededor de los derechos individuales y sociales, le producía un gran desprecio.
> —Todo eso del derecho es una farsa —le oí decir varias veces—; la moral cambia según las circunstancias y el tiempo.
> ... ...
> Unicamente el utilitarismo le atraía un tanto; pero en el fondo era un casuista. *(El amor, el dandismo y la intriga, IV: 15-16)*

Despite Aviraneta's comments and the description of his moral attitude in the texts, his actions in the fictional world show him implicitly to be much closer to traditional morality than Baroja explicitly indicates. In his first experience with war, Aviraneta condemns the savagery of the French and Spanish patriots alike and war in general as an institution.

He maintains throughout the series an uncompromisingly hostile attitude towards hypocrisy of any kind and on any social level, and he refuses to abandon his beliefs to benefit himself. Aviraneta shares the author's soft spot for children, animals, and young lovers. He leads the search for a kidnapped little boy in *Los caudillos de 1830,* he brings his pet dog with him into hiding in *El escuadrón del «Brigante»,* and he engineers the plan to reunite the lovers La Clavariesa and Urbina in *La ruta del aventurero.* When Aviraneta does act violently, Baroja presents the victim in a dehumanized or depersonalized way. Baroja usually gives no characteristics describing the individual —he is merely a wooden obstacle eliminated by the hero and has the function of moving the plot forward, but remains somewhat removed from the more abstract, philosophical level of the text. Others characters perform the most cruel, animalistic actions in the novels: the Count de España in *Humano enigma* and *La senda dolorosa,* María Visconti in *Los caminos del mundo,* Fermina in *El escuadrón del «Brigante»,* and the Iturmendi brothers in *Las mascaradas sangrientas.* Often Aviraneta is the mastermind behind disruptive and violent plots, but is removed from the scene when havoc breaks loose. And Baroja associates these plots with ideals and a higher good. In this sense, the banker's reference to Aviraneta as a man of moral probity in *Crónica escandalosa* (IV: 1033) rings true and is perfectly consistent with the poetic justice I mentioned in Chapter IV. Templin has discussed the issue of casuistry in relation to Baroja's heroes. According to him, Baroja was basically a moralist whereas casuists maintain simultaneously an inner morality of pity and an outer morality of action (which can often seem amoral). Baroja's men of action maintain a healthy harmony of opposites (similar to the casuist), a balance of self-indulgence/self-discipline, civilization/primitivism, self-destruction/self-fulfillment, etc. Those who cannot establish this harmony become the neurotics of Baroja's fictional world. As examples of the men of action, Templin offers Zalacaín, who combines the child of nature image with aristocratic elegance, and Chimista, who alternates energetic periods with moments in which he bows to fate and combines an inner core of morality with public amorality.[18] Aviraneta fits the pattern Templin describes and like the other men of action, represents Baroja's attempt to overcome traditional bourgeois moral codes, with which he had little patience and for which he had no respect. As Nietzsche strives to overcome the accepted moral values in his philosophical essays and drives towards a morality that has its basis in human values and on strictly human terms, Baroja tackles the same problem in his novels. Neither the philosopher nor the novelist arrives at an easy, pat solution, but both point to the conclusion

[18] TEMPLIN, «Three Pivotal Concepts», pp. 317-21.

169

that it is an issue that must be resolved by each individual in accordance with his convictions and as a reflection of an inner core of integrity.

Aviraneta's occasional posture as the butt of a joke and his central role in some farcical situations also seems incompatible with Baroja's presentation of him as a hero. He appears completely ludicrous in some of his disguises, especially dressed as a priest in *Los caminos del mundo.* In the same novel during «Conspiración del triángulo», he becomes drunk at the dangerous climax of the story and acts like a fool while he and his friends run for their lives. He seems ridiculous in his role as aid to the young lovers in *La ruta del aventurero,* a parody of bourgeois romances of the day, when he uses his military skills to plan an assault on the convent where the young woman is imprisoned. Aviraneta the hero runs away like a frightened stray dog when the aged father of his former beloved Fermina threatens him vocally. He leads the amusing «Auto de Fe» in *Con la pluma y con el sable,* an obvious parody of the trial of the books in *Don Quijote,* in which he and his men decide which religious books to burn while they spend the night in an old monastery. In the latter part of the series, Aviraneta sometimes assumes the manner of a crotchety, querulous old man, especially in the pamphlets and letters he writes in his own defense (a tone Baroja borrows from the writings of the historical Aviraneta), which offers a whining, weak Aviraneta in contrast with the vigorous, energetic adventurer of most of *Memorias de ·un hombre de acción.* Yet these all-too-human images of Aviraneta do not ιhreaten his heroic stature. As I have already pointed out, *Memorias de un hombre de acción* is a fundamentally ironic, subversive work and quite commonly in such texts irony snowballs to the point that it threatens to undercut the few people and things of value that the author actually wishes to praise and uphold. Baroja the ironist could not let the hero escape his critical eye. In the same vein, it is not surprising to see Aviraneta at the ironic heart of parodic episodes. Baroja also did not want his protagonist to be a larger-than-life classical hero, but rather a human being with flaws and failures despite his superior integrity and capacity for action. In *La estructura mítica del héroe en la novela del siglo XX,* Juan Villegas modifies the mythical-anthropological structure of a hero's adventures as outlined by Mircea Eliade and Joseph Campbell in light of the twentieth-century novel. According to Villegas, the contemporary novel maintains the three phases of the hero's adventure (separation, initiation, and return), but there is considerably less physical displacement and more internalized displacement, the hero's sense of alienation and loneliness is greatly increased, and the final return phase is more complex. For many heroes of modern novels, adventure ends with defeat, dissatisfaction with life (thus return to society is blocked, or he discovers a margin of freedom that permits him to live both within and outside of society).[19] The point is that while the mythic pattern remains basically intact, but with inevitable displacements to adapt it to modern circumstances, the hero has become a very different figure —torn, vulnerable, alienated, approachable, identifiable, human. When Baroja manipulates and victimizes Aviraneta and makes him the object of his irony he demythifies the hero. But rather than add more fuel to the fire of Baroja's detractors, I want to indicate that this process neither proves Baroja's ineptitude as an author nor makes him strange, but rather ties him to general philosophical changes taking place at the time and their corresponding literary expression. Baroja was neither the first nor the last novelist to have scapegoats, marginals, semi-ridiculous, or ambiguous figures as heroes although unquestionably his own attitude towards and distance from them varied in the course of the novels. Baroja wrote at a time when Western man was questioning the entire structure of his world —its values, organization, the existence of God, his own nature. If his heroes often seem frail, insecure, and neurotic this is a reflection of the times. Their struggles and actions represent the search for solutions to the existential dilemma.

Yet another explanation is to see Aviraneta as a literary counterpart of the «absurd man» described in *The Myth of Sisyphus*. Camus begins by explaining modern man's perception of the absurd. According to him, man is alienated in a universe with no hope and meaning. He yearns for order and illusion in a world that offers only chaos, indifference, and the irrational in response. The absurd arises from the confrontation and schism between desire and reality.[20] But the absurd man does not respond with despair to this situation. He chooses the life of the actor (remember Aviraneta's love of role-playing) or of the adventurer, going out into the world with neither illusion nor hope, but he still acts, experiences the world with all its limits and frustrations (pp. 77-90). He shows the heroism of Sisyphus, who bested the gods by facing with courage and persistence the eternally futile task of rolling a boulder uphill only to watch it fall back down again (pp. 119-23). Aviraneta shows the same tenacity and devotion in the futile task he takes on of defending liberalism and freedom in the criminal and chaotic society of nineteenth-century Spain.

---

[19] JUAN VILLEGAS, *La estructura mítica del héroe en la novela del siglo XX* (Barcelona: Planeta, 1978).

[20] ALBERT CAMUS, *The Myth of Sisyphus and Other Essays*, trans. Justin O'Brien (New York: Alfred A. Knopf, 1967), pp. 24-30. Subsequent references to this edition of *The Myth of Sisyphus* will be cited parenthetically in the text by page number. See also «Recognition and Engagement», in HAZEL E. BARNES, *The Literature of Possibility: A Study in Humanistic Existentialism* (Lincoln: University of Nebraska Press, 1959), pp. 155-271.

LEGUÍA: THE PASSIVE HERO

Besides this man of action, however, Baroja includes several major figures in *Memorias de un hombre de acción* characterized by inactivity, resignation, and a comfortable bourgeois life: Miguel Aristy, Pepe Carmona, J. H. Thompson, Alvarito Sánchez de Mendoza, and Leguía. He does not submit these individuals to a strong, critical viewpoint, although none entirely escapes his irony. Longhurst has noticed that the passive, reflective characters outnumber the men of action in the series. He believes that Baroja creates more convincing characters in Thompson, Aristy, and Sánchez de Mendoza than in his men of action and concludes that the author can identify with them on account of his own passive nature. Longhurst thinks that Baroja views action through passive eyes and that the man of action represents a curiosity that fascinates him, but that he cannot understand. Alberich similarly states that Baroja contemplates and views adventure as a spectacle, from an intellectual stance.[21] These views are an inaccurate assessment of the active and inactive men in *Memorias de un hombre de acción*. I do not agree that Baroja's passive characters are more convincing than his men of action, although clearly it is a matter of personal judgment. But more importantly, Baroja gives no indication in the novels that his sympathies lie with one group as opposed to the other nor does he exalt Aviraneta at the expense of Leguía or Alvarito or vice versa. To return to Templin's concept of the harmony of opposites, it seems more likely that Baroja wishes to explore varied modes of being and possibilities, different ways of responding to the challenge of finding meaning and direction in life. Baroja's entire artistic style is based on opposition, contrasts, paradox, and dichotomies and it seems quite natural that he would balance off his man of action hero with a number of passive characters. Undoubtedly Baroja is closer in temperament to many of these characters, but he shows no marked preference for them. They simply represent different methods of coping with reality.

Leguía, the fictional editor of *Memorias de un hombre de acción,* is by far the most important passive character of the novels. His work mirrors that of Baroja and he often functions as a mouthpiece for the author's ideas (as do Aviraneta and many of Baroja's major characters). The reader sees him again and again as the collector, organizer, and imaginative expander of notes and papers. At the beginning of *Crónica escandalosa* Leguía compares his work to that of a naturalist who reconstructs an entire animal of an extinct species from fossils and a few bones and he confesses that he has invented some of the material to clarify

[21] LONGHURST, pp. 112-18 and ALBERICH, pp. 109-11.

points. He apologizes for the repetitive aspects of his works, but sees it as the inevitable consequence of old age (IV: 979-80). The passage offers an interesting testimony of Baroja's awareness of his own artistic endeavors in the series and presents a kind of ironic, self-mocking comment on its nature. Leguía remarks on his function in the series as a counterpoint to Aviraneta:

> ... creo que de Aviraneta he hablado bastante y que a las cosas y a los hombres hay que compararlos para apreciar sus caracteres; y en esta narración, Aviraneta y yo estamos con frecuencia frente a frente, no como enemigos, sino como tipos de modalidad espiritual distinta. *(El amor, el dandismo y la intriga,* IV: 13)

He makes this comment at the point at which he picks up his life story after dropping it at the end of *El aprendiz de conspirador.* His changing, evolving nature contrasts with Aviraneta's sameness. With this character Baroja shows that one man's reality is not another's and that in the process of self-realization, one must discard the inauthentic Selves one assumes on the way to discovery of one's true Self. The reader first sees Leguía as a naive, romantic young man who yearns for the adventurer's life: «Recorrer tierras y tierras a caballo, cambiar de paisajes constantemente, comer aquí, dormir allá, no volver nunca la mirada atrás, éste hubiera sido su ideal» *(El aprendiz de conspirador,* III: 30). A chance encounter and involvement with Aviraneta, the godfather of his beloved Corito Arteaga, leads to his active pursuit of the conspirator's life style. When his story continues in Bayonne in volumen thirteen of *Memorias de un hombre de acción,* Leguía begins speaking in the nostalgic, melancholy tone of an elderly man. His retrospective stance and his talk of writing as therapy for sadness and boredom is reminiscent of that of the older Shanti Andía. But Leguía quickly shifts to a more lively recounting of his amorous adventures, evenings in fashionable salons, and cultivation of aristocratic friendships. In a comparison of himself with Aviraneta, Leguía indicates some of the basic differences between them that ultimately determine their different life styles. He describes his life as «más completa que la suya» *(El amor, el dandismo y la intriga,* IV: 13). While Aviraneta enters into undertakings on blind impulse, «Yo siempre tuve más prudencia que él, y no olvidé jamás las dificultades de una empresa» (IV: 14). Leguía never presumes to dominate fate and never feels Aviraneta's unfailing faith in his resourcefulness. Unlike his mentor's life, his own had not been shaped by obstacles and he found himself supported by influential figures. He lacks Aviraneta's self-assurance: «Yo, además de transformarme, tenía dudas acerca de mi vida y momentos de depresión; experimentaba muchas veces un vago sentimiento de no haber seguido una línea más recta, más pura» (IV: 15). Leguía cannot share the adventurer's morality. He has broader sentiments of compassion and love:

> En lo que sí me separaba de él era en que yo tenía un sentido de humanidad más agudo y más amplio.
>
> ... ...
>
> para mí la vida de cualquiera era respetable y no podía ser sacrificada por una idea o por una conveniencia de la mayoría.
>
> Jugar con la vida propia me parecía cosa de valientes; jugar con la ajena es lo que me parecía ilícito. (IV: 15)

Leguía soon begins to tire of the life of intrigue and the emptiness and hypocrisy of the dandy's world. He realizes that this way of living cannot last forever: «'Por ahora, me divierte el peligro, la aventura, pero nada más; dentro de poco me gustará la vida tranquila y la buena mesa'» (*El amor, el dandismo y la intriga,* IV: 112). A disastrous, poverty-stricken stay in Paris makes him see the error of his ways: «Todo mi dandismo era vanidad, humo. Era un pobre majadero presuntuoso» (*El amor, el dandismo y la intriga,* IV: 131). Aviraneta sends him on a dangerous mission to gather information on the split in the Carlist camp. Leguía nearly dies during the assignment and ends up contracting a fever and subsequently renouncing his ambitions: «La idea de exponerme y correr aventuras y peligros no me seducía. Mi impulso por la acción había desaparecido» (*El amor, el dandismo y la intriga,* IV: 167). Leguía finally withdraws from the active life, marries, and becomes a comfortable bourgeois bureaucrat, «espectador de las luchas políticas» (*El amor, el dandismo y la intriga,* IV: 169). Baroja obviously goes to great pains to give a detailed account of Leguía's sentimental education and the changes in his life. He makes the fictional editor a softer, more malleable character than his hero and a man more vulnerable to human emotions and suffering. The adventurer's life is merely a mask or role that Leguía assumes and then discards in the process of self-recognition. He functions, however, not only as a counterpoint to Aviraneta, but as his counterpart in Baroja's existential quest for endowing life with order and meaning. Leguía and Aviraneta represent complementary and undefinitive approaches to the existential dilemma. In Aviraneta, Baroja presents a man whose total, intense, and completely subjective engagement with life generates a general unawareness of surroundings, time and his fellow man. His total commitment to his ideals and the active life generate the atmosphere of spiritual intensity that Baroja has identified with heroes. The tone of resignation and position of distance that Leguía and others like Alvarito and Miguel Aristy adopt as a means of coping with life are more readily identifiable with the passive and often ironic spectator. Baroja seems to suggest that an acceptable existential position lies around two opposing yet complementary poles: that of complete engagement, envelopment in action in which self, ideas and action are one, and that of distanced observation, in which one watches, weighs, and judges.

Baroja explored these solutions to man's existential dilemma through the protagonist of *El árbol de la ciencia*. Andrés Hurtado's movement back and forth from action to contemplation corresponds to the constant philosophical shifting from Nietzsche to Schopenhauer in the novel. These skeptics, who had the greatest impact philosophically on Baroja, offer opposing views regarding the ideal mode of living. Nietzsche celebrates this world and man's will in his dancing prophet Zarathustra. He proposes a vitalistic approach to life and praises man's irrational as well as rational powers. Schopenhauer, on the other hand, advocates an ascetic life of self-denial and mortification of the will. It is a celebration of nihilism rather than an affirmation of life. Baroja would explore again and again in his fictional heroes the possibilities and limitations of these two existential stances and the chance of reconciling them. In a sense, he transfers the abstract philosophical challenge of endowing life with order and meaning to the more individualized, everyday level of personality, self-creation, and self-realization in his fiction.

In fact, here these two existential positions correspond to the vacillating perspective of Baroja the narrator who moves in and out of his characters' point of view, one moment narrating in first person or as if in first person and the next moment moving outside of his characters and judging them or ironically undercutting them. It explains the oscillation in Baroja's point of view and the inconsistency in distance of the narrator. One minute he is at one with the actor and the next he withdraws and tends to view and judge the character as a spectator. Baroja's perspective is similar to Aviraneta's action with his spyglass. By focusing sharply he can see far away things close up and in great detail, but with an unfocused spyglass or without it, he sees things only in broader, more general, typological terms (part of Baroja's tendency to abstract his fictional material).

THE WRITER AS MAN OF ACTION

Leguía offers the best example of the Baroja character who crosses over from man of action to passive spectator and writer, yet Baroja's fictional world suggests that there is a certain similarity between the man of action and the writer. Templin first pointed out the connection between the collectors and the men of action in Baroja's novels and Baroja's own method of creation as the same «approach to the manipulation of reality».[22] Much stronger parallels exist, however, between the man of action

22 TEMPLIN, «Three Pivotal Concepts», pp. 309-10.

and the writer. Throughout *Memorias de un hombre de acción* characters refer to Aviraneta's activities as a form of art. The title of one novel, *Con la pluma y con el sable*, implies the dual image of the hero presented in the novel: the administrator, record-keeper, and something of a man of letters and the dynamic fighter and defender of the liberal cause, the man of action. And let us remember that Aviraneta's elasticity of spirit was referred to as the «literatura de un hombre iliterato» (*Con la pluma y con el sable*, III: 395). At times Aviraneta shows a surprising awareness of the artistic nature of his endeavors. In a discussion with Thompson, the hero points out that their plan offers an alternative aesthetic experience to the architecture of the convent that the Englishman will miss: «'¡Qué arte! No sea usted amanerado, Thompson. ¿No es una obra de arte el intentar, como intentaremos nosotros, si se puede, robar una señorita de un convento?'» (*La ruta del aventurero*, III: 680).

In a comparison between the Count de España and Aviraneta, Hugo Riversdale describes the hero as a storyteller and an artist: «un inventor de fábulas; hombre que forjaba una creación artística y la lanzaba al enemigo para que la devorase» (*Humano enigma*, IV: 670). Even more striking are the reappearance in a fictional context and in relationship with seemingly non-artistic things of Baroja's attitudes towards art as expressed in his own writings. In a conversation between Aviraneta and his fellow conspirator Tilly, the young man discusses intrigue as an art form:

> «... yo creo que el arte de conspirar, el arte de crear pueblos y de suble-varlos no tiene reglas, como no las tiene el arte de esculpir, ni el de escribir, ni el de pintar.
> ... ...
> Sobre el impulso, sobre la intuición, no se pueden dar reglas como sobre la manera de hacer relojes.» (*La Isabelina*, III: 1050)

Tilly's comments recall Baroja's opposition to a normative, Classical approach to writing novels and his emphasis on the irrational aspect of artistic creation, «impulso» and «intuición». The high value Baroja places on spontaneity reappears as a comment on a segment of Spanish society, the common people: «El pueblo era lo genial entre los españoles; lo demás valía poco o no valía nada. Así, en las guerras, los guerrilleros daban la nota, lo espontáneo, lo improvisado» (*Humano enigma*, IV: 593). All these quotations point to a vision of action and an intense and spontaneous life as equivalent to art. But Baroja also moves in the other direction as well, suggesting that art replaces and equals the life of the man of action. Aviraneta tells Leguía: «'Los hombres de mi tiempo no leíamos tantas novelas como los de ahora. Buenas o malas, las hacíamos en la vida'» (*Los contrastes de la vida*, III: 801). Aviraneta's statement implies that novels have replaced a mode of existence that is no longer possible for the men of Leguía's (and Baroja's) time. In describing his own literary temperament Baroja identifies himself with the man of action:

> Este conjunto de particularidades instintivas: la turbulencia, la aspiración ética, el dinamismo, el ansia de posesión de las ideas, el fervor por la acción, el odio por lo inerte y el entusiasmo por el porvenir, forman la base de mi temperamento literario, si es que se puede llamar literario a un temperamento así que, sobre un fondo de energía sería más de hombre de acción que de otra cosa. («Prólogo» to *La dama errante*, II: 231)

Many of the characteristics here displayed are identical to those displayed by Aviraneta. The lines suggest a tentative identification of art (writing in particular) with an ethic of action, a connection made by Sartre:

> Thus the prose writer is a man who has chosen a certain method of secondary action which we may call action by disclosure...
> The «engaged» writer knows that words are action. He knows that to reveal is to change and that one can reveal only by planning to change. He has given up the impossible dream of giving an impartial picture of Society and the human condition.[23]

Sartre's constant use of writing as an example of action is even more telling in this regard. At the end of *Nausea,* Roquentin concludes that doing something creates existence and being. He commits himself to writing as an act of faith in life and man. The hero considers writing a superior activity because it has the power to condense and express the essence of life. Camus, too, gives art a significant existential role. He sees art as a means of living doubly by permitting man to maintain his consciousness and his adventures in a more permanent form (*Sisyphus,* p. 94). According to him, ironic philosophers produce the most passionate works of art because they abandon unity for diversity. Camus realizes that irony and negation are important components of the absurd creator's work (*Sisyphus,* pp. 114-16). «Irony», «negation», «absurdity», «diversity», «lack of unity» —all these terms have become familiar and identifiable elements of Baroja's fictional world in *Memorias de un hombre de acción* and make clear the connection between existential thought and the series.

Baroja stops short of making a direct association between writing and action, but the fictional world of *Memorias de un hombre de acción* offers ample proof that he had a similar belief. Baroja, Aviraneta, and Leguía have in common the fact that they are all subjective, imaginative orderers of reality even though their media of communication and engagement differ. Aviraneta's life does not represent the author's desire to enjoy vicariously the life of the man of action, but rather another means of coping with a common existential dilemma. Leguía acts as the

[23] JEAN-PAUL SARTRE, «What is Writing?», in *Essays in Existentialism,* introd. Jean Wahl, ed. Wade Baskin (Secaucus, N. J.: Citadel Press, 1979), 303-31 at p. 320.

pivotal figure, the middle man, between the writer and the man of action. Baroja's belief in the fundamentally subjective nature of human experience made him realize that each individual must find a solution to the existential problem for himself and that that solution would be a viable solution only for himself. This lonely subjectivity has its philosophical counterpart in existential thought:

> All these commonplace, everyday values, derive their meaning from an original projection of myself which stands as my choice of myself in the world... I do not have nor can I have recourse to any value against the fact that it is I who sustain values in being... I have to realize the meaning of the world and of my essence, I make my decision concerning them —without justification and without excuse. *(Being and Nothingness,* pp. 77-78).

Aviraneta never completely emerges from the underworld society of *Memorias de un hombre de acción,* unlike a traditional hero, nor does he consistently maintain a cynical spectator's distance from that world. He remains in the realm of human activity, at times caught up in a whirl of transcendent activity generated by a strong will, resourcefulness, and imagination, and yet coping with and entrapped by everyday circumstances and problems beyond his control. He shares with his author the ambiguous status of total involvment with the world and aloof withdrawal created by his own core of integrity that distinguishes him from other men. It is a lonely and stoic vision of heroism, but Baroja clings to this vision as the only possible one to have in the modern world. He projects onto his fictional hero his own heroic, aesthetic goal: to create meaning and order out of that which is senseless and chaotic and in the process to transcend one's own all-too-human limitations.

CONCLUSION

> For what is freedom? That one has the will to
> assume responsibility for oneself. That one main-
> tains the distance which separates us. That one
> becomes more indifferent to difficulties, hardships,
> privations, even to life itself. That one is prepared
> to sacrifice human beings for one's cause, not
> excluding oneself. Freedom means that the manly
> instincts which delight in war and victory dominate
> over other instincts, for example, over those of
> pleasure.
>
> (NIETZSCHE, *Twilight of the Idols*)

Baroja's *Memorias de un hombre de acción* owes much to the nineteenth-century novel of adventures, to thrillers, and to other popular
literary forms. The author derives an action-oriented plot and a morally-
polarized universe from these types of romance and schematic, ideological
characterization, and an ironic point of view from satire. He fuses with
this paradoxical amalgam of literary forms a serious philosophical preoccupation with the existential problem of endowing life with order and
meaning in an absurd, meaningless world. The tendency in Baroja criticism has been either to gloss over the paradoxical world view that emerges
inevitably from ambiguities and contradictions in structure, point of view,
and attitude towards his hero in *Memorias de un hombre de acción* and
his other works, or to choose one of the two labels, «pessimistic» or
«vitalistic», and studiously ignore the evidence that disproves the validity
of either label alone. The fact is that the paradoxical dichotomies that
underlie *Memorias de un hombre de acción* —romance/satire, fragment-
ation/unification, demythification/remythification, hero/all-too-human person, are the foundation of his entire novelistic universe and represent the
culmination of tendencies present in his very first novels. Baroja's world
view and the ambiguities and unevenness in tone and point of view that
it produces are the essence of an ironic artistic stance in which the author
maintains the fictional world at a distance and manipulates it for his own
purposes. Yet his moralistic and judgmental attitude constantly threatens
to rupture the fragile illusion of that fiction. Baroja's search for a solution
to the existential dilemma in *Memorias de un hombre de acción* leads to
the skeptical conclusion that order and meaning in the universe rest with

each individual's subjective experience of reality and thus the viability of each solution is limited to that individual's experience.

Despite the bleakness of the vision and the label of «pessimism» that it seems to cry out for, Baroja refuses to relinquish his faith in mankind's strength and ability to survive. In a world characterized by deceit, illusion, and changeability mankind is the only ultimate reality, as one of his characters states: «'Lo único que quedará serán los hombres. Antes no había nada más que los hombres y no quedará más que los hombres. Es una mala raza..., pero fuerte'» (*Las mascaradas sangrientas,* IV: 511). In a section from that same novel, «Moral y etnografía», Baroja the narrator asserts that, «Los diez mil años de la Historia significan muy poco para el millón de años que el hombre vive en el planeta» (IV: 516). For him, the record of social and political conflicts and upheavals seems insignificant beside man's span of time on earth and his consistent moral character across that period —his potential for sinking into animality or rising above his own human limitations and aspiring to a higher moral nature. In his essay entitled «El héroe, el señor y yo» Baroja creates a hypothetical dialogue between a fictional bilious gentleman, an author of a social drama and a proponent of fighting for the common good by embracing social causes, and himself. In the discussion, the man attacks Baroja's motives for writing *Memorias de un hombre de acción* and the values embodied in the series:

> Este hombre del cálculo doloroso me abordó el otro día con cierta afabilidad de pulpo, y me dijo:
> —¿Va usted a publicar otro tomo de Aviraneta?
> —Sí —contesté yo.
> —¿Y qué serie de libros es ésta? —prosiguió, descubriendo el vinagre que llevaba debajo de la crema—. ¿Es un folletín? ¿Es un conjunto de anécdotas? ¿Quiere ser una historia pintoresca de España?
> —¡Pchs! De todo un poco.
> —No comprendo qué se propone usted. ¿Cuál es su idea? Usted no canta la democracia, el derecho, el respeto a la ley, las batallas de la vida moderna...
> —¡Ah!, no; claro que no.
> —No veo por qué.
> —Para mí hay virtudes de ciudad y virtudes de campo... —empecé a decir.
> —Y estas campesinas son las únicas por las que tiene usted entusiasmo.
> —Eso es.
> —¿Para usted Zumalacárregui o Zurbano son más grandes que Castelar y Salmerón?
> —¡Ah!, claro; no tiene duda. Del siglo diecinueve español hemos olvidado los héroes, y no nos acordamos más que de los histriones de la mísera restauración.
> —¿De manera que toda nuestra generación, con su preocupación de derecho y de democracia y de arte, para usted ha sido inútil?
> —Completamente.
> —¿Nuestras luchas no han servido para nada?
> —Para nada.

—Todos esos jurisconsultos, grandes oradores, que a nosotros nos parecen nobles, ¿para usted son unos farsantes despreciables?
—Exacto.
—De manera que Cánovas, Ruiz Zorilla, Martos, Moreno Nieto, Monero Ríos, Maura...
—A mí me parecen gente mediocre. Abogados, charlatanes. Grandes hombres para un pueblo ramplón y decaído. Hombres gesticuladores, buenos para tener estatuas de Querol y de Benlliure.
—¿Estos escultores también le parecen a usted malos?
—Malos, no; vulgares, sin espíritu.
—Y el teatro español del siglo diecinueve, ¿tampoco valdrá gran cosa?
—A mí no me interesa.
—¿Y el libro?
—El libro, poco más o menos, lo mismo que el teatro.
—¿Así que, según usted, aquí todo es pequeño, y únicamente los alborotadores, los sanguinarios, los turbulentos, los Aviranetas son grandes?
—Eso es.
—¿De manera que el pensamiento para usted no es nada?
—Sí, hombre, mucho; cuando es pensamiento.
—¿De manera que la democracia para usted es una farsa?
—Sí; algo de eso.
—¿Y la moral, una mixtificación?
—Algo por el estilo.
—¿Y que queda entonces? *(Nuevo tablado de arlequín,* V: 132-33)

Baroja assumes a negative, skeptical, ironic attitude towards all the traditional concepts, values and goals embraced by his opponent. He denounces them as mediocre, common and insignificant. But from his negation and denial, his ironic view of history and his own time, one positive thing emerges: the potential of each man to rise above the mediocrity of his age, aspire to his own higher set of values, and remain true to himself and to those ideals —to become a lonely, stoic hero like Aviraneta, but a hero nonetheless. Baroja's social awareness does not take the superficial form of his imaginary dialogue companion. He rather advocates a profound social, philosophical, and moral reform that begins with the individual. His response to the bilious gentleman synthesizes the existential stance present in all of his works, but explored most thoroughly in *Memorias de un hombre de acción* and in his hero Aviraneta. It is a call-to-arms to men to commit themselves to self-sacrifice, self-overcoming, and self-realization —to become men of integrity, heroes:

—Queda el hombre, el hombre, que está por encima de la religión, de la democracia, de la moral, de la luz y taquígrafos, de los versos de Núñez de Arce y de las aleluyas de Campoamor...; queda el hombre, es decir, el héroe, que, en medio de las tempestades, de los odios, de los recursos de la mediocridad, de la envidia de los hombres cetrinos con las vejigas calculosas, impone una norma difícil a los demás; sí, queda el hombre, el héroe...

181

¡Oh tú, joven lector! Si te sientes hombre, si te sientes con fortaleza para serlo, no vaciles, no oigas a las sirenas de aspecto hepático que encuentres por las calles; no hagas caso de viejas momias ni de supersticiones cristianas; sacrifica tu dicha, sacrifica a tu prójimo, sacrifica todo lo sacrificable..., porque vale la pena. *(Nuevo tablado de arlequín, V: 133)*

LIST OF WORKS CONSULTED

LITERARY TEXTS

BAROJA, PÍO: *Camino de perfección*. 1920; rpt. New York: Las Américas, n.d.
— *Obras completas*. 8 vols. Madrid: Biblioteca Nueva, 1946-51.

BAROJA CRITICISM

ALBERICH, JOSÉ: *Los ingleses y otros temas de Pío Baroja*. Madrid: Alfaguara, 1966.
ALFARO, MARÍA: «Pío Baroja: El pasado. La raza.» *Cuadernos Americanos*, 16, Nos. 5-6 (1957), 240-49.
ANGELES, JOSÉ: «Baroja y Galdós: un ensayo de diferenciación.» *Revista de Literatura*, 23, Nos. 45-46 (Jan.-June 1963), 49-64.
BAEZA, FERNANDO, ed.: *Baroja y su mundo*. 2 vols. Madrid: Arión, 1961.
BARROW, LEO L.: *Negation in Baroja: A Key to his Novelistic Creativity*. Tucson: University of Arizona Press, 1971.
BOLINGER, DWIGHT L.: «Heroes and Hamlets: The Protagonists of Baroja's Novels.» *Hispania*, 24 (1941), 91-94.
BRETZ, MARY LEE: *La evolución novelística de Pío Baroja*. Madrid: Porrúa Turanzas, 1979.
CAMPOS, JORGE: *Introducción a Pío Baroja*. Madrid: Alianza, 1981.
— «Pío Baroja, corresponsal de guerra (1903).» *Cuadernos Hispanoamericanos*, Nos. 265-67 (July-Sept. 1972), pp. 270-92.
CARENAS, FRANCISCO: «La abrumadora concreción del lenguaje barojiano.» *Cuadernos Americanos*, 202, No. 5 (Sept.-Oct. 1975), 116-27.
CARO BAROJA, JULIO: «Confrontación literaria o las relaciones de dos novelistas: Galdós y Baroja.» *Cuadernos Hispanoamericanos*, Nos. 265-67 (July-Sept. 1972), pp. 160-68.
— Personal interview. 3 May 1982.
CASALDUERO, JOAQUÍN: «Baroja y Galdós.» *Revista Hispánica Moderna*, 31 (1965), 113-18.
— «Sentido y forma de la vida fantástica.» *Cuadernos Hispanoamericanos*, Nos. 265-67 (July-Sept. 1972), pp. 427-44.
CHALLIS, DAVID J.: «Pío Baroja and Disguise as Self-Expression.» Diss. University of Pittsburgh 1973.
CIPLIJAUSKAITÉ, BIRUTÉ: *Baroja, un estilo*. Madrid: Insula, 1972.
CONTE, RAFAEL: «El grado cero de la novela.» *El País*, 30 Oct. 1981, p. 31, cols. 2-4.
CORRALES EGEA, JOSÉ: *Baroja y Francia*. Madrid: Taurus, 1969.
EARLE, PETER: «Baroja y su ética de la imposibilidad.» *El País*, 30 Oct. 1981, p. 31, cols. 2-4.

EMBEITA, MARÍA: «Pío Baroja: una interpretación.» *Cuadernos Hispanoamericanos,* No. 291 (Sept. 1974), pp. 14-30.

— «Tema y forma de expresión en Baroja.» *Cuadernos Hispanoamericanos,* Nos. 265-67 (July-Sept. 1972), pp. 143-51.

FEAL DEIBE, CARLOS: *«Zalacaín el aventurero* y las tres mujeres de Pío Baroja.» *Revista Hispánica Moderna,* 33 (1967), 285-92.

FERRERAS, JUAN IGNACIO: «Tensión y negación en la obra novelesca de Baroja.» *Cuadernos Hispanoamericanos,* Nos. 265-67 (July-Sept. 1972), pp. 293-301.

FLORES ARROYUELO, FRANCISCO: «Baroja y la historia.» *Revista de Occidente,* NS No. 62 (1968), pp. 204-24.

— *Pío Baroja y la historia.* Madrid: Helios, 1971.

— *Las primeras novelas de Pío Baroja: 1900-1912.* Murcia: La Torre de los Vientos, 1967.

FOX, E. INMAN: «Baroja and Schopenhauer.» *Revue de Littérature Comparée,* 37 (1963), 350-59.

GALBIS, IGNACIO: «El lirismo de tono menor en la obra de Pío Baroja.» Diss. Syracuse University 1973.

GINSBERG, JUDITH: «Pío Baroja: The Transformation of Politics into Art (1900-1911).» Diss. City University of New York 1976.

GRANJEL, LUIS: «Autor y personaje en la obra barojiana.» *Cuadernos Hispanoamericanos,* Nos. 265-67 (July-Sept. 1972), pp. 3-10.

HOWITT, D.: «Baroja's Preoccupation with Clocks and his Emphatic Treatment of Time in the Introduction of *La busca.*» In *Hispanic Studies in Honour of Joseph Manson.* Ed. Dorothy M. Atkinson and Anthony H. Clarke. Oxford: Dolphin, 1972, pp. 139-47.

IGLESIAS, CARMEN: «La controversia entre Baroja y Ortega acerca de la novela.» *Hispanófila,* No. 7 (Sept. 1959), pp. 41-50.

— «El 'devenir' y la acción en la obra de Pío Baroja.» *Cuadernos Americanos,* 21, No. 3 (May-June 1962), 263-70.

— *El pensamiento de Pío Baroja: Ideas centrales.* Clásicos y Modernos, No. 12. México: Antigua Librería Robredo, 1963.

KNOX, ROBERT B.: «The structure of *El mayorazgo de Labraz.*» *Hispania,* 38 (1955), 285-90.

LITVAK, LILY: «Baroja y el medievalismo finisecular.» *Revue des Langues Vivantes,* 40 (1974), 269-82.

LONGHURST, CARLOS: *Las novelas históricas de Pío Baroja.* Madrid: Guadarrama, 1974.

— «Pío Baroja and Aviraneta: Some Sources of the *Memorias de un hombre de acción.*» *Bulletin of Hispanic Studies,* 48 (1971), 328-45.

LÓPEZ CAMPILLO, EVELYNE: «Aviraneta: biografía y utopía.» *Cuadernos Hispanoamericanos,* Nos. 265-67 (July-Sept. 1972), pp. 600-09.

LÓPEZ ESTRADA, FRANCISCO: *Perspectivas sobre Pío Baroja.* Sevilla: Universidad de Sevilla, 1972.

MARTÍNEZ PALACIO, JAVIER: *Pío Baroja.* Madrid: Taurus, 1979.

MONTES, JOSÉ ARES: «*Camino de perfección* o las peregrinaciones de Pío Baroja y Fernando Ossorio.» *Cuadernos Hispanoamericanos,* Nos. 265-67 (July-Sept. 1972), pp. 481-516.

NORA, EUGENIO DE: «Pío Baroja.» In Vol. I of *La novela española contemporánea (1898-1927).* Madrid: Gredos, 1958, pp. 97-229.

ORTEGA, JOSÉ: «Andrés Hurtado: un estudio de alienación.» *Cuadernos Hispanoamericanos,* Nos. 265-67 (July-Sept. 1972), pp. 591-99.

ORTEGA Y GASSET, JOSÉ: «Ideas sobre Pío Baroja.» In *El Espectador (1916-1934).*

Vol. II of his *Obras completas.* 4th ed. Madrid: Revista de Occidente, 1957, pp. 69-102.

— «Una primera vista sobre Pío Baroja.» In *El Espectador (1916-1934).* Vol. II of his *Obras completas.* 4th ed. Madrid: Revista de Occidente, 1957, pp. 103-25.

OWEN, ARTHUR L.: «Concerning the Ideology of Pío Baroja.» *Hispania,* 15 (1932), 15-24.

PÉREZ MINIK, DOMINGO: «Al cruzar el siglo XX. Pío Baroja en el panorama de la novela europea.» *Cuadernos Hispanoamericanos,* Nos. 265-67 (July-Sept. 1972), pp. 55-65.

PÉREZ MONTANER, JAIME: «Sobre la estructura de las *Memorias de un hombre de acción.*» *Cuadernos Hispanoamericanos,* Nos. 265-67 (July-Sept. 1972), pp. 610-20.

PLACER, ELOY L.: «Baroja, Flaubert y el estilo.» *Symposium,* 14 (1960), 49-52.

REGALADO GARCÍA, ANTONIO: «Verdugos y ejecutados en las novelas de Pío Baroja.» *Papeles de Son Armadans,* No. 121 (April 1966), pp. 9-29.

ROBLEDO, FIDEL: «Don Pío Baroja y la pintura.» *Papeles de Son Armadans,* No. 175 (Oct. 1970), pp. 31-55.

RODRÍGUEZ ALCALÁ, HUGO: «Ortega, Baroja, Unamuno y la sinceridad.» *Revista Hispánica Moderna,* 15 (1949), 107-14.

ROGERS, EDITH: «Sobre el pesimismo de Baroja.» *Hispania,* 46 (1962), 671-74.

SALGADO, MARÍA A.: «El paisaje animado en *Camino de perfección.*» *Hispania,* 49 (1966), 404-09.

SARRIÁ, F. G.: «Estructura y motivos de *Camino de perfección.*» *Romanische Forschungen,* 83 (1971), pp. 246-66.

SHAW, DONALD L.: «The Concept of 'Ataraxia' in the Later Novels of Baroja.» *Bulletin of Hispanic Studies,* 34 (1957), 29-36.

— «A Reply to *Deshumanización* —Baroja on the Art of the Novel.» *Hispanic Review,* 25 (1957), 105-11.

— «Two Novels of Baroja: An Illustration of his Technique.» *Bulletin of Hispanic Studies,* 40 (1963), 151-59.

SOBEJANO, GONZALO: «Componiendo *Camino de perfección.*» *Cuadernos Hispanoamericanos,* Nos. 265-67 (July-Sept. 1972), pp. 463-80.

SOTO VERGES, RAFAEL: «Baroja: una estilística de la información.» *Cuadernos Hispanoamericanos,* No. 265-67 (July-Sept. 1972), pp. 135-42.

TEMPLIN, E. H.: «Pío Baroja and Science.» *Hispanic Review,* 15 (1947), 165-92.

— «Pío Baroja: Three Pivotal Concepts.» *Hispanic Review,* 12 (1944), 306-29.

TIJERAS, EDUARDO: «El relativismo en Baroja.» *Cuadernos Hispanoamericanos,* Nos. 265-67 (July-Sept. 1972), pp. 363-70.

UGALDE, LOUIS M.: «El supuesto antihistoricismo de Pío Baroja.» *Hispanófila,* No. 36 (May 1969), pp. 11-20.

URIBE ECHEVARRÍA, JUAN: *Pío Baroja: Técnica, estilo, personajes.* Santiago, Chile: Editorial Universitaria, 1969.

URRUTIA SALAVERRI, LUIS: «Baroja ¿un centenario más?» *Revista de Occidente,* NS No. 117 (Dec. 1972), pp. 274-94.

VILA SELMA, JOSÉ: «La conciencia histórica en Pío Baroja.» *Cuadernos Hispanoamericanos,* No. 265-67 (July-Sept. 1972), pp. 249-69.

YNDURAÍN, DOMINGO: «Teoría de la novela en Baroja.» *Cuadernos Hispanoamericanos,* No. 233 (May 1969), pp. 355-88.

LITERARY AND HISTORICAL BACKGROUND

ARJONA, DORIS KING: «*La Voluntad* and *Abulia* in Contemporary Spanish Ideology.» *Revue Hispanique,* 74 (1928), 573-671.

BLANCO AGUINAGA, CARLOS: *Juventud del '98*. Madrid: Siglo XXI, 1970.

CARR, RAYMOND: *Spain: 1808-1939*. Oxford: Clarendon Press, 1966.

CIPLIJAUSKAITÉ, BIRUTÉ: «The 'Noventayochistas' and the Carlist Wars.» *Hispanic Review*, 44 (1976), 265-79.

— *Los noventayochistas y la historia*. Madrid: Porrúa Turanzas, 1981.

CLAVERÍA, CARLOS: «Unamuno y Carlyle.» In his *Temas de Unamuno*. Madrid: Gredos, 1953, pp. 9-58.

DÍAZ-PLAJA, GUILLERMO: «El modernismo, cuestión disputada.» *Hispania*, 48 (1965), 407-12.

DURÁN, MANUEL: «La técnica de la novela y la generación del 98.» *Revista Hispánica Moderna*, 23 (1957), 14-27.

FERRERAS, JUAN IGNACIO: *Los orígenes de la novela decimonónica (1800-1830)*. Vol. I of his *Estudios sobre la novela española del siglo XIX*. Madrid: Taurus, 1973.

— *El triunfo del liberalismo y de la novela histórica (1830-1870)*. Vol. II of his *Estudios sobre la novela española del siglo XIX*. Madrid: Taurus, 1976.

— *La novela por entregas 1840-1900. (Concentración obrera y economía editorial)*. Vol. IV of his *Estudios sobre la novela española del siglo XIX*. Madrid: Taurus, 1972.

FOX, E. INMAN: «Two Anarchist Newspapers of 1898.» *Bulletin of Hispanic Studies*, 41 (1964), 160-68.

GULLÓN, RICARDO: *Direcciones del modernismo*. Madrid: Gredos, 1971.

— *Galdós, novelista moderno*. Madrid: Taurus, 1960.

— «Indigenismo y modernismo.» *Papeles de Son Armadans*, No. 67 (Oct. 1961), pp. 15-31.

— «La invención del 98.» In his *La invención del 98 y otros ensayos*. Madrid: Gredos, 1969, pp. 7-19.

JESCHKE, HANS: *La Generación de 1898 (Ensayo de una determinación de su esencia)*. Trans. Y. Pino Saavedra. Madrid: Editora Nacional, 1954).

LAÍN ENTRALGO, PEDRO: *La generación del noventayocho*. Madrid: Diana, 1945.

LANDON, SARA B.: «Galdós and his Fictional Historians: Views of Nation and Self in the *Episodios nacionales*, Series IV and V.» Diss. Northwestern University, 1978.

LITVAK, LILY: *A Dream of Arcadia, (Anti-Industrialism in Spanish Literature, 1895-1905)*. Austin: The University of Texas Press, 1975.

— «La sociología criminal y su influencia en los escritores españoles de fin de siglo.» *Revue de Littérature Comparée*, 48 (1974), pp. 12-32.

LIVINGSTONE, LEON: «Interior Duplication and the Problem of Form in the Modern Spanish Novel.» *PMLA*, 73 (1958), 393-406.

MONTESINOS, JOSÉ F.: *Introducción a una historia de la novela en España, en el siglo XIX*. 2nd ed. Madrid: Castalia, 1966.

NEVIUS, JANET D.: «The Intellectual Hero in Spanish Fiction: Galdós, Unamuno, Baroja.» Diss. New York University, 1975.

ONÍS, FEDERICO DE: «Sobre el concepto del modernismo.» *La Torre*, 1, No. 2 (Apr.-June 1953), 95-103.

RAMSDEN, HERBERT: *The 1898 Movement in Spain: Towards a Reinterpretation with Special Reference to «En torno al casticismo» and «Idearium español»*. Manchester: Manchester University Press, 1974.

REDING, KATHERINE P.: «The Generation of 1898 in Spain as Seen through its Fictional Hero.» *Smith College Studies in Modern Languages*, 17, Nos. 3-4 (April-July 1936).

RIBBANS, GEOFFREY: «Riqueza inagotada de las revistas literarias modernas.» *Revista de Literatura*, 13, Nos. 25-26 (Jan.-June 1958), 30-47.

SALINAS, PEDRO: «El concepto de generación literaria aplicado a la del 98.» *Revista de Occidente,* 49-50 (1935), 249-59.

SEELEMAN, ROSA: «The Treatment of Landscape in the Novelists of the Generation of 1898.» *Hispanic Review,* 4 (1936), 226-38.

SHAW, DONALD L.: *The Generation of 1898 in Spain.* New York: Barnes & Noble, 1975.

— «Modernismo: A Contribution to the Debate.» *Bulletin of Hispanic Studies,* 44 (1967), 195-202.

SIEBENMANN, GUSTAV: «Reinterpretación del modernismo.» In *Spanish Thought and Letters in the Twentieth Century.* Ed. Germán Bleiberg and E. Inman Fox. Nashville: Vanderbilt University Press, 1966, pp. 497-511.

SILVA CASTRO, RAÚL: «¿Es posible definir el modernismo?» *Cuadernos Americanos,* 24, No. 4 (July-Aug. 1965), 172-79.

TAYLOR, ALAN CAREY: *Carlyle et la pensée latine.* Paris: Boivin, 1937.

TUCKER, PEGGY LYNNE: *Time and History in Valle Inclán's Historical Novels and Tirano Banderas.* Valencia: Albatrós Hispanófila, 1980.

TZITSIKAS, H.: *El sentimiento ecológico en la generación del 98.* Madrid: Hispam, 1977.

VARELA JÁCOME, BENITO: *Renovación de la novela en el siglo XX.* Barcelona: Destino, 1967.

VÁZQUEZ BIGI, A. M.: «El pesimismo filosófico europeo y la Generación del 98.» *Revista de Occidente,* NS Nos. 113-14 (Aug.-Sept. 1972), pp. 171-90.

ZAVALA, IRIS: *Fin de siglo: Modernismo, 98 y bohemia.* Madrid: EDICUSA, 1973.

ZELLER, GUILLERMO: *La novela histórica en España, 1828-1850.* New York: Instituto de las Españas, 1938.

PHILOSOPHY AND ANTHROPOLOGY

BARNES, HAZEL, E.: *The Literature of Possibility: A Study in Humanistic Existentialism.* Lincoln: University of Nebraska Press, 1959.

BARRETT, WILLIAM: *Irrational Man: A Study in Existential Philosophy.* Garden City, N.Y.: Doubleday, 1958.

CAMUS, ALBERT: *The Myth of Sisyphus and Other Essays.* Trans. Justin O'Brien. New York: Alfred A. Knopf, 1967.

ELIADE, MIRCEA: *Cosmos and History: The Myth of the Eternal Return.* Pantheon Books, 1954; rpt. New York: Harper Torchbooks, 1959.

— *The Sacred and the Profane: The Nature of Religion.* New York: Harcourt, Brace, Jovanovich, 1959.

GOODHEART, EUGENE: «Nietzsche and the Aristocracy of Passion.» In *The Cult of the Ego: The Self in Modern Literature.* Chicago: University of Chicago Press, 1969, pp. 114-32.

GRENE, MARJORIE: *Introduction to Existentialism.* Chicago: University of Chicago Press, 1959.

ILIE, PAUL: «Nietzsche in Spain: 1890-1910.» *PMLA,* 79 (1964), 80-96.

KAUFMANN, WALTER: *Nietzsche: Philosopher, Psychologist, Antichrist.* Princeton: Princeton University Press, 1974.

— trans. and ed. *The Portable Nietzsche.* New York: Penguin Books, 1976.

KERN, EDITH: *Existential Thought and Fictional Technique: Kierkegaard, Sartre, Beckett.* New Haven: Yale University Press, 1970.

KNIGHT, EVERETT W.: *Literature Considered as Philosophy: The French Example.* London: Routledge and Kegan Paul, 1957.

LEE, DOROTHY: «Codifications of Reality: Lineal and Nonlineal.» In *Freedom and Culture*. Englewood Cliffs, N. J.: Prentice-Hall, 1959, pp. 105-20.

McELROY, DAVIS DUNBAR: *Existentialism and Modern Literature: An Essay in Existential Criticism*. New York: Greenwood Press, 1968.

NIETZSCHE, FRIEDRICH: *On the Genealogy of Morals and Ecce Homo*. Trans. and Ed. Walter Kaufmann. New York: Vintage Books, 1969.

ORTEGA Y GASSET, JOSÉ: «Historia como sistema.» In his *Obras completas*. Vol. VI. 4th ed. Madrid: Revista de Occidente, 1958, pp. 11-50.

— «Meditaciones del Quijote.» In his *Obras completas*. Vol. I. 4th ed. Madrid: Revista de Occidente, 1957, pp. 309-400.

SARTRE, JEAN-PAUL: *Being and Nothingness*. Trans. Hazel E. Barnes. New York: Washington Square Press, 1966.

— *Essays in Existentialism*. Introd. Jean Wahl. Ed Wade Baskin. Secaucus, N.J.: Citadel Press, 1979.

SCHOPENHAUER, ARTHUR: *The World as Will and Representation*. Trans. E. F. J. Payne. 2 vols. New York: Dover, 1966.

SOBEJANO, GONZALO: *Nietzsche en España*. Madrid: Gredos, 1967.

HISTORIOGRAPHY AND HISTORICAL NOVEL

BAKHTIN, MIKHAIL: «Epopée et roman.» *Recherches Internationales à la Lumière de Marxisme*, No. 76 (3° trimestre 1973).

BARANTE, M. DE: Préface. *Histoire des Ducs de Bourgogne: de la Maison de Valois, 1364-1477*. Bruxelles: Société Typographique Belge, Adolphe Wahlen et Compagnie, 1838. 2 vols., 7-28.

BARTHES, ROLAND: «Le Discours de l'histoire.» *Information sur les Sciences Sociales*, 6, Pt. 2, No. 4 (Aug. 1967), 65-75.

BUTTERFIELD, HERBERT: *The Historical Novel*. Cambridge: Cambridge University Press, 1924.

COLLINGWOOD, R. G.: *The Idea of History*. Oxford: Clarendon Press, 1946.

DARBY, WILLIAM D.: «Sir Walter Scott and the Historical Novel: Intellectual Values and the Definition of a Genre.» Diss. Wayne State University 1974.

DASPRE, ANDRÉ: «Le Roman historique et l'histoire.» *Revue d'Histoire Littéraire de la France*, 75 (1975), 235-44.

FLETCHER, MADELEINE DE GOGORZA: *The Spanish Historical Novel: 1870-1970*. London: Tamesis, 1973.

GOSSMAN, LIONEL: «History and Literature: Reproduction or Signification.» In *The Writing of History: Literary Form and Historical Understanding*. Ed. Robert H. Canary and Henry Kozicki. Madison: University of Wisconsin Press, 1978, pp. 3-39.

HARTMAN, GEOFFREY H.: «History-Writing as Answerable Style.» *New Literary History*, 2 (1970-71), 73-83.

LE GOFF, JACQUES: «Naissance du roman historique au XIIᵉ siècle?» *La Nouvelle Revue Française*, Nos. 237-40 (Sept.-Dec. 1972), 163-73.

LEWIS, C. S.: «Historicism.» *The Month*, 4 (1950), 230-43.

LUKÁCS, GEORGE: *The Historical Novel*. Trans. Hannah and Stanley Mitchell. London: Merlin Press, 1962.

MÉNARD, JACQUES: «Lukács et la théorie du roman historique.» *La Nouvelle Revue Française*, Nos. 237-40 (Sept.-Dec. 1972), pp. 229-38.

MAY, GEORGES: «L'Histoire a-t-elle engendré le roman? Aspects français de la question au seuil du siècle des lumières.» *Revue d'Histoire Littéraire de la France*, 55 (1955), 155-76.

METTRA, CLAUDE: «Le Romancier hors les murs.» *La Nouvelle Revue Française,* Nos. 237-40 (Sept.-Dec. 1972), pp. 5-29.

MILLER, J. HILLIS: «Narrative and History.» *English Literary History,* 41 (1974), 455-73.

MOLINO, JEAN: «Qu'est-ce que le roman historique?» *Revue d'Histoire Littéraire de la France,* 75 (1975), 195-234.

OLDENBOURG, ZOÉ: «Le Roman et l'histoire.» *La Nouvelle Revue Française,* Nos. 237-40 (Sept.-Dec. 1972), pp. 130-55.

PATRIDES, C. A.: *The Grand Design of God: The Literary Form of the Christian View of History.* Toronto: University of Toronto Press, 1972.

RÉMY, PIERRE-JEAN: L'Histoire dans le roman.» *La Nouvelle Revue Française,* Nos. 237-40 (Sept.-Dec. 1972), pp. 156-60.

SHAW, HARRY E.: *The Forms of Historical Fiction: Sir Walter Scott and his Successors.* Ithaca: Cornell University Press, 1983.

SIMMONS, JAMES C.: *The Novelist as Historian: Essays on the Victorian Historical Novel.* Paris: Mouton, 1973.

TURNER, JOSEPH W.: «The Kinds of Historical fiction: An Essay in Definition and Methodology.» *Genre,* 12 (1979), 333-55.

WHITE, HAYDEN: *Metahistory: The Historcial Imagination in Nineteenth-Century Europe.* Baltimore: The Johns Hopkins University Press, 1973.

LITERARY THEORY AND CRITICISM

ARNHEIM, RUDOLF: *Entropy and Art: An Essay on Disorder and Order.* Berkeley: University of California Press, 1971.

AUERBACH, ERICH: *Mimesis: The Representation of Reality in Western Literature.* Princeton: Princeton University Press, 1953.

BAKHTIN, MIKHAIL: *Rabelais and his World.* Trans. Hélène Iswolsky. Cambridge, Mass: The M.I.T. Press, 1965.

BARTHES, ROLAND: «L'Ecriture du roman.» In his *Le Degré zéro de l'écriture.* Paris: Editions du Seuil, 1972, pp. 25-32.

BENJAMIN, WALTER: «The Storyteller: Reflections on the works of Nikolai Leskof.» In his *Illuminations.* Ed. Hannah Arendt. New York: Harcourt, Brace, and World, 1968, pp. 83-109.

BLOOM, EDWARD A., and LILLIAN D. BLOOM: *Satire's Persuasive Voice.* Ithaca: Cornell University Press, 1979.

BLOOM, HAROLD, et al.: *Deconstruction and Criticism.* New York: Seabury Press, 1979.

BOOTH, WAYNE C.: *The Rhetoric of Fiction.* Chicago: The University of Chicago Press, 1961.

BROOKS, PETER B.: *The Melodramatic Imagination: Balzac, Henry James, Melodrama, and the Mode of Excess.* New Haven: Yale University Press, 1976.

COOPER, LANE, ed.: *Aristotle on the Art of Poetry.* Ithaca: Cornell University Press, 1947.

DE MAN, PAUL: *Allegories of Reading: Figural Language in Rousseau, Nietzsche, Rilke, and Proust.* New Haven: Yale University Press, 1979.

DEMETZ, PETER: «The Uses of Lukács.» *The Yale Review,* 54 (1964-65), 435-40.

DERRIDA, JACQUES: *Spurs: Nietzsche's Styles.* Trans. Barbara Harlow. Chicago: University of Chicago Press, 1979.

ELLIOTT, ROBERT C.: *The Power of Satire: Magic, Ritual, Art.* Princeton: Princeton University Press, 1960.

FOLEY, BARBARA: «History, Fiction, and Satirical Form: The Example of Dos Pasos' *1919.*» *Genre,* 12 (1979), pp. 357-78.

FRYE, NORTHROP: *Anatomy of Criticism: Four Essays.* Princeton: Princeton University Press, 1971.

— *Fables of Identity: Studies in Poetic Mythology.* New York: Harcourt, Brace, and World, 1963.

— *The Secular Scripture: A Study of the Structure of Romance.* Cambridge, Mass.: Harvard University Press, 1976.

GENETTE, GÉRARD: *Figures III.* Paris: Editions du Seuil, 1972.

GILLET, JOSEPH E.: «The Autonomous Character in Spanish and European Literature.» *Hispanic Review,* 24 (1956), 179-90.

GIRARD, RENÉ: *Deceit, Desire, and the Novel: Self and Other in Literary Structure.* Trans. Yvonne Freccero. Baltimore: The Johns Hopkins University Press, 1976.

GOLDMANN, LUCIEN: *Pour une sociologie du roman.* Paris: Gallimard, 1964.

HAMBURGER, KÄTE: *The Logic of Literature.* Trans. Marilynn J. Rose. Bloomington: Indiana University Press, 1973.

HIGHET, GILBERT: *The Anatomy of Satire.* Princeton: Princeton University Press, 1962.

KENNER, HUGH: *The Stoic Comedians: Flaubert, Joyce, and Beckett.* Berkeley: University of California Press, 1974.

KERNAN, ALVIN B.: *The Plot of Satire.* New Haven: Yale University Press, 1965.

MENDILOW, A. A.: *Time and the Novel.* 1952; rpt. New York: Humanities Press, 1972.

MEYERHOFF, HANS: *Time in Literature.* Berkeley: University of California Press, 1955.

MUIR, EDWIN: *The Structure of the Novel.* 1928; rpt. New York: Harcourt, Brace, and World, 1969.

POULET, GEORGES: *Studies in Human Time.* Trans. Elliot Coleman. Baltimore: The Johns Hopkins University Press, 1956.

RALEIGH, JOHN HENRY: «The English Novel and the Three Kinds of Time.» In his *Time, Place, and Idea: Essays on the Novel.* Carbondale: Southern Illinois Press, 1968, pp. 43-55.

RIFKIN, JEREMY: *Entropy: A New World View.* New York: Viking Press, 1980.

SCHOLES, ROBERT, and ROBERT KELLOGG: *The Nature of Narrative.* New York: Oxford University Press, 1966.

TOBIN, PATRICIA DRESCHSEL: *Time and the Novel: The Genealogical Imperative.* Princeton: Princeton University Press, 1978.

TODOROV, TZVETAN: *The Poetics of Prose.* Trans. Richard Howard. Ithaca: Cornell University Press, 1977.

VILLEGAS, JUAN: *La estructura mítica del héroe en la novela del siglo XX.* Barcelona: Planeta, 1978.

INDEX